World Wisdom
The Library of Perennial Philosophy

The Library of Perennial Philosophy is dedicated to the exposition of the timeless Truth underlying the diverse religions. This Truth, often referred to as the *Sophia Perennis*—or Perennial Wisdom—finds its expression in the revealed Scriptures as well as the writings of the great sages and the artistic creations of the traditional worlds.

The Perennial Philosophy provides the intellectual principles capable of explaining both the formal contradictions and the transcendent unity of the great religions.

Ranging from the writings of the great sages of the past, to the perennialist authors of our time, each series of our Library has a different focus. As a whole, they express the inner unanimity, transforming radiance, and irreplaceable values of the great spiritual traditions.

Timeless in Time: Sri Ramana Maharshi appears as one of our selections in the Spiritual Masters: East & West series.

Spiritual Masters: East & West Series

This series presents the writings of great spiritual masters of the past and present from both East and West. Carefully selected essential writings of these sages are combined with biographical information, glossaries of technical terms, historical maps, and pictorial and photographic art in order to communicate a sense of their respective spiritual climates.

Timeless in Time

Sri Ramana Maharshi

A.R. Natarajan

Foreword by
Eliot Deutsch

World Wisdom

Timeless in Time: Sri Ramana Maharshi

The text and Introduction to the 2002 edition of *Timeless in Time* published by arrangement with
V.S. Ramanan, President, Board of Trustess, Sri Ramanasramam, Tiruvannamalai 606 603.
© Sri Ramanasramam. All rights reserved.
Publisher's Preface, Foreword, Glossary of *Timeless in Time*
© 2006 World Wisdom, Inc.

All photographs © Sri Ramanasramam, except photographs on pages 9, 10, 17, 32,
80-81, 121, 122 © Michael Oren Fitzgerald

On the Cover: Sri Ramana Maharshi and Arunachala

Book design by Susana Marín

Library of Congress Cataloging-in-Publication Data
Natarajan, A. R.
  Timeless in time : Sri Ramana Maharshi / by A.R. Natarajan ; foreword by Eliot Deutsch.
    p. cm. -- (The library of perennial philosophy) (Spiritual masters. East & West series)
  Previously published: Bangalore : Ramana Maharshi Centre for Learning, 1999.
  Includes bibliographical references.
  ISBN-13: 978-1-933316-15-4 (pbk. : alk. paper)
  ISBN-10: 1-933316-15-2 (pbk. : alk. paper) 1. Ramana, Maharshi. 2. Gurus--India--Biography. I.
Title. II. Series. III. Series: Spiritual masters. East and West series.

BL1175.R342N37 2006
294.5092--dc22

                                    2005031951

*World Wisdom would like to thank V.S. Ramanan and the Sri Ramanasramam
for their assistance in making this book possible.*

Printed on acid-free paper in China.

For information address World Wisdom, Inc.
P.O. Box 2682, Bloomington, Indiana 47402-2682
www.worldwisdom.com

Contents

Publisher's Preface

Timeless in Time, a biography of the great Hindu sage of world-renown, Bhagavan Sri Ramana Maharshi, was written by A.R. Natarajan, the President of the Ramana Maharshi Center for Learning, Bangalore, and has the official authorization of Ramanasramam, the hermitage where Sri Ramana lived for many years.

The new World Wisdom edition of *Timeless in Time* is the first to appear outside of India. It is not, however, a mere reprinting of the Indian edition, for it contains an extensive collection of additional photographs; includes a new Foreword by Eliot Deutsch, eminent scholar, professor, and author of *The Essential Vedanta: A New Source Book of Advaita Vedanta*; reproduces Sri Ramana's words in italics and in a distinctive red font; and is brought out as a full-color illustrated edition (where the Indian version was only in black-and-white). But in order to produce this new full-color version with a manageable page count, it was necessary to reduce the number of pages by editing out some of the less significant biographical details of Sri Ramana's life (mostly about individuals associated with him at the *asram*); it was also necessary to present the copious bibliographical references in an abbreviated form.

Timeless in Time draws on a wealth of sources not available to earlier biographers of Sri Ramana, but also includes extensive excerpts from these same biographies. Readers will find that *Timeless in Time* contains a fascinating selection of Sri Ramana's autobiographical reminiscences of key events in his life, events which are fittingly complemented by Ramanasramam's collection of the most essential photographs of the Maharshi, as well as the people and places associated with him. Readers will also find a select choice of question-and-answer sessions wherein Sri Ramana expounds his Vedantic teaching in its most essential manner, continually drawing the questioner back to his key question of spiritual introspection: "Who am I?"

What can the West learn from the life and teachings of Bhagavan Sri Ramana Maharshi? What has *Timeless in Time* to teach it? To quote the incisive words of Frithjof Schuon: "Sri Ramana was as it were the incarnation, in these latter days and in the face of the modern activist fever, of what is primordial and incorruptible in India. He manifested the nobility of contemplative 'non-action' in the face of an ethic of utilitarian agitation, and he showed the implacable beauty of pure truth in the face of passions, weaknesses, and betrayals. The great question 'Who am I?' appears, with him, as a concrete expression of a reality that is 'lived,' if one may so put it, and this authenticity gives to each word of the sage a flavor of inimitable freshness—the flavor of Truth when it is embodied in the most immediate way. The whole Vedanta is contained in the Maharshi's question 'Who am I?' The answer is: the Inexpressible."[1]

WORLD WISDOM
October 2005

Foreword

Timeless in Time, a biography by A.R. Natarajan of the remarkable life and teachings of Ramana Maharshi (1879-1950), is a beautifully written and illustrated work which offers a vivid account of the person "Ramana" (as the author prefers to refer to him) and a choice selection from his sayings and writings. It also includes numerous excerpts of talks with Ramana and his Indian disciples and devotees, among them Gambhiram Seshier, Sivaprakasam Pillai, and Vasishta Ganapati Muni, and also Western admirers such as Paul Brunton and Arthur Osborne, including interviews with them regarding their relations with him.

Ramana was not a learned pundit or an accomplished academic philosopher; he was rather a living exemplar and embodiment of the deep spirituality and wisdom of the Advaita, or non-dualist, Vedantic tradition which has extended from the early Vedic writings, primarily the *Upanisads*, to the present. From early childhood, Ramana seemed obsessed with the central Advaitic question "Who am I"? and was able to answer it, as it were, in terms of his own state of realized consciousness of the undifferentiated oneness of being. He is said to have become enlightened when he was only sixteen years old.

*Who can understand the state of the one
Who has dissolved his ego and
Is abiding always in the Self?
For him the Self alone is.
What remains for him to do?*

Living the life of a modern-day *sadhu*, Ramana spent long periods of time dwelling in silence. His world may be summed up in his own words:

*Can there be space, can there be time, except for me?
Space and time bind me, only if I am the body.
I am nowhere, I am timeless,
I exist everywhere and always.*

ELIOT DEUTSCH

Introduction

B.V. Narasimha Swami examined several devotees and took depositions from them about their relationship with Ramana to ensure authenticity. Above all he had several interviews with Ramana, the most important of which was his enlightenment. He stayed in a cave adjacent to the *asram* in order to be present during many of the question and answer sessions which Ramana had with devotees. It was after sustained research extending over two years that he wrote his biography of Ramana, *Self-Realization*, which was published in 1931. Its appeal is undimmed nearly seventy years later. In 1954, Arthur Osborne wrote his biography, *Ramana Maharshi and the Path of Self-Knowledge*. His basic data was drawn from the earlier biography. He himself says so. But what makes his book fascinating is his style of writing, his acceptance of Ramana as his guru, and the account of the three years spent in Ramana's physical presence. Many have been drawn to Ramana and are still being drawn by this powerful presentation.

T.S. Ananthamurthy has written a very appealing biography in 1972, *Life and Teachings of Sri Ramana Maharshi*. In 1974, Professor K. Swaminathan wrote a biography-cum-teachings book, *Ramana Maharshi*. The biography portion is only fifty-four pages. Therefore, though the book has a special fragrance, written as it is by one soaked in Ramana, its coverage was limited due to space constraints. The same holds good for T.M.P. Mahadevan's *Ramana Maharshi*. This biography, published in 1977, is scholarly but short being only seventy-seven pages. The rest of the book is devoted to the teachings. In 1980, Ramana's birth centenary year, Joan Greenblatt and Mathew Greenblatt wrote their pictorial biography, *Bhagavan Sri Ramana*. The design and presentation, backed by their love and reverence for Ramana, have made this book very attractive.

To all these earlier biographers, each great in their own way, I offer my humble salutations.

I also offer my salutations to the vast and growing circle of disciples and devotees of Ramana. They are scattered all over the world. It is their collective spiritual power which has to be the backing for this new biography.

Over the past several decades we have vast, varied, and authentic material about Ramana which was either not available to or could not be used by the earlier biographers. It is now nearly seventy years since the first biography was written. There is need for new insights and fresh perspectives as there is a growing awareness of the power of Ramana's presence. One is able to relate more directly to him. Readers in the new millennium need to savor and enjoy the sweetness of the fresh discoveries and new material which has unfolded since then. But where is the need to justify? The sweetness of his life itself is enough reason. It draws one irresistibly to him. For, "once the Maharshi's story is heard or read, who would care to listen to or read any other?"[1]

The story of Sri Rama was written by Valmiki, *Mahabharata* by Sage Veda Vyasa, and *Bhagavatam* on Sri Krishna, by Suka Brahmam. They were all *jnanis*. Dante wrote his *Divine Comedy* and Milton *Paradise Lost* and *Paradise Regained*. Both were immersed in their devotion to Jesus Christ. One wishes that there was someone of their stature to write a biography of Ramana, whose story is of epic proportions, at this juncture when there is so much of material available.

This book is one of a trilogy planned as a homage to Bhagavan Ramana on the occasion of his centenary of enlightenment. The first of these, *Radiance of the Self*, with over 170 photographs, including some from the archival films, was published last year. This sacred biography is the second one. The third book, *Arunachala—From Rgveda to Ramana Maharshi* is expected to be ready by the middle of next year.[2]

Many refer to Bhagavan Sri Ramana Maharshi as "Bhagavan," some others refer to him as "Maharshi." I have preferred to use the word Ramana throughout for it casts a magic spell beyond the reach of words and the mind.

Though my heart does not melt with love for Ramana, as a candle near fire would, often he makes me a captive of his love. I can feel strongly his boundless grace at work as this biography is being written, as each event falls in place in the proper perspective. Is he not the master of "Proper Placing"?[3] The words too seem to order themselves. There is no other way of expressing my gratitude than to place this biography as an offering at Ramana's time-transcending sacred feet.

It is my prayer to him that readers may be recipients of his ever-flowing grace.

A.R. NATARAJAN
December 14, 1999

Section I: Who are you Ramana?

Who are you Ramana?

In the recesses of the hearts of all, beginning with Hari, the pure intellect shines as the Self, as Arunachala Ramana. When the mind melts in love for him, the subtle eye of pure intellect opens and reveals himself as pure consciousness.[1]
— *Bhagavan Ramana*

The light of lights that shines within
The deep heart's core,
All in one and one in all
True seer in whom all truth is seen.[2]

— Muruganar

Ramana was a student in the tenth standard, staying in his uncle's house in Madurai. It was July 17, 1896. He was studying in the rooms upstairs when it happened. A sudden, gripping fear of death made him question, intensely, his true identity. It took the form of the query "Who am I?" Such was his passion to know that straightaway the enquiry merged him in the source of consciousness, in the divine current. "I" being a divine current, fear ended once for all. This awareness of the natural "I"-consciousness remained steadily thereafter unaffected by the outer activities in which he might be engaged. He became the Enlightened One when he was only sixteen years of age.

*Who can understand the state of the one
Who has dissolved his ego and
Is abiding always in the Self?
For him the Self alone is.
What remains for me to do?*[3]

Then why had he to move to Arunachala?[4] For its call was irresistible and had to be obeyed. Ramana had been aware of the glory of Arunachala from the age of innocence and he felt its presence in the heart.[5] Providence had cast him in the role of a universal *guru*, a role that he had to perform there. Consequently he never left the place after he arrived on September 1, 1896. The entire period of his guidance as *sadguru* for fifty-four years, till his *mahanirvana* on April 14, 1950, was at this one place. There is no parallel to this.

In 1899, Ramana shifted to the Virupaksha Cave on the Arunachala hill. Till 1907 he remained outwardly silent as well. However, the radiance of his Self-knowledge,

the power of his penance, was so evident that it attracted seekers, visitors, and even children. Just to be in his peace-filled presence was enough. He was golden-hued and handsome with large, powerful, and lustrous eyes. Who could resist his magnetism and fail to recognize his unique spiritual state?

An ascetic, Amritanatha Yati took the liberty of requesting Ramana to clarify as to which of the great Hindu Gods had incarnated in his human form. He wrote in Malayalam a verse imploring Ramana to reveal whether he was Vishnu (Hari) or Siva Guru (Kartikeya), Yativara (Siva), or Vararuchi.

Ramana replied in the same Malayalam meter, on the same paper. The answer was altogether at a different level. Ramana was no particular form nor any of the Gods. Who was he then? Arunachala Ramana is the pure intellect shining in the hearts of all. He is the life of lives, the fullness of consciousness in each and every one. As Muruganar had sung, "He is the light of lights that shines within the deep heart's core."

Ramana would hint at this truth time and again. Here one could refer to the vision which a devotee, Raghavachari, had round about the year 1910. This devotee wished to know the true form of Ramana. He told him, "Just as Arjuna wished to see the form of Sri Krishna, I wish to have the vision of your real form." Then he saw the form of Ramana disappear, as also that of the picture of Dakshinamurti which was behind him. "There was just empty space." After some time he saw these forms reappear preceded by a blazing light. Such was the impact of this vision that for one month he did not go back. When he did, he picked up the necessary courage to ask Ramana the true meaning of this experience. Ramana told him. *"You wanted to see my form. You saw my disappearance. I am formless. So, that experience might be the truth. Further visions may be according to your conception derived from the study of* Bhagavad Gita.*"*[6]

Ramana would also assure devotees that he was not bound by time or space. They could feel his presence in their hearts wherever they were. Eleanor Noye while traveling in Kashmir and north India, under unimaginable conditions, could hear Ramana's assurance *"I am always with you wherever you go."* She writes, "His dear face was ever before me, no matter what I was doing. His presence filled my heart."[7]

Due to compelling family circumstances Sundaresa Iyer had to seek a job in another place and was distraught at the thought that he had to leave Ramana's presence. Ramana reassured him by remarking to devotees, *"Here is someone who has been with me for forty years and is now saying that he is going somewhere away from Bhagavan."*[8] Subbaramayya would attend Ramana's *jayanti* (birthday) celebrations every year. However, he could not do so in 1943. When he came later another devotee mildly chided him saying that on such occasions one should be in Bhagavan's presence. Ramana promptly told him, *"The feet of Bhagavan are everywhere! So where can we gather except at his feet?"*[9] What reassurance through a simple statement of fact that Ramana is available to every in-turned mind seeking his presence in the heart.

Ganapati Muni had many intense spiritual experiences while he was staying at Sirsi far away from Ramanasramam. Initially he was depressed at the fact that he was away from his *guru* at this juncture. But soon this depression passed away because of his strong faith "in the space-transcending might of Ramana's glory like the rays of the sun."[10]

Ramana is the all-pervasive Self ever present everywhere. Even so he revealed himself in various perceptions to some of his ardent devotees.

To Muruganar, Ramana was the supreme power. Therefore, for him, all the Gods of the Hindu pantheon radiated only Ramana's power though named differently. He says so categorically in some of the verses of *Tiru Undiyar*.[11] In this composition there are also some verses on Ramana relating him to Lord Buddha, the upholder of the value of compassion, and Lord Jesus Christ, suffering from crucifixion, on to expiate the sins of others.[12]

Later in 1917, while composing *Ramana Gita*, Ganapati Muni records that he had several visions which repeatedly confirmed his belief. To him only the name was different, but the power was the same.[13] In *Chandogya Upanishad*, the science of the Self was taught to sage Narada by Sanatkumara. Drawing a parallel from his own life the Muni felt that Ramana's role was identical. It was not only to reveal to him the direct path to Self-knowledge but also to make the path easily accessible to all.

Here it may be mentioned that there are some indications in Ramana's statements which lend support to this view. After his enlightenment, while leaving his home for Arunachala, Ramana left a note beginning with the words, *"I have, in search of my father and in obedience to his command, started from here."*[14] On reaching Arunachala he went straight to the *sanctum sanctorum* of the Arunachaleswara temple and reported, *"Father, I have come."*[15]

To appreciate the perception of Muruganar, Muni, and many others like Viswanatha Swami, and Swami Sankarananda Bharathi, one has to have a background of Hindu beliefs. Veda Vyasa identified Sri Krishna, the leader of *Bhagavad Gita*, as an incarnation of Vishnu. Similarly Adi Sankara has been regarded as the incarnation of Siva.

There have been other perceptions of Ramana as well because he defies all the time-honored classifications. Many found that their mental conceptions about him were far removed from reality.

Swami Siddeswarananda was under the general belief that *jnanis* were devoid of devotion till he himself saw Ramana's state while reading some devotional poetry. He reported the same to Paul Brunton. "One morning at 7 o'clock when I was sitting in the hall, I asked the Maharshi about a certain verse by Nammalwar embodying his vision of cosmic consciousness. The Maharshi replied, *'I shall recite some similar verses from another poet of the Tamil language. Pay attention to my way of repeating the words and you will be able to understand, even though you are a Malayali from the west coast.'* The verse referred to

divine love. A shaft of sunlight fell through the window onto his face. He had read out barely two lines, when I noticed tears trickling down his face. Then he stopped speaking, as though he felt too keenly and emotionally the meaning of the words. There was an atmosphere of love around him. For two or three hours he remained silent, the rest of the poem unread, the book resting on his knee, his eyes open in a trance of divine emotion."[16]

Yet another angle of perception would be to look at him as a perfect human being. Viewing him thus Ganapati Muni finds him to be an ideal held out before mankind. Why? For he combined in himself the vast peace of the silent mind while being at the same time the repository of all power as well. His extraordinary dispassion was combined with a heart which melted in love. Truly he was a "Purushottama, a man among men."[17]

Muruganar too expresses the same feeling in one of his soul stirring poems.

No form he has, no name, no quality.
Still there besides the holy hill he dwells
In human form, known by the comely name
Of Ramana, marked by the primal power
Of love: with moist eyes showering grace for all
To see.[18]

Such was his exalted state that his very presence was a benediction to mankind "enough to bless the whole world, like the sun, which by its mere presence gives us light and life."[19]

All said and done, a *jnani* like Ramana must remain an enigma. He once told Subbaramayya, *"However much a* jnani *might talk, he is still a silent one. However much he might work, he is still a quiet one. His voice is the incorporeal voice. His walk is not on the earth, it is like measuring the sky with the sky."*[20] Therefore while attempting to comprehend the true stature or glory of Ramana one is reminded of one of his own verses which reads:

Master, you have till this day kept me at your feet
And Master, when people ask me,
What is your nature? you make me stand with
Head hung down, a speechless statue.[21]

Tiruchuzhial: Birth Place of Sri Ramana

Self that dances as unbroken bliss in devotees' hearts. Siva unique, the light supreme that shines unceasing in bright Tiruchuzhi, bestow your grace on me and shine as Heart within my heart.[1]
—*Bhagavan Ramana*

Bhuminatha temple tank in Tiruchuzhi

Tiruchuzhi is an important place of pilgrimage from ancient times. The temple dedicated to Lord Siva as Sri Bhuminatha is noted for its antiquity and held in deep veneration. There is a separate shrine for the consort of Lord Siva named Sahayavalli.

This temple has been visited by ancient Tamil saints famous for their devotion—Sri Appar, Sri Sundarar, Sri Manickavachagar, and Sri Vageeshar. Here they spontaneously poured forth-beautiful classical Tamil songs in praise of this God and his consort.[2]

Among these the most famous compositions are by Sundarar. The English translation of a few of these verses is given hereunder:

Verse 1: Tiruchuzhial has groves in which swarms of bees, longing for honey, hum melodiously. It is the residence of the Lord Who abides as body, as soul living in it (body), as wide-open space, as sky discharging rain, and as the intellect (*buddhi*) which experiences the fruits of deeds (*karma*). The attendants of Yama will not torment those who, in various ways, think of Tiruchuzhial.

Verse 5: The Lord's abode is Tiruchuzhial. He is our Relative. He wears the waxing moon on His matted hair. His mind has mastery over the five senses. He is pleased to reside forever in Tiruchuzhial. Those who have learnt to chant His sacred Name fare well on the path of salvation. It is our duty to chant His Name.[3]

There is a holy tank in front of the temple. This is called Trisula Tirtham as it was created by a mere stroke of Lord Siva's weapon, the *trisulam*. In the Tamil month of Masi (Feb-March) the waters of this tank rise noticeably just before the full moon day.

Ramana once recalled this feature of the temple tank when Suri Nagamma reported to him about her visit to Tiruchuzhi. *"The water will not be so good at this time of the year. In the month of Magha, on the day of the star Magha, it swells and the water rises. The* abhisheka *festival of the Deity is celebrated on that day, that is, on the 10th day of the Brahmotsavam. That day, the Deity is brought to the* mandapam *there and the* abhishekam *is done with the water of the Trisula Tirtham. After the* abhishekam *is over, all the people bathe in that tank. In my boyhood days, all of us used to join together and draw on the steps some signs in order to see how much water rose everyday. It used to be amusing. The rising of the water used to start ten days earlier and used to submerge the steps at the rate of one step per day. The tank would become full by the full moon day. To us it was great fun."*[4]

Tiruchuzhi is a small town and administrative center in Ramanathapuram district in South India. It is about 38 miles from the city of Madurai where later Ramana was to become an Enlightened One.

Ramana's father's house in Tiruchuzhi

Tiruchuzhi has become a hallowed place because of the birth of Ramana here on December 30, 1879. He was born as the second child to the pious couple Sundaram Iyer and Azhagammal.

The house in which Ramana was born is in Kartikeyan Street in Tiruchuzhi very near to the main temple. By divine grace the house in which he was born has been acquired by Sri Ramanasramam and is called Sundara Mandiram. There is special worship for Ramana daily in the room in which he was born.

Tamil scholars have pointed out a significance for the name Tiruchuzhi. In Tamil *Karuchuzhi* means *karma*-bound destiny. *Tiruchuzhi* is grace-bound destiny. Therefore it is believed that a transformation takes place if one remembers Ramana, who made this sacred place incomparable by his birth. Those who do so would be freed from *karma*-bound destiny and be shielded by the bounty of his grace.

Blissful Parents

"I was reading in the Third Standard in the Taluk Board School at Tiruchuzhi when Maharshi was reading in the Fourth Standard. He was about ten or eleven then. His father, Sundaram Iyer, was well-known as a prominent *va-kil* (pleader) of the town. There were no certified pleaders then. He was obliging, sweet, and agreeable in speech and manners. He was also handsome. His complexion was very fair and he was of medium stature. Those who want-ed to have a meal or quarters to stay for a while would go to him and be invited as a matter of course. His house was terraced and had two compartments (portions)."[1]

Sundaram Iyer was a private *vakil* at Tiruchuzhi in the 1880s. He did not have any degrees or diplomas in law. Yet, on account of his intelligence and common sense, by his clever advocacy and winning manners, by his character, personality, and integrity, he commanded a lucrative practice in the court of the sub-magistrate of Tiruchuzhi and also won the love, esteem, and confidence of the people of the locality. He was truly regarded as a benevolent master by the oppressed and downtrod-den. To the poor and distressed, he was verily the Lord and Master. Even the so-called criminals looked upon him as their protector and benefactor.[2]

Once Sundaram Iyer had to appear in some cases in the magistrate's camp in a village a few miles from Tiruchuzhi. The magistrate too had to reach the village in his double bullock cart, which sped along pompously. It overtook Sundaram Iyer's cart and moved on without keeping company with the *vakil*'s cart. The modest *va-kil* was left far behind as the "magistrate, amidst official pomp and the jingling of bells, disappeared around the bend of the road."

He could have hardly foreseen what awaited him there. Thieves surrounded his cart. The magistrate's personality, his threats, and the protests of the liveried servant were all in vain. "The cart driver stood rooted to the spot in terror. The thieves snatched the despatch box and were about to retreat in good order. But Lo! behind the hedge came a shout, 'Oh! The *vakil sami* is coming!' The box was left on the road and the thieves took to their heels. The magistrate didn't hurry on but waited for the other cart. He got down from the cart and with folded hands apologized to Sundaram Iyer for leaving him behind. 'Hereafter I will understand whom the people love and esteem. It is a lesson for me and it has made me shed my official pride and learn humility,' he said, and for the rest of the way they kept company."[3]

The Raja of Ramnad once camped at Tiruchuzhi to arrange for the work of reclamation and renovation of the sacred shrine of Bhuminatha at Tiruchuzhi. All the local officials and people of repute called on him and paid their respects. Having heard about Sundaram Iyer the Raja was keen on meeting him and inviting him to help in the sacred task. Much to the Raja's disappointment, Sundaram Iyer did not call on him even though he had camped at Tiruchuzhi for three days and three nights. Finally the Raja himself sent for Sundaram Iyer. The Raja asked him whether he had offended him in any way, for among all the important people of Tiruchuzhi he alone had not called on him. Sundaram Iyer was surprised. He explained that being an ordinary person he had not thought of calling on the Raja. He had no business with the Raja and had not imagined that the Raja would have any need for him either. The Raja was overjoyed to meet this great man who in his humility did not realize his own importance and that nothing could be done at Tiruchuzhi without him. The Raja requested Sundaram Iyer to cooperate with him in his efforts to renovate the temple. The work went on well and he proved to be of great help to the Raja.[4]

T.P.R. writes, "Bhagavan rarely spoke about his father. But what little he told me about him is worth recording. He told me that his father was a courageous

and generous man. All day and night, his house would be filled with guests, poor and needy. He was never tired of feeding people. In his office he commanded very great respect and as a lawyer he had to move about places and conduct his cases. The magistrates, wherever he went, paid him great respect. His fame was so great and he was so much renowned for his upright character that both the parties, the accused and those who accuse, would come to him with a request to represent them. On several occasions what he told them was law and both the parties reconciled with equal happiness."[5]

Sundaram Iyer and Azhagammal were a united couple. Ramana himself has immortalized their relationship in his verse: *"O! Arunachala, may I and you, like Azhagu and Sundaram, become one and remain indivisible."*[6]

It may be mentioned that Azhagu means beautiful in Tamil and Sundaram connotes beautiful in Sanskrit.

Born With a Purpose

In Tiruchuzhi, the holy town of Bhuminatha, I was born to Sundara and his good wife Sundari. To rescue me from this barren worldly life, Arunachala Siva in the form of a Hill famous throughout the universe, gave me His own state of bliss, so that His heart might rejoice, so that His own Being as Awareness might shine forth and His own Power might flourish.[1]

—*Bhagavan Ramana*

It was Monday, December 30, 1879. It was the Tamil month of Margazhi, which has been set apart tradition-

Ramana's parents, Sundaram Iyer and Mother Azhagammal

ally for remembering God's power and protection through visits to temples, going around the streets in the early morning singing songs full of devotional fervor and so on. The holy Christmas season was being celebrated all over the world. The sacred village of Tiruchuzhi, and the devotees of Siva, God of gods, Mahadeva, were celebrating the holy Ardra Darsana day. The procession of Bhuminatheswara was slowly returning to the temple at 1 a.m. The star in the constellation was Punarvasu, also considered to be special. It was at that time that Ramana was born. It was the birth of the birthless, born for the welfare of the world.

He was the second son of his parents and was named Venkataraman. Among those present at the time of his birth was a blind lady who was blessed with a vision of light. She told others present there, "He who is born today in your house must be a divine being."[2] How true indeed were these words, how prophetic! Later events and the years to come were to prove this beyond doubt.

Osborne remarks, "The child was born a little later, both in the time of the day and year than the divine child of Bethlehem, nearly two thousand years ago. The same coincidence marked the end of earthly life also, for Sri Ramana left his body in the evening of April 14, a little later in time and date than Good Friday."[3] The analogy might be because like Jesus, Ramana was a pathfinder. He revealed a way of life by following which one could be born anew.

In the autobiographical quotation at the beginning of this chapter, Ramana himself has declared the purpose of his birth. What was it? It was to proclaim the power, the glory of Arunachala Siva in the form of a hill. What was that power? The power to guide on the path of Self-knowledge and to bestow it. This power is hidden but can be discovered by everyone whose inner eye of wisdom has opened. It is only in a still mind that the truth is revealed and the very thought of Arunachala stills the mind. In his hymns on Arunachala, Ramana says, *"Look, there it stands as if insentient. Mysterious is the way it works, beyond all human understanding. From my unthinking infancy, the immensity of Arunachala had shone in my awareness. But even when I learnt from someone that it was only Tiruvannamalai, I did not realize its meaning. When it stilled my mind and drew me to itself and I came near, I saw that it was stillness absolute."*[4]

"Though lacking in luster in its appearance as a hill, is in fact fiery."[5]

Room of Ramana's birth

Through the centuries the hill has been beckoning seekers of truth and has become the home of many seers and sages.

Having declared the purpose of his birth Ramana also writes about how the power of Arunachala operated on him to fulfill its purpose. Firstly from his age of innocence it made him aware in his innermost heart of *"the immensity of Arunachala."* Its grace was operating on him all the time. He refers to this in one of his hymns: *"As mother and father both, you gave birth to me and tended me. And before I could fall into the deep sea called* jaganmaya, *and get drowned in the universal illusion, you came to abide in my mind, you drew me to yourself, O Arunachala, you whose being is all Awareness. What a wonderful work of art your Grace has wrought, my Mother-Father-Lord!"*[6]

Ramana was born in the lineage of the ancient *rishi* Parasara. There is also considerable significance in this. Parasara was the first among those who recognized the all embracing nature of the Vedic God, Agni. In one of his compositions he says, "Agni glows in every heart and whoever perceives this indweller in the heart cave becomes one with the fullness of consciousness."[7] The reference to the heart and fullness of consciousness is significant for Ramana's role as a universal *guru* was to awaken source consciousness and some have termed his teachings as the "Science of the Heart." Besides, Self-knowledge is referred to as the fire which burns away *karma*, the accumulated tendencies which obstruct awareness of the truth. The first form of Arunachala was also of a blazing column without beginning and end. This pillar of light cooled into the form of a hill in answer to the prayer of great gods.[8] Arunachala is renowned as the "Agni-Linga."

Kalayar temple on the Koundinya river near Tiruchuzhi

Early Years

Ramana had an elder brother Nagaswami, a younger brother Nagasundaram, and a sister Alamelu. The children grew up happily. Ramana's ways were so endearing that he was a hot favorite among the men and women of Tiruchuzhi, more so of those who did not have children of their own. Among those who loved him dearly were Tasildar Ganapati Aiyar and Sub-Registrar Narayana Swami Aiyar.[1]

Maharshi used to call his father, *"Nayana,"* the corresponding word in Telugu and not "Appa" which is the Tamil word. The reason for this is that a relative of his, Lakshmana Aiyar, knew Telugu. As a result Ramana learnt to speak Telugu. This relative also used to call him "Ramana," the name by which he is famous the world over.[2] Later when the family shifted from Tiruchuzhi,

this pet name fell into disuse until it was revived by Ganapati Muni on that epoch-making day, November 18, 1907. Because Ramana called his father Nayana, the other members of the family followed suit and gradually Sundaram Iyer came to be called Nayana by the entire village for they held him in great regard.[3]

Once his uncle Subbier found fault with Ramana on the occasion of a marriage and Ramana went straight to the temple of the goddess Sahayambal to pour out his heart and derive solace from her.[4]

In school Ramana was noted for his phenomenal memory, and his knowledge of Tamil grammar. His handwriting used to be like print. This is seen from the notebook of his classmate Kathirvelu at whose request he had written down his name, class, and school in English, and added "Madras Presidency" in Tamil and numbered the pages.[5]

There is no photograph of his boyhood. Ramana recalled that once a group photograph was taken and he was asked to hold a heavy book in his hand to look studious. Just when the photograph was about to be taken a fly settled on him and he raised his arm to brush it off. No copy of the photograph is available.[6]

It is believed that once an ascetic who was not given a meal by Sundaram Iyer's ancestors left them with the curse that in each generation one member of the family would turn ascetic and live on alms begged for sustaining the body. The curse held till then. For one of Sundaram Iyer's paternal uncles had renounced home and turned an ascetic. His own elder brother Venkateswara Aiyar had developed dispassion while young and left the village on a pilgrimage and never returned. Would the curse hold good for one of the three brothers? Would one of them too renounce home for an inward way of life, in search of truth? The answer to this question lay in the lap of the future.

On the outskirts of Tiruchuzhi was a river Koundinya whose sands used to be the playground for Ramana and his friends. He once recalled, *"We used to bathe in the river and pour a vessel full of water on the linga in the Kalayar temple nearby, offer the food and then eat it."*[7]

Dindigal—Self-Enquiry Begins

When he was eleven years old Ramana shifted to Dindigal for his studies, since his uncle Subbier was working there. With his photographic memory Ramana has recalled some of the happenings of those years. There was a big fort in the place which served as an ideal playground. But entry into it was barred by a sentry standing at the gate. So Ramana and his friends would quietly slip in by scaling the wall at the end and jumping down for the fun of it. They would get out by a hole at the back of the wall after enjoying themselves.[1]

Often his sleep in those years was so sound that it is difficult to call it such. It was more akin to *samadhi* for he had no body consciousness even when soundly thrashed. He just could not be woken up. Later, at Ramanasramam, Ramana narrated dramatically what happened one night when all the family members had gone out for a marriage leaving him behind.

In the afternoon, Bhagavan saw a young relative of his, in the hall. He said: "*Seeing you reminds me of something that happened in Dindigal when I was a boy. Your uncle, Periappa Seshaiyar, was living there then. There was some function in the house and all went to it and then in the night went to the temple. I was left alone in the house. I was sitting and reading in the front room, but after a while I locked the front door and fastened the windows and went to sleep. When they returned from the temple no amount of shouting or banging at the door or the window could wake me. At last they managed to open the door with a key from the opposite house and then they tried to wake me up by* beating me. All the boys and your uncle beat me to their heart's content, but without effect. I knew nothing about it till they told me next morning."[2]

This situation continued even in Madurai, where he shifted when his uncle was transferred there. "*The same sort of thing happened to me in Madurai too. The boys didn't dare touch me when I was awake, but if they had any grudge against me they would come when I was asleep and carry me wherever they liked and beat me as much as they liked and then put me back to bed, and I would know nothing about it until they told me in the morning.*"[3]

When Ramana was twelve years old, in 1892, his father Sundaram Iyer died. On the day of the cremation, for several hours Ramana enquired into the meaning of life and death. Paul Brunton has recorded what Ramana told him about his enquiry on that tragic day.

"On the day his father died he felt puzzled by death and pondered over it, whilst his mother and brothers wept. He thought for hours and after the corpse was cremated he got by analysis to the point of perceiving that it was the 'I' which makes the body to see, to run, to walk and to eat. '*I now know this "I" but my father's "I" has left the body*'"[4]

Quite obviously the constant awareness of Arunachala-Siva in his heart was cutting at the illusion of a separate individuality, his ego-sense. One can also say that this was an indication of the things to come, a fore-runner of his enlightenment, which was to happen four years later at Madurai.

Tank and *gopurams* of the Meenakshi temple in Madurai

The thousand-pillared hall of the Meenakshi temple in Madurai

Madurai

On the death of Ramana's father Sundaram Iyer, in 1892, the family split up. Azhagammal, and the younger children went to Manamadurai, to live with Nelliappa Iyer. Nagaswami and Ramana stayed with their other uncle Subbier, in Chokkappa Naicken Street, near the Minakshi temple. Ramana studied initially in the Scott's Middle School and later in the American Mission High School. He was not studious but his memory helped him through. He was a natural leader and he excelled in every sport, particularly football and swimming. A schoolmate, Subbiah Thevar, recalls how at night both Ramana and his brother would manage to leave the house along with them and spend several hours either playing in the sands of the Vaigai river or engaging in swimming contests in Pillaiyarpaliam tank.[1]

Another classmate Sab Jaan recalls how Ramana was injured once in a football game and made his friends anxious because of the resultant high fever. Sab Jaan also recounts that during the weekends they would visit a renowned temple of Lord Subrahmanya and that Ramana would say, *"God's creation is alike and there is no differentiation in creation. God is the same. The apparent differences were created by man."*[2]

Another side of Ramana is mentioned by his classmate Narayanaswami. He recalls that the terrace of the house and the small room on the first floor[3] were va-

cant and rarely used by the families in the ground floor. Narayanaswami remembers that "he used to see his friend sit still for long stretches of time in the small room on the first floor."[4] On one occasion he asked if he could do likewise. On hearing this Ramana made him squat on the floor with his legs crossed and pressed a pencil midway between the eyebrows. Narayanaswami was lost in a trance for about half an hour. When he got up he saw Ramana smiling at him brightly.[5]

Ramana and his friends would often play hide and seek and other games in the third-story of Varada Perumal temple.[6]

In his younger years Ramana used to be called "Tangakkai" (one with golden hands). Once he explained how he got this name. *"At all times and in all games, I used to win invariably, were it wrestling or swimming or even domestic chores. If my aunt began preparing appalams, or such like, she would call me and ask me to put my hand on it first. She had great faith in me because I would do everything according to her wishes and never told lies."*[7]

Ramana got a small helping of a particular sweet dish, prepared as an offering, on one of his visits to Alagar Koil near Madurai. He enjoyed it very much and wished to have more of it. On his next visit after the worship was over, a priest, who had a large quantity of this dish as his share, off-loaded it on Ramana to be carried to his house, which was some distance away. Ramana was thus forced to trudge a long way with a heavy load of the sweet dish on his head. Recalling it Ramana remarked, *"You know how heavy it was! All the muscles of my neck began to ache.... I felt it was a punishment for my wanting to have some more pongal last time I came."*[8]

In 1895, when Ramana was fifteen years old, the first call of Arunachala came. He was not aware that Arunachala was a sacred hill in Tiruvannamalai. He met an elderly relative from Tiruchuzhi at Madurai and asked where he was coming from. "From Arunachala," was the reply. For the first time he became aware that it was a place on earth. Excited by the knowledge he asked the relative, *"What! From Arunachala? Where is that?"*[9] The relative wondering how he could be so ignorant informed him that it was Tiruvannamalai. Ramana was to be drawn there, irresistibly, less than a year later, under a divine compulsion.

At about the same time, *Periyapuranam*, the lives of sixty-three Saivite saints, came into Ramana's hands. *"The book happened to be in our house and coming across it, I looked into it out of curiosity and then becoming interested, read the whole book."*[10] It moved and inspired him no end. They were stories filled with yearning for God, as the saints were soaked in devotional fervor and faith.

The Day Before

You have withheld from me all knowledge of gradual attainment while living in the world setting me at peace; such care indeed is blissful and not painful, for death in life is in truth glorious.[1]
— Bhagavan Ramana

The day before Ramana's enlightenment, therefore, assumes great importance. What was Ramana's state of mind on July 16, 1896, just a day before his enlightenment? Narasimha Swami, his first biographer, has recorded a statement of Ramana about this. Ramana had told him, *"At that time, I had no idea of the identity of that current of my personality with personal God or Iswara as I used to term him. I had not even heard of Bhagavad Gita or other religious works. Except Periyapuranam and the Bible class texts, the Gospels and Psalms. I had not read any other religious books. I had just seen, with my uncle, a copy of Vivekananda's Chicago address but had not read it. I could not even correctly pronounce the Swami's name but pronounced it Vyvekananda giving the 'i' the 'y' sound. I had no notions of religious philosophy, except the current notion of God that he is an infinitely powerful person, present everywhere, though worshipped in special places in images representing him and other ideas which are contained in the Bible text or Periyapuranam which I had read."*[2]

From this it is clear that Ramana had deep faith in God and his omnipotence. However, he had not studied any of the scriptures in a systematic manner nor had he received any special instructions from his elders. In later years he could refer to certain fundamental passages in the Bible while clarifying the doubts of the seekers because of the Bible classes which he had attended while at school. His study of the *Periyapuranam* covering the life of sixty-three Saivite saints had left a great impact on his mind about the devotional fervor of these saints. Even so it is clear that his scriptural knowledge and the practice of it was hardly enough to prepare him for the enlightenment which happened the next day.

This is quite surprising because when the fullness of knowledge dawns one is completely taken over by the divine and is in its total embrace. Technically called *sakti-patana*,[3] one's body and mind, one's sense of separate individual existence, would be lost in the infinite ocean of bliss. One would have become "food unto God." Thereafter every single pore of one's body would be permeated by that supreme presence. Unless one is ready to receive this overwhelming manifestation of the divine grace, both the body and mind would go haywire. Therefore one has to go deeper and find out the factors responsible for this great awakening of Ramana.

The Ramana *mandiram*: house in which Ramana achieved enlightenment

Attention is to be drawn to his *samadhi*-like sleep when he was totally oblivious to the existence of his body for many hours.[4]

One should also remember Ramana's first association with death and what its implication was, when his

The small upstairs room in Ramana *mandiram*

father died in 1892. At that time by deep introspection he had arrived at the conclusion that his father's "I" had left the body while his "I" was in his body making for the difference between life and death.[5]

One must give due significance to the fact mentioned by Ramana in one of his autobiographical verses on Arunachala that from his "*unthinking infancy the immensity of Arunachala had shone in his awareness.*"[6] Here one has to remember that Arunachala is regarded as the embodiment of Lord Siva, the greatest of *Yogis*. It is said that even the thought of Arunachala has the power to liberate a person. In Ramana's case he was in constant awareness of it from his infancy. In his mind Arunachala surpassed all grandeur. It may be because of this that in later years Ramana referred to Arunachala as his *guru*. For it is the *guru* who guides one on the path to Self-realization.

Therefore, despite appearances to the contrary, Ramana was already totally ripe and ready for the

awakening of Self-knowledge which happened next day spontaneously. His enlightenment, on the following day, July 17, 1896, has served to demonstrate to the entire humanity that, given the necessary passion for the goal of Self-knowledge and Ramana's guidance for it through the direct path of self-enquiry taught by him, discovery of the truth about oneself would be *"very easy," "very easy"* indeed.

❧

Enlightenment—July 17, 1896

There is a first person account by Ramana of his enlightenment. "*One day I was alone in the first floor of my uncle's house. I was in my usual state of health. But a sudden and unmistakable fear of death seized me. I felt I was going to die. Why I should have so felt cannot now be explained by anything felt in the body. I did not however trouble myself to discover if the fear was well grounded. I did not care to consult doctors or elders or even friends. I felt I had to solve the problem myself then and there.*"[1]

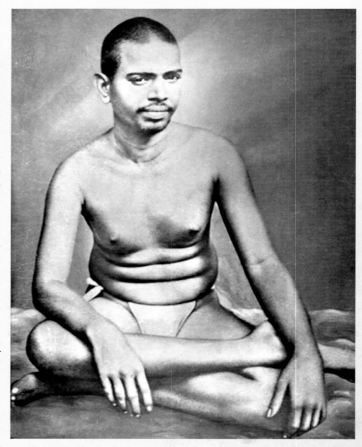

"*The actual inquiry and discovery of 'Who am I?' was over on the very first day, after a short time. Instinctively I held my breath and began to dive inward with my inquiry into my own nature…. I stretched myself like a corpse, and it seemed to me that my body had actually become rigid— 'I' was not dead—'I' was on the other hand conscious of being alive, in existence. So the question arose in me, 'What was this "I"?' I felt that it was a force or current working, despite the rigidity or activity of the body, though existing in connection with it. It was that current or force or center that constituted my personality, that kept me acting, moving etc. The fear of death dropped off. I was absorbed in the contemplation of that current. So further development or activity was issuing from the new life and not from any fear.*"[2]

Ramana explained in later years that as soon as he commenced his "*Who am I?*" enquiry "*some force, call it the atmic power or anything else, arose in me and took possession of me.*"[3]

What happened thereafter has also been narrated by Ramana to Narasimha Swami. "*That changed my mental attitude and habits. I had formerly some preferences and aversions. All these dropped off and all food was swallowed with equal indifference. I would put up with every burden imposed on me at home, every slight at my expense by the boys. Studies and duties became a matter of utter indifference and I was going through studies turning over pages mechanically.*"[4]

His awakening gave him the continuous feeling of awareness of the force in which he was "perpetually absorbed, whatever he did, whether he read, walked, spoke, or rested."[5]

The obsession also led to his visiting the temple of Minakshi Sundaresa every day. He would stand, emotion-charged, for a long time before Siva, Nataraja, Minakshi, and sixty-three saints.[6]

The enlightenment was possible because of a massive upsurge of divine grace whose flood-tide swept away all limitations, springing from the ignorance of one's true nature. He was illumined by the powerful grace of Arunachala. Was he not born with the constant remembrance of its grandeur?[7]

After his enlightenment, there was no change in the state of Ramana's steady Self-abidance. It is necessary to clarify this point. For, to the observer, his outward conduct might appear different from time to time. For instance he was visiting the Minakshi temple every day for six weeks, but after reporting his arrival to Arunachaleswara he never stepped inside the temple again. For eleven years from September 1896 to November 1907 he remained silent. For many years he was absorbed inwardly so fully that he did not seem to have any body consciousness at all. In later years he was accessible all the time and has clarified more than thirty thousand doubts. A devotee sought Ramana's explanation for these outward appearances. "We note so many outward changes in you." "*Yes,*" replied Bhagavan, "*that is because you see me as this body. So long as you identify yourself with your body, you cannot but see me as an embodied being.*" He also explained, "*I am ever the same. There is neither* sankalpa, *desire, nor change in me. Till I reached the Mango Cave I remained indifferent with my eyes shut. Afterwards I opened my eyes and am actively functioning. Otherwise there is no change whatsoever in me.*"[8]

Ramana was categoric about the completeness of his experience. Nothing further was revealed. He made this position clear to philosophy professor D.S. Sarma.

Sarma: In Western mysticism three definite stages are often spoken of—viz. purgation, illumination, and union. Was there any such stage as purgation—corresponding to what we call *sadhana*—in Bhagavan's life?

Bhagavan: *I have never done any* sadhana. *I did not even know what* sadhana *was. Only long afterwards I came to know what* sadhana *was and how many different kinds of it there were. It is only if there was any object or anything different from me that I could think of it. Only if there was a goal to attain, I should have made* sadhana *towards that goal. There was nothing which I wanted to obtain. I am now sitting with my eyes open. I was then sitting with my eyes closed. That was all the difference. I was not doing any sadhana even then. As I sat with my eyes closed, people said I was in samadhi. As I was not talking, they said I was in mauna. The fact is I did nothing. Some Higher Power took hold of me and I was entirely in Its hands.*[9]

What happened in 1912 near Tortoise Rock is most significant for understanding the natural state of Ramana since his enlightenment, his uninterrupted awareness of the "I"-consciousness in the heart. His respiration had stopped, his body had become cold, death slowly crept on his body. This happened for about some ten or fifteen minutes. While narrating this incident Ramana said, *"Yet my usual current was continuing, without a break in that state also."*[10]

The Father's Command

The moment I thought of your name, you caught and drew me to yourself.
Who can know the greatness of your grace Arunachala?[1]

—*Bhagavan Ramana*

It was on August 29, 1896, about six weeks after his enlightenment. Ramana's indifference to his studies thereafter received numerous reprimands from his uncle and jeers from his brother Nagaswami. That day he began writing the imposition given to him to copy certain portions from *Bain's English Grammar*. He had to do so thrice. After he wrote it twice the futility of it struck him with great force. He stopped writing and lapsed into meditation drawn by the divine current within. Seeing this his brother remarked, "Why should one, who behaves thus, retain all this?" This was not the first occasion that he had taunted him thus. But this time the truth of the remark went home. Ramana regarded it as the command from his father Arunachala. He could no longer stay at home. So Ramana decided to leave his home for Tiruvannamalai.

He informed his brother Nagaswami that he had to attend a special class in electricity at school. He said, "Well then, do not fail to take five rupees from the box below and to pay my college fees in the college near your school." Arunachala had provided him with the money needed for the journey. He went down, gulped a quick meal served by his aunt who gave him five rupees. Then he hastily looked up an atlas which, unfortunately, was outdated, and thought that the nearest station to

Tiruvannamalai was Tindivanam. Actually in 1892 itself the Villipuram-Tiruvannamalai-Katpadi branch line had been opened. He then estimated that three rupees would be sufficient for the fare. He left the balance of two rupees in the box itself along with a parting letter[2] which reads:

in search of my Father and I have, in obedience to his command, started from here. THIS is only embarking on a virtuous enterprise. Therefore none need grieve over THIS affair: To trace THIS out, no money need be spent.

Your college fee has not yet been paid. Rupees two are enclosed herewith   *Thus,*

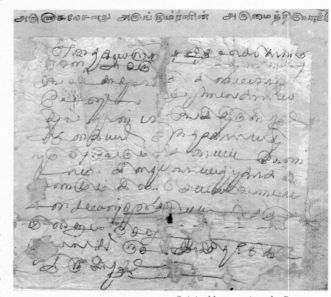

Original letter written by Ramana

The letter was not signed, for his separate identity as Venkataraman had been lost after the discovery that his true identity was the divine current in the heart. The omission of a signature is clearly not due to lack of time in the hurry to catch the train. There has been time to inscribe a series of dashes in lieu of the signature, and thereafter to add even a postscript, to inform the brother about his unpaid college fee, and the balance of money left. Even these later lines are all impersonal, *"Your college fee has not been paid"* says the postscript, but does not add by whom. There is no such phrase as "by me" or "by this." And lastly about the two rupees left, reference is made to the inert silver lying with the letter. It is purely impersonal. How eloquent are these indications of the alteration in his personality! Later Ramana told Kapali Sastri in 1929, *"You see in the letter at home at the time of starting, I first wrote 'in obedience to his command' and interposed above it 'in search of my father and' because it is he who drew me. I wrote that and started. The finding of funds was not my act. My brother of his own accord did it.*"[3]

The word "search" might appear dualistic. But one must remember in this context that Ramana had heard about Tiruvannamalai for the first time from a relative and no further data about how to reach the place. His looking up the old atlas for locating the place is indicative of this. Ramana had never traveled on his own to any new place and the journey also indicates that he had to make enquiries to reach the destination. The words *"in obedience to father's command"* are used, for after his enlightenment, Ramana had no will or volition of his own, and was acting only according to the dictates of providence.

After writing the letter, Ramana hurriedly walked to the station as the scheduled time of departure for his train was 11.45 a.m. and it was already 12 noon when he could leave. Since Ramana had left home as per the divine commandment it was its duty to ensure that he reached the destination. Hence, though he was late, the train too was late. He bought a ticket to Tindivanam and three annas was returned to him as the balance. Had he looked at the railway timetable he would have noticed that a few stations below, Tiruvannamalai had been mentioned and the fare was exactly three rupees which he had taken. His body had to suffer more hardships though his mind was immersed in bliss.

One or two stations after Madurai an old Maulvi with a flowing beard asked him, "Where are you going Swami?" Ramana replied. *"To Tiruvannamalai and I have a ticket up to Tindivanam."* Hearing this the co-passenger told him, "You are a queer passenger to go to Tindivanam for Tiruvannamalai. I am also going there and we should change the train at Villipuram." The Father had provided the requisite information. Ramana recalled later that this person had told him that he was going to Tirukoilur but strangely enough he missed him when after some stations he looked in the carriage.[4]

Then, till about sunset he remained absorbed in the Self. When the train reached Tiruchirapalli junction he felt hungry and purchased two country pears. But strangely his hunger was satisfied with just a little bite of one of the fruits. He had a hearty appetite. This was therefore quite surprising. He went back to his state of natural *samadhi*. At about 3 a.m. the train reached Villipuram, where he alighted. After day break he went round the streets of the place to find the direction to Tiruvannamalai for it was obvious that he had to walk the rest of the distance. The sign posts indicated only the place Mambalapattu, which was en route. Tired by his wanderings he felt hungry and went to a hotel but had to wait for several hours for the lunch time which was at noon. The owner of the hotel was greatly impressed by the golden complexioned teenager, with asceticism writ large on his face, with ruby earrings, and jet black locks

Ariyaninallur temple

of hair. After his meal Ramana offered the little change he had. The hotel owner waived the amount due for the meal. Ramana returned to the station and with the change left with him he purchased a ticket to Mambalapattu which he reached by 3 p.m. in the afternoon. Thirty miles still separated him from his Father's home. He had no option except to walk the distance. By nightfall he reached the Ariyaninallur temple after walking ten miles. Tired by the walk and heat he waited for the temple to be opened. When it was opened, Ramana entered and sat down in the pillared hall, the only portion which was not yet quite dark. He immediately beheld a brilliant light covering the whole temple. He thought that it must be from the main shrine of the deity but found it was not. It disappeared and he continued in his usual state. After worship he asked the priest for something to eat. He was told that he might get some food at the nearby temple in Kilur. So he went there, where again after the worship the priest refused to give him food. But the drummer, seeing the boy's plight and his ascetic behavior, offered his share to him. Ramana was thirsty and he was asked to go to

a nearby place to get water. As he walked there with the rice on a leaf plate, overcome by exhaustion he fainted. When he came around shortly thereafter, a small crowd had gathered. He drank the water given to him, collected the scattered rice, ate it, and then lay down on the bare ground and slept. Even the most stone-hearted cannot but be moved to tears at the plight of this illumined one's body that night.

The next morning, August 31, was Gokulashtami, an important festival day in honor of Lord Krishna. Ramana stopped at random at a house which happened to be that of Muthukrishna Bhagavatar and asked for food. The couple were delighted to have a *brahmin* youth with luminous eyes as their guest on that day. The lady of the house gave him a large meal right away and insisted affectionately on his having the whole of it. The only possession which Ramana had was his earrings which he pledged for four rupees with the Bhagavatar, who insisted on giving him a receipt and his address. Ramana tore up the slip after leaving his house. Before Ramana left, he was lovingly given lunch as well as a packet of sweets for the journey. Since there was no train till the next morning he slept at the station. What hardships his sacred body had to undergo for obeying his Father's command.

Advent at Arunachala

Arunachala, my loving lord, place your garland on my shoulders and wear this my garland on your own.[1]

—*Bhagavan Ramana*

It was the morning of September 1, 1896, when Ramana reached his Father's home, Arunachala. The command had been obeyed. The search had ended. Thereafter there was no parting ever.

Heart brimming with love, Ramana went straightaway to the Arunachaleswara temple. This temple was the very center of attraction of the pilgrims. But strangely it was empty though all the doors were open. None was there in the inner shrine too. The Lord was waiting to receive his son, born to proclaim his glory and power, to proclaim the direct path for Self-knowledge. Ramana

View of Arunachaleswara temple

Ritual shaving of hair at the Ayyankulam tank as performed today

could go into the *sanctum sanctorum* unhindered. Just the Father and the son together in holy union never again to part physically. *"Father, I have come,"* Ramana said. More words were superfluous. Thanks to the overflowing grace of Arunachala the schoolboy became the enlightened *jnani* Ramana at Madurai. This had happened on July 17, 1896. Now the physical separation too ended. It could not be otherwise as his task as a universal *guru* was to be performed from this one place.

As Ramana left the temple, someone accosted him and wished to know if he would like to have his hair cut. When he said "yes," he was taken to Ayyankulam tank where there was a congregation of barbers. One of them completely shaved off his lovely locks of jet-black hair. This was symbolic of Ramana having renounced the world. Then Ramana threw away his sacred thread and balance of money which he had and the sweets which had been given to him the previous day by the pious couple at Kilur. He never again touched money in his life. By his actions Ramana had renounced attachment to caste and to money, outwardly as well.

Ramana then took off the *dhoti* he was wearing, tore a portion of it to serve as his cod-piece and threw the rest away. Even when he was exposed to the elements, to the sun, rain, and cold, Ramana wore only a cod-piece for the rest of his life.

Though traditionally one would have a bath after a shave, Ramana simply thought it was an unnecessary luxury for his body. But a sharp shower drenched him before he re-entered the temple. That night there was a heavy downpour.

While talking about the rain on the night of the Golden Jubilee of his arrival,[2] Ramana recalled, "*I remember the same thing happened on the night of 1.9.1896 when I arrived here. It seems they had no rains for a long time then. But on that night there was a heavy downpour. I was then staying at the* mandapam *in front of the Big Temple. Only that morning for the first time I had discarded all my clothes, except a cod-piece, and on account of the rains beating in, and the cold winds blowing about, I found the cold unbearable; and so I ran from there and took shelter on the pial of the house nearby. About midnight some inmates of the house came out opening the street door and I ran into the Big Temple. For some days after that, too, it rained!*"[3]

As days passed, the thick growth of hair, which had got matted and woven like a basket, made his head heavy. When a suggestion was made for having his head shaven Ramana readily agreed. This was about a year-and-a-half after his arrival. For awhile he had a feeling of having no head![4]

Ramana also recalled some other incidents relating to the early period of his stay in the temple. In the first four months of his stay he had no bath. One day the wife of a devotee forcibly gave him a bath. "*After I came to this place, Tiruvannamalai, I had no bath for four months. One day, when I was in the compound of the Arunachala temple, the wife of a devotee by name Ponnuswami came unexpectedly, pulled me along, made me sit, cleaned my head with soap-nut powder and gave me a bath. She had been coming to the temple every now and then: so I had thought that she had come as usual, but that day she had come there prepared! That was my first bath.*"[5]

Similarly while he was staying in Gurumurtam another lady, Minakshi, also forcibly gave him a badly needed bath as his head got matted due to neglect. "*After that Palaniswami came and everything was adjusted into a routine of daily baths.*"[6]

View of Arunachaleswara temple

The son had returned home. People were to witness the intensity of his penance, the immensity of his silence, his utter absence of body consciousness, and his total unconcern for the body. The devotees could see it for themselves since he remained in the various parts of the Arunachaleswara temple itself for nearly a year after reporting his arrival to his Father, Arunachala.

Section II: Penance

Penance

The natural state is free from sloth. One established firmly in it is incessantly performing the most difficult penance, spontaneously.[1]
—*Bhagavan Ramana*

From the onlooker's point of view, Ramana's state seems to have three or four distinct outward landmarks. The first period was the first six weeks after his enlightenment, when he was virtually hiding his momentous experience and supreme wisdom. The mantle of the student was not discarded, and the family members were not allowed to have any idea of his state. Whenever possible Ramana would be immersed in the Self.

The next stage may be said to be the period from his arrival at Tiruvannamalai on September 1, 1896, till November 18, 1907, when he broke his silence to instruct Ganapati Muni on the meaning of *tapas*. The doubts of all earnest seekers would be answered, but their numbers were not large. There were long spells of immense and powerful silence.

The third and final stage was in the forties when seekers from all over the world and of all religions came in their thousands to seek Ramana's counsel—the doors were always open to one and all. In this period too there would be those indrawn hours but they were less frequent.

The fourth is the post-*nirvana* years when his continued presence as the unfailing "living *guru*" is apparent to seekers of truth.

It is necessary to make the point clear for one is apt to be misguided by the outer appearances into thinking that there are some differences in Ramana's state of natural *samadhi*. Ramana himself has clarified the correct position categorically, when specifically questioned about his *sadhana*.[2]

The outward differences in Ramana's conduct should not be taken to indicate any need for or any change in Ramana's state after his enlightenment. It was always the same steady abidance in the Self. It is against this background that one is to view Ramana's life story after his enlightenment. As mentioned before, whatever differences there may be for the onlookers, Ramana was steadily in the natural state. One who is so firmly established is in the constant state of penance. Such penance, however, is spontaneous and effortless.

The first place where he did this spontaneous penance was in the thousand-pillared hall in the front portion of the Arunachaleswara temple. There he sat oblivious to his body, fully immersed in the bliss of the Self. He was not aware either of the passage of day or night. However, since he was still a teenager, the urchins around the temple could not understand his state. They would attempt to disturb him by pelting stones at him and enjoy troubling him. Seshadri Swami, who had come to Tiruvannamalai earlier, tried to protect him but it was not of much help.

In order to avoid this Ramana just moved into the Patalalingam, an underground vault in the thousand-pillared hall. It was dark and damp. The rays of the sun

Inside the Patalalingam shrine

21

never penetrated its darkness. It was seldom that any human beings entered that place. Only ants, vermin, and mosquitoes flourished there. They preyed upon him and his thighs were covered with sores that ran with blood and pus. The underground vault served to free him from stone missiles of the misguided youth and he remained immersed in the bliss of being. However, after some

The thousand-pillared hall

time the urchins were emboldened and started pelting stones into the pit. Fortunately this was noticed one day by Venkatachala Mudali who reports thus: "One day, going near the thousand-pillared hall, I found a group of boys hurling stones in the direction of the pit. Enraged at the sight, I seized a twig, and ran towards the young scamps who fled promptly. Suddenly from the dark recesses of the hall there issued forth the figure of Seshadri. I was taken aback, but soon recovering myself, enquired of the Swami if the stones pelted by the boys had hurt him. 'Oh no,' replied the Swami, 'but go and see the Chinnaswami there.' He pointed towards the pit and went away. Proceeding inside, I could make out nothing for a while, as I was coming from the glare into the darkness. In a few minutes, the faint outlines of a young face became discernible in that pit. Somewhat frightened, I went out to the adjoining flower-garden where a *sadhu* was working with his disciples. Mentioning the facts to them I took some of them with me. Even then the youthful figure sat motionless

and with closed eyes, despite the noise of our footsteps. Then we lifted the Swami from the pit, carried him from the hall up the flight of steps and deposited him in front of a shrine of Subrahmanya. The Swami still remained unconscious, his eyes closed, evidently he was in deep *samadhi*. We noticed the large number of sores on either side of his thighs and legs, with blood and pus flowing from some of them, and wondered how anyone could remain unconscious of his body amidst such torture. Regarding it as irreverence, nay impertinence, to make any further noise in such a presence, we bowed and came away."[3]

Ramana stayed at the Subrahmanya shrine for a couple of months. He would sit motionless in *samadhi* and was looked after by one of the mendicants in the temple, the Mouni Swami. Ramana then moved to a place of tall oleander bushes, a dense alley of oleander (arali trees) with cut off stems projecting. *"Occasionally I would sit under one tree and wake up much further inside. I must have passed through these projecting stems in my unconscious condition. Yet I was not hurt at any time."*[4]

The Vahana Mantapam

Ramana then moved to Vahana Mantapam or the place reserved for the temple vehicles. He recalls, *"I would edge through the narrow passage between the vahanas, the tallest in that mantapam or the interiormost, to escape attention. I would seat myself under the belly of a vahana. I would lose consciousness of the body then and sometimes find, when awake, that I had got to the 10th row. I must have crept into it like a lizard. Whether I did so or some-*

thing carried me in I did not know. Strangely enough, on not a single occasion did these crawlings or movements produce even a scratch on my person.[5]

Gurumurtam

In November/December 1896, a large crowd gathered in Tiruvannamalai and in the Arunachaleswara temple during the Kartigai festival. Consequently large gatherings used to surround the silent youthful sage Ramana. Among them was one Uddandi Nayanar. Seeing Ramana immersed always in *samadhi*, unaware of his body, he felt that he could attain peace of mind by association with

Though Uddandi Nayanar took upon himself the duty of being Ramana's attendant he was often forced to be away, during which time Ramana remained uncared for and unattended. The mischievous boys would take this opportunity of troubling Ramana again. "One day, while he was engrossed in *samadhi* at the foot of the illupai tree, a mischievous boy noticing that no one was around, eased himself on Ramana's body, dirtying and wetting his cod-piece. The young Swami was quite unaware of what had happened. Sometime later, when his consciousness revived he wondered why the rags should be wet. Then from the smell he gathered that some little fellow must have played a prank upon him though no boy was by his side at that time. There was no anger at such treatment."[2]

Gurumurtam

him. Therefore he took upon himself the job of being an attendant to protect Ramana from the crowd of sightseers and prevent persecution by urchins. We may say he was the first attendant of Ramana.

Uddandi Nayanar hailed from Tiruvani village near Tiruvannamalai. A well-built rustic, he made a modest living by plying his double bullock cart moving people and goods between towns. He was very pious and well versed in reciting Vedic texts in Tamil like *Jnana Vasistam* and *Kaivalya Navanitam*.[1]

At this stage the divine took a hand in protecting Ramana from such a situation. One Annamalai Tambiran noticed Ramana. He was immediately impressed by the luster of the Self radiating from the face of Ramana. Tambiran was in charge of his *guru's* tomb, Gurumurtam, near Tiruvannamalai. He consulted Nayanar and both of them decided that it would be best that Ramana should shift to Gurumurtam where he could be better looked after. When this suggestion was made to him he attempted to get up. Noticing this "they happily helped him to his feet and took him to Gurumurtam."[3]

Bhagavan has given a detailed account of his stay in Gurumurtam when questioned about it by Narasimha Swami. This is what he has told him.

"Days and nights would pass without my being aware of their passing. I entertained no idea of bathing or clean-

திருவண்ணாமலை பிராஹ்மணசுவாமிக ளென்கிற
ஸ்ரீ ரமண மஹார்ஷிகள்.

ing of teeth or other cleansing activities even when I had defecated and had no baths. The face got begrimed, the hair had become one clotted mass like wax and the nails grew long. When anyone thought that I should have food, I would stretch a hand and something would drop on my hand. My hands were not useful for any other purpose. I would eat and rub my hand on my head or body and drop

again into my continuous mood. This was my condition for some years from the time of my arrival. For many years I ate only off my hand without using any leaf plate.

"While at Gurumurtam, I had a fairly large number of persons calling to see me and in a sense a reputation had been established. A number of persons wished that I should eat what each of them had brought every day. The difficulty of eating all was solved this way. A bit of what each of them had brought, be it solid or liquid, sweet or salted, fruit or rice, all would be taken up and mixed into a sort of sauce and given to me as a cupful. This would be my night meal and I would drink it not minding how this compound mixture tasted.

"I was very much constipated while at Gurumurtam. I would pass hard, solid, steel-like square blocks. I would just sit somewhere and after some time try to get up. I would raise myself from my haunches, half a foot at a time and at once feel faint and giddy and resume my old position. Sometime later I would try to get up and raise myself a foot or so then feel the same reeling sensation and sit down again. On one such occasion after many such failures I got up and tried to go out and was clutching the front door. Then Palaniswami came and held me in his embrace. I turned to him and asked him (through sign language) why he behaved thus. He said that he noticed that I was about to fall and so he had seized me to prevent the fall. But I was holding to the door with both my hands outstretched and was not aware that I was about to fall. This difficulty of getting up on account of reeling was a constant feature of my life at Gurumurtam."[4]

Narasimha Swami continues the narration thus: "As Swami continued to neglect his comfort, and even cleanliness, he rose in popular esteem. His body was besmeared with unwashed dirt, his hair became a clotted mass, and his fingernails grew so long and curly that his hands were not useful for any purpose. He sat for some weeks on a floor which was always infested by ants, and despite their constant crawling and biting, he sat for hours with eyes closed, leaning against the wall in *samadhi*, and left on it the imprint of his back. The visitors could not endure for even a few minutes the ants, which he endured for hours, days, and weeks, losing his body consciousness. The Swami was therefore provided after some time with a stool in a corner, the feet of the stool being placed in water. But even then his leaning on the wall gave the ants their access to him. People swarmed to see this height of self-neglect. Some said: 'This Swami must be very old,' and pointed to the length of his nails as proof. Many people jumped to the conclusion that, being so saintly, he could grant them all the boons they desired, such as wealth, health, issue, and salvation, and poured praises into his ears and offerings at his feet."[5]

Once Tambiran overdid his reverence. He wished to perform *abhisheka* (worship by pouring water on the head, which is done for deities). His living deity was Ramana. He gathered the requisite material required for it, namely oil, sandal paste, etc. Noticing this Ramana took a piece of charcoal and wrote on the wall nearby his seat thus. *"This (food) alone is service needed for this body."* Ramana meant that looking after his body was sufficient. Tambiran understood the wishes which were clearly written on the wall and he refrained from any outward show of his inner feelings towards Ramana. Since Ramana had written in correct Tamil, people understood for the first time that he was educated and this was the first step towards his being discovered by his relatives.[6]

Amongst the people who held Ramana in great reverence there was one Venkatarama Aiyer, Head Accountant in the Government Taluk Office at Tiruvannamalai. Having discovered that Ramana was educated he decided to find out more about his birthplace and other details. For this purpose he insistently stayed at Gurumurtam and went on a hunger strike to achieve his object. Ramana was always compassionate. Perhaps he also felt that it was the correct time for the news about his whereabouts to be known to his mother who must have been in anguish without any information about him. In this sense he allowed himself to be discovered. The hunger strike provided a good reason to reveal his birthplace. Ramana wrote on the wall, "Venkataraman, Tiruchuzhi." When Venkatarama Aiyer wondered where Tiruchuzhi was, Ramana picked up a copy of *Periyapuranam* which was nearby. It related an account of the visit of Sundaramurthy, one of the famous Saivite saints, to the temple of Siva called "Bhuminatha" in that village. This disclosure led before long to his being discovered by his relatives.[7]

A little after Ramana shifted to Gurumurtam, Palaniswami joined him as the permanent attendant. Anyone who knows the life story of Ramana would feel indebted to Palaniswami for the more than mother's care given by him in protecting Ramana's body. From Gurumurtam days till Ramana shifted to Skandasramam in 1917, for seventeen long years he was the instrument of the divine for protecting Ramana's body.

Ramana would be without any consciousness of the body lost in the inner bliss most of the time. At those times this protection was very valuable. Palaniswami would also regularly beg for alms and cook for himself and Ramana.

The story of how Palaniswami joined Ramana is interesting. He was from Kerala and was worshipping the image of Lord Ganesa in Tiruvannamalai town. One Srinivasa Iyer, seeing his capacity for devotion and also being aware of the need to protect Ramana's body, advised him thus, "What is the use of spending your life with this stone swami? There is a young swami in flesh and blood at Gurumurtam. He is steeped in austerities like the youthful Dhruva, mentioned in the *puranams*. If you go and serve him and adhere to him, your life would serve its purpose." Others also mentioned to Palaniswami about the glorious state of Ramana, who needed a full-time attendant to look after his body. At his very first visit itself, Palaniswami was certain that he had discovered his *guru* and savior. For a little while he continued his worship at the temple of Ganesa. Later he felt that Ganesa himself had led him to Ramana and spent his full time with him like a shadow.[8]

Palaniswami

Arunagirinathar Temple—
Pachaiamman Koil

Ramana has crossed the fearsome ocean of misery and stands on its other shore, uses His hands soft as lotus to serve Him as a bowl, chases away fear from those who take refuge at His lotus-feet, by a single refreshing glance.[1]

—Ganapati Muni

There were two short spells when Ramana begged for alms in the streets. The first was before he shifted to Gurumurtam and the other after he left it. The first time he begged for alms, he stood before the house of one of the younger priests. Though there was no feeling of abasement, due to his upbringing and habit, he felt bashful. Sometimes he would get only stale gruel at a house. He would take it even without salt or any other flavoring, in the open street, then wipe his hands on his head and pass on happily.

The second period was in August-September, 1898, when he begged for alms after he left Gurumurtam. At that time he was staying in the Arunagirinathar temple. The first person whose house he visited was that of one Krishna Iyer who was playing cards when Ramana clapped his hands. He hurriedly mixed some rice and gave him alms. Ramana would mostly beg at night. He would accept only two or three handfuls of food from a few houses and return. Ramana had become well known even in his Gurumurtam days. Hence people used to wait hoping that he would come to their house for alms.

To avoid disappointing them he would cover different portions of the street each day. As a result he practically covered every single house in the street opposite the temple.[2]

Ramana also had two forced lunches. The first was in the house of the grandfather of T.P. Ramachandra Iyer. It happened in 1896. At that time Ramana was staying in one of the temples in the Arunachaleswara temple complex. T.P.R.'s grandfather would come daily and stay for a while and leave. There was no conversation since Ramana was silent.

Ramana recalled what happened one afternoon. *"In the noon, before meal time, he came to me with another person. Standing on either side they said, 'Swami, get up. Let us go.' 'Why?' I enquired by signs. They told the purpose. I refused. But would they go? They were prepared to carry me in their arms forcibly.... I knew they were inviting me with great devotion. So, thinking it was no use arguing with them I walked with them."*[3] The other forced meal was at the Isanya Math. This was in his Virupaksha years. Ramana labeled it a "funny story" and narrated it humorously. *"One day when Palaniswami and myself went round the hill and came near the temple it was 8 p.m. As we were tired, I lay down in the Subrahmanya temple. Palani went out to fetch food from the* choultry. *He (the head of the* mutt*) was going into the temple. As usual there were a number of disciples around him. One of them saw me and*

Pachaiamman shrine

told them about it. That was enough. While returning, he came with ten of his disciples and stood around me. He began saying, 'Get up Swami. We shall go.' I was in mouna then, so I showed by signs that I wouldn't accompany them. Was he the man to listen to me? 'Lift him up bodily, lift,' he said to his disciples. As there was no alternative, I got up. When I came out, there was a bandy ready. 'Get in, Swami,' he said. I declined and showed them by signs that I would prefer to walk and suggested that he should get into the bandy. He took no notice of my protestations. Instead, he told his disciples, 'What are you looking at? Lift Swami and put him in the cart.' There were ten of them and I was alone. What could I do? They lifted me bodily and put me into the cart. Without saying anything more, I went to the mutt. He had a big leaf spread out for me, filled it with food of all kinds, showed great respect and began saying 'Please stay here always.' Palaniswami went to the temple, enquired about me, and then came to the mutt. After he came, I somehow managed to escape from them."[4]

After Ramana moved over to Virupaksha Cave in 1899, for about six months he had to shift to Pachaiamman Koil, due to the outbreak of plague in Tiruvannamalai. One is almost reduced to tears while reading about the tattered condition of the only cod-piece and towel Ramana had at that time. To Ramana of course it was a matter of indifference as could be seen from the humorous way he has narrated this fact. *"When I was at Pachaiamman Koil, I had a small towel which was tattered and torn, almost to rags, with threads having come out in most places. Once a cowherd boy made fun of this torn rag by telling me, 'The governor wants this towel.' I replied, 'Tell him I won't give it to him!' I never used to spread it out in public. I used to keep it rolled into a ball and wipe my body, hands, or mouth as the occasion demanded with the towel so rolled up into a ball. I used to wash it and dry it in a place between two rocks, which place was never visited by any of those who were with me. Even my cod-piece was tattered. When the top end used to become worn out, I would reverse the cod-piece and use it with the bottom end topmost. When going into the forest*

I would secretly mend my cod-piece with thread taken out of it with prickly pear thorn for needle."[5]

When the devotees discovered the sorry state of his towel and the cod-piece they were filled with remorse at their neglect.

During the plague, the staff in charge of disinfection used to visit Ramana frequently. They had invited Ramana for a session of devotional singing after their work was over. All of a sudden they turned up after making elaborate preparations for the same. Ramana had to go and was duly garlanded and honored. This is the only public function Ramana attended in his fifty-four years stay at Tiruvannamalai.

Section III: Virupaksha Years

Virupaksha Years, 1899-1916

The formless and imperishable Real stands revealed in the Aruna Hill, the embodied Presence of the three-eyed God. Since the Cave named Virupaksha sustains the very devotees who dwell within the Heart-cave of that God, well may we call it Mother.[1]

—*Bhagavan Ramana*

Ramana stayed in the Virupaksha Cave for seventeen years from 1899 to 1916. Ramana was just a young lad of twenty years when he shifted from Gurumurtam to the Virupaksha Cave. Ramana's feelings towards this cave are expressed in the stray verse extracted above. He considers it appropriate to call it "Mother" because it sustains the very devotees who give themselves wholly to the Aruna Hill, the embodied form of Lord Siva.

This cave is situated on the eastern slopes of the Aruna Hill. It is a unique cave, which has the shape of the mystic syllable "Om." It is named after Virupaksha Deva, a saint who lived and has been buried there in the 13th century. Many momentous events in Ramana's life took place during the years of his stay here. It was here that his mother Azhagammal came to live with him permanently in the last years of her life. She surrendered herself totally to him and was guided by him on the inward path. Her liberation at the sacred hands of Ramana is an epoch-making event.[2]

Another event of immense significance is Ramana's "first spoken *upadesa*" to a disciple, which was given to Ganapati Muni in 1907.[3] Till then Ramana had remained silent outwardly as well.

It was again at Virupaksha that Ramana communicated the experience of his enlightenment through his spiritual instructions to Gambhiram Seshier and Sivaprakasam Pillai.[4]

In writing about the Virupaksha years of Ramana, one might say that it is not a biographer's account but almost an autobiographical account by Ramana himself.

Hornets

In the initial years an attempt was made by the trustees of the Virupaksha Math, who owned the cave, to levy a small charge for the entry. Ramana did not want any kind of interference with his accessibility. Hence he moved out of the cave to a level path of ground outside it and sat under the shade of a tree there. When the agent tried to levy a fee there also, Ramana shifted to the nearby Sadguruswami cave for a short time. The trustees, realizing the inconvenience caused, stopped levying the fee so that Ramana could return to the Virupaksha Cave.

An event while at this cave as narrated by Ramana is fascinating. *"In those days I used to go all by myself. For answering calls of nature I used to stroll along taking no water with me, but going wherever water may be available.*

Virupaksha Cave

It was on one such occasion, on one morning, that I came across the banyan tree of which I have spoken often.

"As I was walking on the bed of a hill stream, I saw a big banyan tree on a boulder, with big leaves. And crossing the stream, I wanted to get to the other bank and view from there this big tree. When I accidentally put my left foot near a bush on the way to the other bank, so that the hornets clustered round my left leg up to the knee and started stinging it. They never did anything to my right leg.

I left the leg there for some time, so that the hornets could inflict full punishment on the leg which had encroached on their domain. After a time, the hornets withdrew and I walked on. The leg got swollen very much and I walked with difficulty and reached 'Ezhu Sunai' (Seven Springs) about 2 a.m.

"Jadaswami, who was camping there then, gave me some buttermilk mixed with jaggery, which was all that he could provide by way of food. This is what actually happened. But afterwards, people have gone and written that I had purposely set out to explore and find the banyan tree described in the purana as the one on the northern peak of the Hill, where Arunachala is said to be residing as a siddha. I never had any such idea. When I saw for the first time a remarkable banyan tree on a huge and precipitous boulder, I was prompted by curiosity to have a look at it. Meanwhile, the hornets stung me and I forgot all about the tree."[5] The last words, *"I forgot all about the tree,"* show Ramana's sense of humor.

Ramana also composed a stray verse on this incident, which is extracted below:

Apology to Hornets

*When I was stung by hornets in revenge
Upon the leg until it was inflamed,
Although it was by chance I stepped upon
Their nest, constructed in a leafy bush,
What kind of mind is his if he does not
At least repent for doing such a wrong?*[6]

Composition of the *Five Hymns*

We have an account of how the *Decad on Arunachala* and *Eight Verses on Arunachala* came to be composed by Ramana spontaneously.

"One morning, when he was sitting on the verandah in Virupaksha Cave, the words *'Karunaiyal Ennai'* came to him very insistently, but he took no special notice of them. It seems the same thing happened the following morning also. Then Bhagavan composed the first stanza of *The Decad on Arunachala*. The next morning the words beginning the second stanza similarly came to him and he composed the second stanza; and so the thing went on every day, till the last two stanzas were composed on one day. On that day, after composing the two last stanzas, Bhagavan, it seems, started for *giripradakshina* (going round the hill). One of his disciples, Aiyaswami, brought a piece of paper and pencil and told another disciple who was going with Bhagavan, 'Bhagavan has been composing one stanza every morning for some days now, and today he has composed two stanzas. More may come to

him today. In case they do, have this paper and pencil with you so that the same may be recorded.' Bhagavan actually composed the first six stanzas of the *Arunachala Ashtakam* (*Eight Verses on Arunachala*). It seems Echamma first got "The Marital Garland of Letters" published. Narayana Reddi came to know of the *Padikam* and *Ashtakam* soon afterwards and wanted to publish them. Then Bhagavan composed two more stanzas for completing the *Ashtakam* and the *Decad* (*Padikam*) and *Eight Verses* (*Ashtakam*) were published by Narayana Reddi. This is how the *Padikam* and *Ashtakam* in the *Five Hymns on Arunachala* came to be composed."[7]

The most famous of Ramana's *Five Hymns on Arunachala* is "The Marital Garland of Letters" with the refrain *Arunachala Siva*. This was also mostly composed during Ramana's circuits of Arunachala. The story of the need for composing these 108 verses has been mentioned by Ramana. In order to feed Ramana and the fellow devotees at the Virupaksha Cave it became necessary to beg for alms in the streets of Tiruvannamalai. Palaniswami wanted Ramana to compose a new devotional hymn so that Ramana's group may be identified by the people of the town. After it was composed a party of four led by Palaniswami would start out to town, blow a long blast on their conches, and start chanting "The Marital Garland of Letters." This was an announcement to the town's people that Bhagavan's party had left the cave on their begging mission. The party would give another blast when they reached the foot of the hill. A third call would be sounded at the entrance of the street. All the residents of the street would be ready with their offerings and the party would march along the street singing and some collecting the offerings. The food collected was ample, it seems, for all who gathered near Bhagavan and even all of the monkeys etc. "The Marital Garland of Letters" was specially composed for use by the begging party. Bhagavan humorously added, "'Marital Garland of Letters' *fed us for many years.*"[8]

Ramana with Children

Even though Ramana remained silent in the first years of stay at Virupaksha Cave, many children would climb up to the cave and sit for long periods just to be in his presence. After 1907, sometimes Ramana would join the children in their play. He played marbles with them and referred to this later as follows: *"The holes dug for the purpose must be there even now. Those children sometimes used to bring packets of sweetmeats and we all used to share them. During Deepavali they used to put aside my share of the crackers and bring them up to me. We used to fire the crackers together."*[9]

Ramana has also narrated how two children were emotionally moved when he was about twenty-two and living in the Virupaksha Cave. It seems he was sitting on a rock near the cave and a boy about 8 or 10 came there, looked at Bhagavan and, not being able to bear the sight of such a young and bright person taking to such a hard life of penance, was so moved by compassion that he started to sob and sobbed violently for some time.

Bhagavan said, *"Who could say what was the reason for his sobbing and why tears flowed out of him merely at his seeing me?"* Bhagavan continued in a reminiscent mood later in the day and added that another boy, also about 8 or 10 years old, met Bhagavan another day at Virupaksha Cave. He took such pity on Bhagavan that the following conversation took place between them. Bhagavan was sitting on a rock near the cave, all alone, and the boy met him there.

Boy: Why are you here all alone, like this?

Bhagavan: *I had some trouble at home and so have come away like this.*

Boy: Then how about your food?

Bhagavan: *I eat if anybody gives me anything to eat.*

Boy: I have a good master. I shall take you to him. First, you may have to volunteer your services free. If he approves of your work, he will give three pies a day and gradually increase it to six pies, and so on.

Bhagavan added, *"There was no doubt that the boy was very much concerned over what he considered my sad plight and that he was moved by great and genuine pity."*[10]

Some Other Incidents

One day Ramana was doing a small masonry job when some visitors came up in order to see the Swami. He told them, *"Swami has gone out."* When they were returning down the hill, they met Echamma who told them that the person whom they had met was none other than the Swami. She later asked Ramana why he had misled the men, to which Ramana replied, *"Do you want me to go about with a bell around my neck announcing 'I am the Swami' or to have a label on my forehead that 'I am the Swami'?"*[11]

In 1912, a group of devotees headed by Vasudeva Sastri, wished to celebrate Ramana's birthday for the first time. Ramana opposed it saying that the true birth is only when one becomes

The inside of the Virupaksha Cave as it is today

Self-aware. But Vasudeva Sastri pleaded with him saying, "It is for our sake and Bhagavan should not object."[12] Thus they celebrated it that year for the first time. Since then the celebration known as *jayanti* has been a very important occasion for all the disciples and devotees of Ramana. Once Ramana's grandmother came to see him. This is Ramana's account of it. *"She came while we were there and said that she would cook food for herself. We told her that she could do so in the cave nearby. She agreed and started cooking. She said to me, 'Venkatarama, I am cooking today. You should not take any other food!' I said yes, but after she left, I ate with the others as usual. When she had cooked, I ate that food also."*[13]

An old relative of Ramana's known for his abusive tongue came along. He was really a good-natured man and meant no ill to anybody. Soon after he came, he asked jocularly, "What Venkataraman, it seems you have become a big Swami! Have you grown horns on your head?"[14]

While at Virupaksha, Ramana also wrote in prose a Tamil translation of *Vivekacudamani*, a sacred scripture composed by Adi Sankara. Right from Gurumurtam days, Palaniswami used to bring Ramana spiritual books from the library in the town. At Virupaksha also he continued to do so. Thus Ramana became more and more acquainted with the sacred lore of Vedanta. In his early years in Virupaksha Cave, he would occasionally visit Padmanabha Swami, popularly called Jatai Swami because of his matted hair. The Swami had several Sanskrit books through some of which Ramana would glance, and remember all that he had read. We have already seen that even

Samadhi of Virupaksha Deva

as a boy at school he was remarkable for his prodigious memory. A scholar once came to the cave and left a copy of Sankaracharya's *Vivekacudamani*, a metrical manual of Vedanta, which expounds the truth of Advaita in a clear and comprehensive manner. Ramana read it and also a metrical Tamil version produced by Palaniswami. Then it occurred to him that a prose translation would be very useful for aspirants who did not know Sanskrit, so he undertook the translation which came to be printed and published under the following circumstances. "Uddandi Nayanar, who was the first regular devotee to be attached to Ramana, was called away in 1897 to the headquarters of the ascetic order to which he belonged. Seven years later, he returned with a hundred rupees as his offering. The Master refused to accept it, since he had no use for money and would not touch it. Nayanar left the money with a devotee asking him to utilize it for any good cause of which the Master approved. It was spent on printing the translation of the *Vivekacudamani*."[15]

In those years there used to be tigers and leopards on Arunachala. Ramana had no fear because the sign of a *jnani* is desirelessness and fearlessness. Hence the wild animals would not be frightened of him. An interesting incident is recorded by Vasudeva Sastri. "In the broad daylight Swamiji and I were seated on the rock outside the cave. In the valley below, a tiger and a leopard were playing with each other and Bhagavan was smiling as he watched the friendly movements of the two animals. I was however in a terrible fright and requested Bhagavan to come into the cave. He was adamant and sat there motionless. As for myself, I sought the shelter of the cave. The two animals played about for a while, looked at Swamiji in the same way pets do, and without any fear or expression of anger went their own way, one going up the hill and the other down. When I came out of the cave and asked, 'Swamiji, weren't you afraid when the two animals were playing so close to you?' Bhagavan said with a smile, *'Why have fear? I knew as I saw them that, after a while, one of them would go up the hill and the other down. And they did. If we get frightened and say, "Oh! A tiger!" They will also get frightened and say, "Oh! A man!" and will rush forward to kill us. If we do not have fear, they too will not have any fear, and will then move about freely and peacefully.'"* In spite of all that Bhagavan had said, Sastry added, "My fear never left me."[16]

Ramana would never take anything without sharing it with all those present. As a result often there would not be enough food to go around. Ramana has narrated what used to happen. *"When I was in Virupaksha Cave, Sundaresa Iyer used to go out into the town for* bhiksa *and bring us food. At times, there used to be no curry or chutney. People to eat were many while the food obtained was limited. What were we to do? I used to mix it into a paste and pour hot water over it to make it like gruel, and then give a glassful to each and take one myself. Sometimes we all used to feel that it would be better if we had at least some salt to mix with it. But where was money to buy salt? We should have had to ask someone for it. If once we began to ask for salt, we would feel like asking for dhal, and when we ask for dhal, we would feel like asking for payasam, and so on. So we felt that we should not ask for anything, and swallowed the gruel as it was. We used to feel extremely happy over such a diet. As the food was sattvic, without spices of any kind, and there was not even salt in it, not only was it healthy for this body, but there was also great peace for the mind."*[17]

The entrance to Virupaksha Cave

The Most Significant Event After Enlightenment

The first biographer, B.V. Narasimha Swami, had interviewed Ramana about an incident which happened in 1912 while he was staying at the Virupaksha Cave. This interview is given as an appendix to Narasimha Swami's biography under the heading, "A strange and remarkable incident in the life of Sri Maharshi."[1] The significance of this event is therefore likely to be lost sight of.

In 1912, Ramana, Palaniswami, and Vasudeva Sastri, and a few others went from Virupaksha Cave to Pachiamman Koil for taking an oil bath as facilities for such a bath were available in plenty in that place. After bathing they returned cutting a path across the hill for themselves.

The sun was fairly hot even at about 10 a.m. when they reached the tortoise rock. Ramana began to feel faint and what happened is best stated in his own words. *"Suddenly the view of natural scenery in front of me disappeared and a bright white curtain was drawn across the line of my vision and shut out the view of nature. I could distinctly see the gradual process. At one stage I could see a part of the prospect of nature yet clear, and the rest was being covered by the advancing curtain. It was just like drawing a slide across one's view in the stereoscope. On experiencing this I stopped walking lest I should fall. When it cleared, I walked on. When darkness and faintness overtook me a second time, I leaned against a rock until it cleared. And again for the third time I felt it safest to sit, so I sat near the rock. Then the bright white curtain had completely shut out my vision, my head was swimming, and my blood circulation and breathing stopped. The skin turned a livid blue. It*

was the regular death-like hue and it got darker and darker. Vasudeva Sastri took me in fact to be dead, held me in his embrace and began to weep aloud and lament my death. His body was shivering. I could at that time distinctly feel his clasp and his shivering, hear his lamentation, and understand the meaning. I also saw the discoloration of my skin and I felt the stoppage of my heartbeat and respiration, and the increased chilliness of the extremities of my body. Yet my usual current was continuing without a break in that state also. I was not afraid in the least, nor felt any sadness at the condition of my body. I had closed my eyes as soon I sat near the rock in my usual posture but was not leaning against it. The body which had no circulation nor respiration maintained that position still. This state continued for some ten or fifteen minutes. Then a shock passed suddenly through the body, circulation revived with enormous force, as also respiration; and there was perspiration all over the body at every pore. The color of life reappeared on the skin. I then opened my eyes, got up and said, 'Let us go.' We reached Virupaksha Cave without further trouble. That was the only occasion on which both my blood circulation and respiration stopped."[2]

At the time of enlightenment, which happened on July 17, 1896, Ramana had only the sudden fear of death. However, in order to go through the experience of what death means, "he stretched himself like a corpse as though rigor mortis had set in and held his lips tightly together and his breath." It was not a physical death but an experience of death intensely felt as part of investigation to find out and discover *"Who am I? Still I felt within myself the 'I' was there, the sound was there, the feeling itself 'I' was there. What was that? I felt that it was a force or current, a center of energy playing on the body working on despite the rigidity or activity of the body though existing in connection with it."[3]* This experience that the true "I" was a current or a force or center that constituted the real "I" stayed with him for the rest of life.

The second experience is different in that there was a physical death for 10 or 15 minutes. The heart beat and the blood circulation had stopped and the body had become cold and blue. But the experience of awareness of the heart current as the "I" remained. This is the most significant aspect of this experience. Even while narrating the experience Ramana has clearly stated, *"Yet my usual current was continuing as usual without a break in that state also."*

Ramana himself has referred to this incident in the course of his conversation with B.V. Narasimha Swami, years later, in 1937. The relevant portion reads as follows: *"I used to feel the vibrations of the Heart, which resemble those of a dynamo, even in school. When I developed rigor mortis many years ago in Tiruvannamalai, every object and sensation disappeared, except these vibrations. It was as if a dark screen was drawn before my eyes and shut the world completely from me, but of course I was all along conscious of the Self, with a vague feeling that someone was crying near me. This state continued till just before I regained physical consciousness, when I felt something rush from the Heart to the left chest and re-establish life in the body."*[4]

One shudders at the thought as to what would have happened if the life force had not re-established itself in Ramana's body.

But then it had to happen only in that way in the divine scheme of things. One who is aware of the life of Ramana will also be aware that the earmarked role for Ramana in the divine scheme was to guide seekers of truth, as the inner and outer *guru*, on the direct path of self-enquiry for Self-knowledge. This role as the *sadguru* was to be for about another five decades in the body from

35

the date of this experience. Ramana's steady Self-awareness and accessibility ensured this.

Arunachala

The Ancient Legends

"Although he had a luster on a par with hundreds and crores of midday suns and rising world destructive fires, he became approachable to living beings (as Arunachala)."[1]

"I can rarely be seen in Kailasa, peak Meru, or in my abodes in various Kula mountains. I myself am Arunachala. On seeing the peak, all the sins of the people will be destroyed and their eye of wisdom would be opened by vision born of Knowledge."[2]

Sage Gautama—*Skanda Purana*

The *Skanda Purana*, III, proclaims in unqualified terms the glory of Arunachala. This is set out in different ways, through the words of Sage Suta, from the lips of great Gautama Muni, and through Nandikeswara (the divine bull of Lord Siva).

In the days of yore a dispute arose between the Creator, Lord Brahma, and the Preserver, Lord Vishnu, as to which of them was superior. Each claimed superiority over the other based upon their respective functions. In their ego-ridden state they forgot their own true nature which was the auspicious state of Self-abidance bestowed on them by Lord Siva. Out of compassion Lord Siva, the great *Yogi*, decided to appear before them as a column of light. He appeared as a blazing fire which enveloped the universe and which appeared to have no beginning or end. A celestial voice in the sky said, "Why are you fighting your nature? Siva will himself decide. Therefore he stands before you as a fiery column. Whoever will be able

to see the beginning or the end is superior in strength." This was in the Tamil month of Margazhi, on the Ardra Darsana day sacred to all the devotees of Siva, sacred too as Ramana's day of birth.

Thereupon Lord Vishnu took the form of a boar and went farther and farther down the bowels of the earth tearing layer after layer. Soon he was overcome with fatigue and realized the futility of his quest. In desperation he prayed to Lord Siva who restored his strength by making him lose false pride. Lord Brahma flew high in the sky as a swan. Despite being enfeebled and dispirited his mind did not accept the impossibility of success in his quest. However, ultimately he too became crestfallen and reported his failure to Lord Siva. They realized that their true strength was Lord Siva, the supreme *Yogi*. They eulogized him and prayed to him to take the form of a *linga* by name Arunachala, in order to bless the world. They pleaded that if they themselves could not bear the effulgence it would be impossible for the ordinary mortals to worship Siva in that form. Out of his love for the world Siva manifested himself as Arunachala. The delighted Gods proclaimed that whoever circumambulated Arunachala slowly and in reverence, singly or in groups, singing and dancing the Lord's praise would be blessed in every way by Lord Siva, the perpetual granter of boons.

The second story relates to the penance of Goddess Parvati at Arunachala and her reunion with Lord Siva. Once Goddess Parvati playfully closed the eyes of Lord Siva as a result of which the whole universe was plunged in darkness, for the eyes of Siva are the Light of the universe. This caused untimely destruction even though the closure of Siva's eyes was only for a few seconds. Hence, Parvati was asked to do penance in the world and bless it. Her *tapas* was sure to ennoble the world. Her penance was first done at Kasi, then at Kanchi and there Siva ad-

vised her through an ethereal voice to go to Arunachala and continue her *tapas*. Siva also asked her to become aware of the glory of Arunachala from Gautama Muni before embarking on her *tapas*. Gautama humbly narrated to her the incomparable and matchless wonder of Siva standing as a hill Arunachala. Gautama said: "All the *Vedas* eulogize you, the body of Siva thus: This one who is copper colored or reddish brown or tawny-colored is highly auspicious." "Obeisance to the copper-colored pink Siva, the supreme Lord whose form can be comprehended through the Vedas, who is accompanied by Uma and whose form is happiness."[3]

Continuing in this strain Gautama says, "The entire greatness of Arunachala cannot be expressed by a crore of mouths." Gautama also elaborated at length the virtues of going round Arunachala emphasizing that all worldly desires and also Self-knowledge would result from such circumambulation.[4]

The third aspect is the story of mother Gauri's *tapas* at Arunachala with full awareness of Arunachala's glory and its redeeming radiance. The demonical forces headed by Mahishasura tried to destroy her *tapas*. They were defeated because no one could match her fiery power with her constant penance and incomparable power of Arunachala. The auspicious Lord Siva was pleased with her *tapas* and appeared before her in the month of Kartika on the day when the constellation of Krittika appears which is the star pertaining to the holy fire, Agni. Then Gauri, the mother of the universe, bowed down to Siva and prayed that they should never again be separated. For she had suffered the pangs of separation enough from her long spells of penance in three sacred places, Kasi, Kanchi, and Arunachala. She told her Lord that she should never be abandoned whatever offence she may be guilty of. Such was her compassionate heart, she also prayed that the knowing and unknowing offences committed by devotees should be excused by Siva through a single glance. Further she prayed that he should be seen in the world in the pleasing form of Arunachala. Siva readily granted the boons asked for by her. He gave the left half of his physical body to her so that once and for all the question of separation ended. The gods and goddesses, sages and the whole world, rejoiced in the union which was for universal welfare.

In this context one needs to refer to Ramana's deposition on Arunachala in 1938, on a commission from a court. It contains several authoritative pronouncements about the sacredness of the hill which is being regarded as the embodiment of Lord Siva. Ramana gave evidence

The cauldron carried to the summit of Arunachala during the Deepam festival

on behalf of the Arunachaleswara temple authorities in a dispute which arose between the temple authorities and the Government of India. "Until the 1930s the eastern slope of the mountain of Arunachaleswara was administered by the Arunachaleswara temple in Tiruvannamalai. Prior to 1934, its right to do so had been accepted by everyone on and around the hill. From time immemorial the temple authorities had maintained the tanks and temples on the mountain, put out any fires which broke out, and arranged for all the forest produce to be sold in an orderly manner. The unquestioned authority that the

temple authorities had wielded over this area had arisen because of the local tradition that the hill was Siva himself manifest in the form of a *linga*. Since the belief was widespread and largely unchallenged, the local people felt that it was natural and correct that the main temple in Tiruvannamalai should administer all affairs pertaining to the hill.

"The traditional arrangement was challenged by the Government of India in 1934. In May that year the Government issued a notification in the district gazette which stated that the whole of Arunachala was a reserve forest and was thus the property of the Government of India. The temple authorities challenged the Government's order in the court, maintaining that the temple was the legitimate owner of 1,750 acres on the eastern side of the hill. This area included all the tanks and temples on the slope of the mountain which begins at the back of the Arunachaleswara temple.

"One of the temple trustees approached Bhagavan and requested him to give evidence in the court which would support the Arunachaleswara temple's claim to the land. Bhagavan agreed and in 1938 lawyers for the plaintiff and the defendant came to the *asram* to hear this evidence and to cross-examine him on it. Bhagavan's initial evidence took the form of a written deposition. A small part of this deposition was recorded in *Talks with Sri Ramana Maharshi*. Talk No. 492."[5]

In the course of his evidence Ramana went on to describe why in his opinion the temple authorities were allowed to administer affairs pertaining to the hill. *"There is an* aitikya *(tradition) that this hill is* linga swarupa, *that is to say, that this hill itself is God. This* aitikya *is not to be found anywhere else. That is the cause of the glory of this place. The tradition of this place is that this hill is the form of God and that in its real nature it is full of light. Every year the Deepam festival celebrates the real nature of the mountain as light itself. Authority for this is found in the* Vedas, *the* Puranas, *and in the* stotras *(poems) of devotees. Because this tradition maintains that the hill is Siva* swarupa, *the practice of* giripradakshina, *walking clockwise around the mountain as an act of reverence or worship, has arisen. I also have faith in* giripradakshina *and have had experience of it.*

"In accordance with the tradition that the hill is Iswara swarupa, the devasthanam *performs* abhishekam *to the top of the hill in the same way it would do to a* linga. *For the last ten to twelve years the cauldron which contains the*

Deepam light on the top of the hill is carried to the summit every year during the festival. Prior to this, for many, many years, the cauldron was left there throughout the year.[6]

In his deposition Ramana also refers to two compositions of his:

Significance of Arunachala

The sudden rise of the blazing column of Annamalai in front of Brahma and Vishnu, and their utter distress at not being able to know the same, is symbolic of the sphurana *of the heart center as the real Self of the intellect and the ego.*[7]

Significance of the Beacon

Getting rid of the "I am the body" idea and merging the mind into the heart to realize the Self as non-dual being and the light of all, is the real significance of darsan *of the beacon light on Annamalai, the center of the universe.*[8]

Ramana's *Guru*

"O Arunachala, you who stand and shine before me in the form of my guru, *destroy utterly my faults, cure me and convert me, and as your servant govern me."*[9]

"Look at me! Think of me! Touch me! Make me fit, ripen me! Then be my Master, govern me, O Arunachula."[10]

—*Bhagavan Ramana*

The power of Arunachala as the inner *guru* has been felt by all seekers of truth from ages past. It has been beckoning, magnetically, many such earnest persons to itself. But it is only given to a few to regard the hill as their *guru* and establish a disciple-*guru* relationship with Arunachala. This is because one may be taken in by the outer appearance of Arunachala as a hill notwithstanding the legends coming down from the days of *Puranas.* They would not be aware of its true stature as the *guru* who silences the mind and helps in discovering Self-knowledge. This is also expressed by Ramana in one of his verses on Arunachala, the inspired *Eight Verses,* the first of which reads as below. "*Look there it stands as if insentient. Mysterious is the way it works, beyond all human understanding. From my unthinking childhood the immensity of Arunachala had shone in my awareness. But even when I learnt from someone that it was only Tiruvannamalai, I did not realize its meaning. When it stilled my mind and*

drew me to itself and I came near, I saw that it was stillness absolute."[11]

One of the sages who discovered this unique aspect of Arunachala was the 16th century saint Guhai Namasivaya, who made Arunachala his home. There is a cave on the hill, which is named after him. In some of his compositions on Arunachala, he recognizes this guru-dom of Arunachala and gives expression to the fact that he regarded the hill as his *guru.*

"Lord Arunagiri! Form of true knowledge! *Guru* to whom I call out 'Om Namasivaya'. Do not scorn me as one who is devoid of love for you, who is a liar and without self-respect, who is mentally immature and deficient in intelligence, but take me to yourself and be my Lord!

"Taking into my heart as my *Guru* the Red Mountain Lord (Arunachala) who now stands formless before me, I put to flight the unutterable arrogance of my good and evil deeds, my soul's indissoluble threefold impurity, and my unparalleled accumulation of *karma.*"[12]

It will be seen from the very first verse of this chapter that Ramana puts very clearly in focus the fact that

the hill Arunachala shines as *guru*. Here it must be mentioned that there is a contemporary notion that the *guru* should be in human form. Based on this belief people would think that Ramana had no *guru*. This is a misconception. Ramana has made it clear not only in his *Five Hymns* on Arunachala but also in his conversations that he regarded Arunachala as his *guru*.

There is a conversation which took place between him and Dilip Kumar Roy of Sri Aurobindo Ashram in the late forties, which reads as below:

D: Some people report that Maharshi denies the need of a *guru*. Others say the reverse. What does Maharshi say?

B: *I have never said that there is no need for a* guru.

D: Sri Aurobindo often refers to you as having had no *guru*.

B: *That depends on what you call guru. He need not necessarily be in the human form. Dattatreya had twenty-four gurus—the elements. etc. That means that every form in the world was his guru. A guru is absolutely necessary. The Upanishads say that none but a guru can take a man out of the jungle of mental and sense perceptions, so there must be a guru.*

D: I mean a human *guru*. The Maharshi didn't have one.

B: *I might have had sometime or other. And didn't I sing hymns on Arunachala? What is a guru? Guru is God or the Self. First a man prays to God to fulfill his desires, then a time comes when he does not pray for the fulfillment of a desire but for God himself. So God appears to him in some form or other, human or non-human, to guide as guru in answer to his prayer.*[13]

Some believe that it is the same red hill which took the human form of Ramana, in order that those who are not aware of the true nature of it as Arunachala may recognize it in the human form of Ramana. He himself has referred to this in one of his verses in the "Necklet of Nine Gems." *"In Tiruchuzhi, the holy town of Bhuminatha, I was born to Sundara and his good wife Sundari. To rescue me from this barren worldly life, Arunachala Siva in the form of a Hill famous throughout the universe, gave me His own state of bliss, so that His heart might rejoice, so that His own being as Awareness might shine forth, and His own Power might flourish."*[14]

It is the purpose of the *guru* to bestow by his grace his own state of fullness of consciousness on the disciple. The *guru*'s greatest happiness is in his disciple becoming Self-aware like himself. One might add that there are innumerable persons so redeemed, so blessed by Ramana in his role as universal *guru*.

It may be for this reason that Ramana stayed performing his role as universal *guru* at various caves of Arunachala and on its southern slopes. T.M.P. Mahadevan refers to this in his book *Ramana Maharshi*. *"This Rock of Ages which chose to assume the role of Azhagam-* *mal's son for a while was now restored to its original status as immutable Self. There was therefore no parting from Arunachala."*[15] This was said in the context of mother's pleading, requesting Ramana to come back home where he could perform his penance undisturbed. How could he return? For his *guru* Arunachala had commanded him to come to be in His physical presence.

Giripradakshina

The ancient legend about the sacredness of Arunachala has been coming down through the ages to the devout public. Going round the hill, which is considered to be the embodiment of the auspicious Lord Siva, is considered to be very holy and beneficial not only spiritually but also materially. As a result pious crowds keep moving around Arunachala from the early morning to past midnight, particularly on days considered to be sacred.

The circuit is eight miles or thirteen kilometers long and one keeps the hill on the right side during the circuit. A number of bathing places, temples, and places of rest are scattered around this entire circuit. It is therefore recommended that this journey should be done slowly

One of the temples on the circuit around Arunachala

with constant remembrance of the holiness of the hill. The circuit should be performed *"as slowly as the gait of a princess in the tenth month of her pregnancy."*[16] Ramana would recommend that one should keep to the left since the path on the right side is reserved for *siddhas* or those who have already attained realization but are in astral bodies.

Ramana himself used to go around the hill with his disciples regularly from 1900 to 1926. He recalls: *"It used to be very exciting when we were going for* pradakshina. *We started whenever we felt like it and especially on a festival day we used to halt whenever we felt it was late or we were tired, cook for ourselves and eat. There was no anxiety whatsoever as there was no need to stop at any particular place. The state of concentration (dhyana) that you cannot enter while sitting, you get into automatically if you go for* pradakshina. *The place and the atmosphere there are like that. However unable a person is to walk, if he once goes round the hill he feels like doing so again and again. The more you go, the more the enthusiasm for it. It never*

decreases. Once a person is accustomed to the happiness of the pradakshina, *he can never give it up."*[17]

B.V. Narasimha Swami gives a very fine description of the *pradakshina* with Ramana. "When Maharshi starts the entire *asram* starts with him, as everyone is eager to accompany him. Sometimes they start at nightfall after the meal and return just at dawn. Sometimes they start in the morning and take a day or two to return. One may wonder why so many hours or days are required to walk eight miles, which could be done in three hours. But Maharshi goes on these circuits mainly to set an example to and benefit others. Again Maharshi often moves in a state of *samadhi*: such an intense ecstasy implies slow and even breath and absence of haste or exertion. So he moves at the rate of one mile per hour, and rests for some fifteen minutes or so in suitable places which are available at every mile or even half-mile. While engaged in this circuit he enjoys the bliss of the *Atman* and cares not for the sounds and sights. He is in the Universal center, in the only Reality, in the Being of beings."[18]

Those accompanying Ramana would be in a mood of fervent devotion because of Ramana whom they considered to be Lord Siva himself. There would be a joyous sense of detachment, sometimes rising to the heights of ecstasy.

"Some address themselves to Lord Arunachala and according to their varying moods praise and dance or pray and weep. One Gajanana, who stayed for some months with the Maharshi, was full of fervent faith in Sri Hari (Lord Vishnu). He would constantly sing songs from *Srimad Bhagavata* and would them which created such an impression. They asked Bhagavan to direct them to some place where they could find water. As there was no water nearby, he took them some distance. He was then about to proceed on his *pradakshina* but one of the women asked him to be so kind as to partake a little of the food they were going to eat before leaving them. Bhagavan did not like to seem rude, so he consented. But what was his surprise when, after one woman had untied her bundle and given him some food out of it, each of the others also opened her bundle and said: 'You must take a little of mine also.' Bhagavan was placed in such a delicate situation that he had to take something from each in order not to hurt any of them, with the result that he ate much more than he had bargained for.

"After this, he left them and continued on his way round the hill. But after he had gone some miles (Bhagavan used to walk round very slowly, sometimes taking even a whole day, and stopping here and there on the way), about midday the same women again met him. Bhagavan was surprised to see that they had not yet gathered any fuel or leaves in their

dance in his joy most of the way round the hill. Others poured forth their soul in Sanskrit, Tamil, Sivanandalahari, Tevaram, Tiruppugazh, Aksharamana-malai etc., aided by cymbals, tambura, drum (*mridangam*), and fiddle.

"The last, but by no means the least, pilgrim is the one who goes on repeating silently the dear Lord's name (such as the Panchaksari) and by dint of meditation becomes himself the object of his own 'thought.' Then really thought is not. In enjoyment it expires."[19]

Another incident connected with *pradakshina* with Bhagavan mentioned by Ramana himself has been recorded by Devaraja Mudaliar. "One day when Bhagavan was still at Skandasram, his stomach was out of order. So he decided to fast for the day. He thought that he could do this more easily if he left the *asram* on *pradakshina*. When he had gone a furlong or two from where the present *asram* stands he met five or six women who looked like peasant women gathering fuel or leaves for making leaf-plates. They had empty bags with

bags. He told us: *'I thought in the morning they were women who had set out to collect leaves. But their bags were still empty.'*

"They approached him and said: 'We are now going to have lunch. Swami must be graciously pleased to take something with us.'

"So saying, each woman offered some food to Bhagavan and he was obliged to eat it all. The matter did not end even here. When Bhagavan had proceeded further on, he was met by Manavasi Ramaswami Iyer, one of the oldest of his devotees, with food and a new kind of pepper water (*rasam*) which he had specially prepared

for Bhagavan with great care and devotion. He had got a big mango that day and thought that if he put it into the *rasam* it would be both a very palatable and nourishing diet for Bhagavan. So he had made the *rasam* in this way and took it to Skandasramam. Learning there that Bhagavan had gone on *pradakshina* he decided to go round the hill in the opposite direction (*apradakshina* i.e., with his left hand to the hill) so that he could be sure of meeting Bhagavan somewhere or other. He did in fact meet him at two in the afternoon, and when Bhagavan heard of all the trouble he had taken he felt that he could not possibly refuse to take the food thus prepared and

brought to him. Eventually he reached the *asramam* some time in the evening, after having had sumptuous food three times in the course of the day.

"Bhagavan told us: *'I thought I would go without food that day. But this is how it ended.'*"[20]

In his recollections Mudaliar also refers to some other incidents. On one occasion when Bhagavan was going round the hill he saw some luminous bodies moving round with him at about a man's height from the ground. "On another occasion he went into the temple at Adi Annamalai on the way round the hill and heard the *Sama Veda* being chanted near the shrine. I asked whether those who accompanied him on those two occasions saw the lights or heard the sounds, and he said, *'No.'*"[21] It is widely believed that *siddha Purushas* (sages with supernatural powers) live on Arunachala and sometimes go round the hill. "Presumably they must have been *siddhas* who took delight in accompanying Bhagavan."[22]

Ramana would always encourage everyone to go around the hill. Mudaliar had the advantage of being totally free like a child with Ramana. In the beginning he used to question Ramana about the efficacy of the *pradakshina*. Ramana told him, *"For everybody it is good to do* pradakshina. *It does not matter if one has faith in the* pradakshina *or not. Just as fire will burn on touching it, whether they believe or not the hill will do good to all those who go around it."*[23]

People who did *pradakshina* would gradually, but invariably, feel the magnetic pull of the hill. In the beginning they would need company but slowly they would feel the enchantment so strongly, they would without any encouragement or stress voluntarily go around the hill.

After 1926, Ramana did not himself go around the hill. This was because the devotees had swollen in numbers. It was difficult for the residents around the hill to provide food for his party. At the same time the devotees did not wish to remain without offering their homage to Ramana. This was the reason for his refraining from going around the hill. However, he would recommend it to everyone.

One of the most moving incidents during the *giripradakshina* years was the befriending of a poor farmer. This farmer would regularly wait for Ramana and his party near Adi Annamalai temple with some food for them whenever he came to know that the party was circumambulating. Noticing his absence on one of the circuits Ramana took a detour and found him sitting, sadly, under a tree with a small pot in his hand. After much cajoling by Ramana the farmer hesitatingly informed him that he could get only a very small quantity of cooked cold rice. How could he offer it?

Ramana exclaimed, *"Oh! Cooked food is it? That is excellent. Why be ashamed? It will be very good, leave it to me."* So saying he took a vessel available with the party, added proportionate water and lime juice and made a large quantity of the liquid and spiced it with ginger and salt. Then he took a glassful saying, *"Oh! this is delicious!"* Chatting freely with the farmer he took extra glasses and

all of them, brought them to Sri Ramanasramam, and handed them over to Sadhu Natanananda. These notes were later published under the title *Vichara Sangraham, Self-Enquiry*, both in its essay format and question and answer format.[1] This notebook is not available now. When B.V. Narasimha Swami wrote his biography, in 1930, the original notebook was still available. Narasimha Swami made his notes from it for his intended publication to be titled *Talks with Ramana Maharshi*. Perhaps he wished to cover the portion directly relating to various extant spiritual practices on which Ramana also throws clear light.[2]

The value of *Vichara Sangraham* is that even though it is not an exclusive Ramana Way treatise, it was for the first time after his Self-realization that Ramana explained the royal path of self-enquiry "Who am I" to any seeker. In this sense it is a very important document to which one can refer for understanding the experience of Ramana. The very invocation puts one on the trail of self-enquiry. It reads thus: "Is there any way of adoring the Supreme who is all, except by abiding firmly as That!" The first three questions and answers indicate the direct path and are extracted below:

Q: Master! What is the means to gain the state of eternal bliss, ever devoid of misery?

R: *Apart from the statement in the Vedas that wherever there is a body there is misery (the idea that one is the body), this is also the direct experience of all people; therefore, one should enquire into one's true nature, which is ever bodiless, and one should remain as such.*

Q: What is meant by saying that one should enquire into one's true nature and understand it?

R: *Experiences such as "I went," "I came," "I was," "I did" come naturally to everyone. From these experiences, does it not appear that the consciousness "I" is the subject of those various acts? Enquiring into the true nature of that consciousness, and remaining as oneself is the way to understand, through enquiry, one's true nature.*

Q: How is one to enquire, "Who am I?"

R: *Actions such as "going" and "coming" belong to the body. And so, when one says "I went," "I came," it amounts*

told him that it was like nectar. He then gave the farmer a sufficient quantity to take home. "Wiping the tears of joy that were welling up in his eyes he took leave and went off to his cottage."[24]

Gambhiram Seshier

To Gambhiram Seshier, also known as Gambhiram Seshayya, goes the credit of being the first person to systematically question Ramana on various spiritual practices and elicit replies about them. He was a Municipal Office Overseer at Tiruvannamalai in 1900 and began seeking Ramana's guidance from that time. He was a keen student of Swami Vivekananda and had assiduously studied his lectures on *Raja Yoga* and certain spiritual texts like *Ramana Gita* of the *Yoga Vasishta*. Ramana's replies naturally covered some aspects of the subjects dealt with by these books. At the same time he would invariably draw the pointed attention of Seshier to the path of self-enquiry. Fortunately for posterity Seshier noted down the questions and answers systematically in slips of paper which he carefully preserved by pasting them in a notebook. After his death, his brother Krishna Iyer collected to saying that the body is "I." But, can the body be said to be the consciousness "I"? This body was not there before it was born, is made up of the five elements, is non-existent in the state of deep sleep, and becomes a corpse when dead. Can this body, which is inert like a log of wood, be said to shine as "I-I"? Therefore, the "I"-consciousness, which at first arises in respect of the body, is referred to variously as self-conceit (tarbodham), and as individual soul (jiva). Can we remain without enquiring into this? Is it not for our redemption through enquiry into this that all the scriptures declare that the destruction of "self-conceit" is release (mukti)? Therefore, making the corpse-body remain as a corpse and not even uttering the word "I," one should enquire keenly thus: "Now, what is it that rises as 'I'?" Then, there would shine in the Heart a kind of wordless illumination of the form "I-I." That is there and would shine of its own accord. The pure consciousness is unlimited and one. When the limited, with the many thoughts, has disappeared it would be experienced. If one remains quiescent without abandoning that (experience), the egoity, the individual sense of the form "I am the body," will be totally destroyed and at the end the final thought, viz, the "I"-form also will be quenched like the fire that burns camphor. The great sages and scriptures declare that this alone is release.[3]

In this work we also find very valuable information and insights into the essential nature of mind as a reflection of consciousness. In response to the question whether Self-experience is possible to the mind Ramana clearly points out that *"the nature of the mind is pure and undefiled like ether. When it stays in that natural pure state, it has not even the name mind. By erroneous knowledge one mistakes another entity and calls it the mind."* When the mind is rid of its accretions in the form of tendencies, it once again reflects its pure nature as consciousness. Another important aspect covered in Gambhiram Seshier's questions and Ramana's answers is that activity does not disturb the mental peace. One more crucial point made is that one should not examine the contents of the mind or the individual thought or thoughts separately since all thoughts are obstructive of the awareness of the Self. *"One should not give room in the mind for such thoughts as 'Is this good? Or is that good? Can this be done? Or can that be done?' One should be rigid even before such thoughts arise and make the mind stay awake in the natural state. If any little room is given such a disturbed mind will do harm to us by posing as our friend. Like a foe appearing to be a friend it will topple us down."*[4] The important point made here is that self-enquiry, attention, has to be from the beginning of the birth of thought and before its proliferation. Otherwise, if entry is allowed for one "favored" thought, many "unfavored" thoughts will also make their entry and crowd the mind. It will consequently be distracted and divided.

Gambhiram Seshier is one of the devotees who has not received due credit for this valuable contribution which he has made through his question and answer sessions with Ramana spread over three years in the early part of the century. He had also taken the necessary care to preserve the dialogues safely. Anyone who reads the question answer form of *Self-Enquiry* (*Vichara Sangraha*) would realize that this dialogue between the disciple Gambhiram Seshier and *sadguru* Ramana holds a special place in Ramana literature.

Sivaprakasam Pillai

The best known prose work of Ramana is *"Nan Yar?"*, "Who am 'I'?" It has a unique position since the path of self-enquiry has been stated in it by Ramana himself with clarity.

This message was first given in the year 1902 to Sivaprakasam Pillai. Sivaprakasam Pillai was born in August 1875 near the sacred town Chidambaram. Even while at college, fundamental doubts like, "Who is this I who whirls about in attachment to the body?" arose spontaneously in his mind. After completing his degree he joined the Revenue Service in 1900, in the office of the District Collectorate in South Arcot. In the course of his official duties he visited Tiruvannamalai in 1902. There he heard of the saintly and ascetic life of a boy residing on the hill who was then known as Brahmana Swami. At once Sivaprakasam Pillai climbed up to the

Guhai Namasivayar temple where Ramana was staying at that time. Immediately he asked the question which was uppermost in his mind, "Who am I?" Little did he realize that he was asking the most fundamental question around which the teachings of Ramana revolve. In the course of the next few days he put thirteen questions in all to Ramana. At that time since Ramana was maintaining silence, he wrote his replies either on sand or with chalk on a slate. The answer to the last question was immediately copied out by Sivaprakasam Pillai. The other twelve questions and replies were written down by Pillai from memory before the work was published, nearly two decades later in 1923. Some of the answers given to Pillai form a part of Pillai's book *Anugraha Ahaval*, "The Story of Grace" (lines 33-73). The poems in this book describe some of the experiences he had of Ramana's grace. Later in the year on the suggestion of some of his friends, Pillai decided to write another book of poems titled *Sri Ramana Charitra Ahaval* in which he narrates the story of Bhagavan's life. In that book the questions and answers put by Pillai to Ramana in 1902 are printed as an appendix under the title. "Nan Yar?", "Who am 'I'?"

As a consequence it would appear that Ramana himself decided to rewrite "Who am 'I'?" in the form of an essay. In his essay version Ramana had made changes in the structure and content. As a result the essay version could be regarded as an original work of Ramana. Since Ramana himself wrote this essay version it immediately superseded all the versions which were based on the question-answer format.[1] Some extracts from this are given below wherein focus is clearly on the essential teachings of Ramana: *"Every living being longs always to be happy, untainted by sorrow: and everyone has the greatest love for himself, which is solely due to the fact that happiness is his real nature. Hence, in order to realize that inherent and untainted happiness, which indeed he daily experiences, when the mind is subdued in deep sleep, it is essential that he should know himself. For obtaining such knowledge the enquiry 'Who am 'I'?' in quest of the Self is the best means.*

"If the mind, which is the instrument of knowledge and is the basis of all activity, subsides, the perception of the world as an objective reality ceases. Unless the illusory nature of the perception of the world as an objective reality ceases, the vision of the true nature of the Self, on which the illusion is formed, is not obtained.

"The mind is a unique power (sakti) in the Atman, whereby thoughts occur to one. On scrutiny as to what remains after eliminating all thoughts, it will be found that there is no such thing as mind apart from thoughts. So then, thoughts themselves constitute the mind. It is only

through the enquiry 'Who am I?' that the mind subsides and one inheres in the Self."[2]

"Firm and disciplined inherence in Atman *without giving the least scope for the rise of any thoughts other than the deep contemplative thought of the Self, constitutes self-surrender to the Supreme Lord. Let any amount of burden be laid on Him. He will bear it all. It is, in fact, the indefinable power of the Lord that ordains, sustains, and controls everything that happens. Why then should we worry, tormented by vexatious thoughts, saying: 'Shall we act this way? No, that way,' instead of meekly but happily submitting to that Power? Knowing that the train carries all the* weight, why indeed should we, the passengers traveling in it, carry our small individual articles of luggage on our laps to our great discomfort, instead of putting them aside and sitting at perfect ease?"[3]

The main point focused on by Ramana is that happiness is inherent and common to all life. Such happiness is experienced by the mind which is abiding in its source, in the spiritual heart. A mind which abides in the heart is the Self itself. Such a mind is a pure mind. In contrast the mind as we know it is only a bundle of thoughts. If all thoughts are taken away, where is the mind? Of all the thoughts the core thought is the "I"-thought. Self-

enquiry relates to this core "I." When the attention is so focused on this core without paying attention to the rising thoughts the mind subsides in its source. The mind is always aware of the bliss in the heart.

Vasishta Ganapati Muni

Vasishta Ganapati Muni was born on November 17, 1878. He belonged to a very respected family of *brahmins* who had settled down in the village of Kalavarayi in the Vizag

Vasishta Ganapati Muni

district of Andhra Pradesh. His father was Narasimha Sastri and mother was Narasamamba. His parents had three sons and Ganapati Muni was the middle one. He belonged to the lineage of the sage Koundinya. He later changed his name to Vasishta Ganapati because Koundinyas are also known as Vasishtas.

Though Ganapati Muni was born in response to intense prayers of his parents for a special and exceptional child, his childhood was a great disappointment. "He did not articulate, disliked food, swooned often, and was affected with some illness or the other. But suddenly at the age of six, a native treatment of branding with an iron made him alright and his faculties began to shine. A new life started to run in the veins of the child."[1]

Ganapati was precocious and his memory was phenomenal. He became well versed, in a few years, in the intricacies of the sacred syllables (*mantras*), astrology, and ayurveda.

In his twelfth year, Ganapati was married to Visalakshi who was aged eight at that time. Visalakshi's earmarked role was to be a spiritual companion of the Muni in his intense penance (*tapas*).

The lure of penance was so strong in Ganapati that he secretly went with a couple of his friends to a quiet place on the bank of the river Kaushiki near Rajamundry. He was engaged in *tapas* for 45 days before he returned home. On his 20th birthday, Ganapati took the blessings of his father and started for Kasi (Varanasi) for another round of *tapas*. This strong desire for *tapas* was there throughout his life even after he became a disciple of Ramana.

While staying at Kasi, with his skill in extempore poetry, Ganapati attracted the attention of the learned scholars there. They felt his stature was such that he should be selected specially to participate in the grand assembly of Sanskrit scholars which was being arranged at Navadweepa, in Bengal. Since Ganapati was a poet of the same caliber as the renowned Kalidasa, his success at this assembly was foregone. He outmatched everyone in his extempore poetry. He was unanimously awarded the title "Kavayakantha," "One in whose throat poetry resides."

All these might be said to be the backdrop of his strenuous, single-minded, and continuous penance. The fruition was to take place when he turned his attention to the south and decided to come to Arunachala in the beginning of this century. At Tiruvannamalai he completed 1000 verses in praise of Siva and titled the work *Harasahasra Slokavali*. Unfortunately this great work was lost due to the untimely demise of the disciple who had taken it to make a fair copy.

Ganapati Muni and Muruganar stand foremost among the disciples of Ramana. When we think of the Muni the image of the ancient *rishis* of India, like Vasishta, Atreya, and the like comes to our mind. He was a ripe fruit of intense penance (*tapasya*). The *mantra* of five sacred syllables, *Namah Sivaya*, was an *ajapa*, a continuous remembrance which was always with him.

Ganapati Muni "had an air of charm and majesty about him. There was grace in his gait, sureness in his speech. When he spoke, perhaps the gods came down from on high and listened. His voice had an ethereal magnificence which beckoned the soul of the listener.… When the Muni initiated someone into a *mantra*, there was no necessity for that person to carry on with the *japa*. From the moment the initiation was done, the voice of the Muni that articulated the *mantra* continued to reverberate ever afterwards in the heart of the disciple."[2]

All generations of Ramana's disciples and devotees must remain indebted to Muni because it was for his sake and seeing his great spiritual hunger and ripeness that Ramana broke his silence of eleven years and gave the oral *upadesa*. This happened on the epoch-making day, on November 18, 1907. Since then, the relationship between Ramana and the Muni has been a model. Ramana used to affectionately call him "Nayana," which has several shades of meaning in Telugu. It is a term of endearment, it is a term by which one refers to one's father and to a disciple as well.

The Muni was always frank and childlike in his letters to Ramana from Sirsi, which included his spiritual problems. This has led to an opinion that the Muni was not steadily Self-aware because he had *sankalpas*. The mere existence of *sankalpas* does not negate the natural state. Ramana's view is that *"a jnani is a most natural person. He may have* sankalpas *but those* sankalpas *are not binding in nature. They arise either because of* prarabdha *or due to divine promptings. They do not bind a person whose mind is dead."*[3]

Again one should not forget that in the immediate presence of Ramana, while Ramana was staying in the Virupaksha Cave and the Muni in the nearby Mango Tree Cave, the Muni had the ultimate spiritual experience in the path of *Sakti*, worship of the divine Mother. He had what is known as *kapalabhedha*. Prior to this Muni was immersed in deep penance for many days. All distinctions between inner and outer, between day and night disappeared. Yet the Muni would somehow visit Ramana once every day. One day the Muni felt as though his head was pierced and a stream of bliss was shooting from there. The Muni managed to go the next day and report his condition to his *sadguru*. Ramana

passed his hand over the Muni's head with great compassion. He advised him to anoint his head with castor oil before his bath and almond oil after. That night the Muni experienced *kapalabhedha*. Throughout the Muni was surrendered to his Master and Ramana's grace flowed uninterrupted.

Truth Revealed

Muni's penchant for moving from one sacred place to another for penance had become his second nature. And

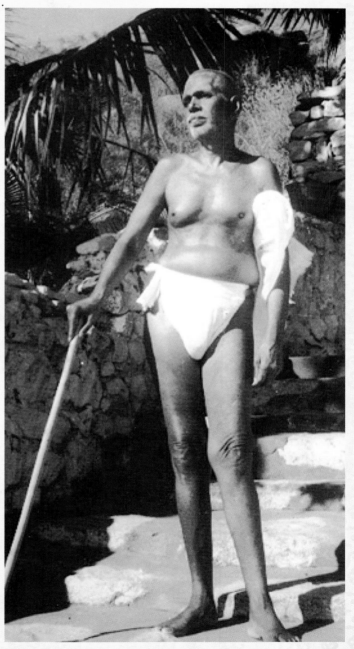

though he was fully endowed with the power which flows from ceaseless penance, though he readily and easily attracted followers, he had the clarity to recognize that somehow his penance was incomplete. He had neither the vision of his favorite God Siva, which he had longed for, nor had he the peace of mind, which must follow from single-minded spiritual effort. Still with faith in his penance and considering that Arunachala was the best place for it he came over there at the turn of the century.

At that time Ramana was known as Brahmana Swami and was staying in the Virupaksha Cave, observing silence. In 1903, on the suggestion of Viswanatha Iyer, the Muni went with him for Ramana's *darsan*. Not finding him at his usual place they went looking for him at an adjacent *asram* of one Padmanabha Swami. They found Ramana there. Though it was their first meeting, the Muni recognized at once that Ramana was "the foremost of sages, lustrous on account of his greatness."[4]

The Muni was greatly attracted to Ramana even at their very first meeting and could quite readily see his glorious state. Yet, the divine time to recognize him as his own *guru*, as also the universal *guru*, had not come. The divine took a hand four years later in 1907, on an epoch-making Monday, November 18, in the Tamil month of Kartigai.

The Kartigai festival was in progress. Hence the Muni came to the town to attend it. After the morning festival, as he was a little tired, he did not return to his place of penance, the Nirrutilinga. Instead, he went to the house of a friend Viswanatha Iyer in order to have his afternoon meal and take some rest. Pondering on the goal of penance he began to be filled with some misgivings. He had performed the Siva *panchaksari* crores of times. He had also subsequently chanted many other *mantras* like *srividya*. He had undergone several austerities including fasting. Yet he did not experience the fruition of his penance. Why was this so? Surely the means prescribed in the scriptures could not be wrong. Then, could there be any deficiency in his understanding of the true meaning of penance? When his mind was caught in this turmoil he suddenly remembered the Brahmana Swami on the hill. He decided to meet him right away in order to fulfill the purpose of his life. No sooner had he decided than he began his climb up the hill reaching there around two o'clock in the afternoon. He could see Brahmana Swami sitting outside the cave. What happened next is best stated in the Muni's own words.

"Those were the days of the Kartigai festival. People, people everywhere. At the dwelling of the Swami also the devotees should have been thronging. It was really a surprise when there was no one there and Swami was sitting alone. I took courage in the thought that this was an indication of divine will. I approached the Swami with jubilation. As soon as I reached him I held his right foot with my right hand and his left foot with my left hand and prostrated with my whole body. Getting up, I appealed thus: 'I have studied and understood the essence of the *Sastras*. I have repeated the great *mantras* with contemplation; many austerities have I performed. Missing still is the Lord's grace. Were there lapses in my *tapas*? Have I missed its very nature? Though learned, I am ignorant. I surrender to you, All-knowing One. Accept me as your disciple and bless me.'[5]

"Thus when I fell at his feet in spiritual agony, desperately pleading for guidance, a soothing stream of his compassionate look flowed into me and encompassed me. He was the foremost among those who had totally conquered his senses. He who comprehended my state and situation in a moment, showered upon me soothing rain of grace and bliss from his fully open compassionate

eyes. Opening a new chapter in both our lives, the words of nectar slowly flowed from him.

"'When the mind enquires from where the notion "I" arises and dissolves right there at the origin of its birth, that is *tapas*. On the enquiry as to the exact origin from where the sound of *mantra* arises, the mind dissolves at the origin itself and that is *tapas*.'

"I was gratified by this teaching…*upadesa* which came directly from a great teacher-*guru*. I had an experience of floating on an ocean of bliss."[6]

It may be noted that the first part of the instructions is in line with what was given earlier by Ramana to Gambhiram Seshier and Sivaprakasam Pillai in 1900-1902, the now famous "Who am 'I'?" enquiry. However,

the second part is new and in a sense equally revolutionary. For, a vast number of seekers are initiated into *mantras*. Their faith in the efficacy of these *mantras* is deep-rooted as the Muni's was then. Ramana draws them gently, yet firmly, to the path of self-enquiry by turning their attention to the source of the *mantra* sound. Thus source consciousness would be awakened.

What was the state of the Muni on that eventful day? He was desperately thirsty for knowing the secret underlying the scriptures. His utter humility is also seen from his remark "though learned, I am ignorant." This fact is heightened if one remembers that a large number of seekers at that time considered the Muni to be their *guru*. His scriptural learning and *tapasya* had made him ripe and ready. What was lacking was the *sadguru*'s grace to light the fire of knowledge. The Self-realized knower of truth, Ramana, provided this. It was his grace which revealed the truth to the Muni.

The Muni remarks that a new chapter had opened up not only for himself but Ramana as well. For eleven years since his arrival at Arunachala in 1896, Ramana had remained silent and had not spoken except to his faithful attendant Palaniswami. True, he had given instructions to his mother, Gambhiram Seshier, and Sivaprakasam Pillai. But it was on sand or slate or paper. Ramana's very first oral instructions were only to the Muni. As a result, Ramana became more openly available to seekers of truth. He had assumed the role earmarked for him, as the universal teacher whose teachings are most appropriate for this age. The world was not to be denied the soft and ambrosial voice of Ramana. What an epoch making breaking of silence it has been!

Let the Whole World Know Him as Bhagavan Sri Ramana Maharshi

The Muni was in a state of ecstatic happiness on receiving Ramana's advice. At last his Herculean penance had borne fruit. A great peace flooded his whole being and he was floating on an ocean of bliss. Till that evening he was meditating sitting right at the holy feet of his *guru*.

On learning that Swami's name was Venkataraman, the Muni turned it into the short and sweet name Ramana. He was not only his *sadguru* but the universal *guru*. Hence the Muni thought that he should also be called "Maharshi." Since he was endowed with all godly qualities, the Muni felt he should be regarded as "Bhagavan." Therefore he proclaimed that henceforth his disciples and the whole world should regard and address the Brahmana Swami as Bhagavan Sri Ramana Maharshi.[7] From then onwards the name Bhagavan Sri Ramana Maharshi has become revered and famous throughout the world. In an inspired mood the Muni immediately wrote to his intimate disciples and well wishers: "I have obtained as my *guru* a supreme sage known as Brahmana Swami, who lives in a cave in Arunachala. He is a great visionary: an epitome of all good qualities; one who deserves the name of Bhagavan Maharshi. I have abridged his name to Ramana in a brief and beautiful manner. Accordingly through my letters I have informed my disciples and well-wishers that they should also call him Ramana."[8]

Ramana Gita—1917

Though the Muni would leave Arunachala for *tapasya* every now and then due to his own inner compulsion, the magnetic pull of his *guru* Ramana would keep pulling him back to Arunachala. During those periods of his stay at Arunachala some significant event or the other would happen. The Muni had come in 1913 and participated in a debate among the scholars on certain Vedantic questions. The nature of the world and spiritual practices relating to the *jnana* path were discussed. When the Muni returned again in 1917, he stayed in the Mango Tree Cave near Skandasramam where Ramana was staying at that time. Proximity to the *guru* made him feel that it was time to obtain authoritative pronouncements from Ramana on all the scriptures and extant religious practices. He felt that Ramana's statements would be authentic being based on his direct experience of Self-awareness and his steady abidance in natural *samadhi*.

In 1917, the Muni spent a few months questioning Ramana directly and through seven of his disciples on problems covering the entire gamut of spiritual practice. Hence through these question and answer sessions we have the authoritative clarifications of Ramana on such important issues. Besides Ramana has also thrown clear light on his direct path termed as "The Science of the Heart." Finding that these rulings were as epoch-making to seekers of truth as the message of Sri Krishna through the *Bhagavad Gita*, the Muni decided to record the questions and answers under the name *Ramana Gita*. Accordingly he arranged the questions and answers recorded in Sanskrit into eighteen chapters covering 300 verses.

One cannot be too grateful to the Muni for this monumental work. For *Ramana Gita* represents the quintessence of wisdom. This work is a pathfinder in many ways. The subjects dealt with, such as "Paramount Duty," "Science of the Heart," "Mind Control," "Self-enquiry," "Cutting the Knot," just to mention a few, are significant for truth seekers. A bird's eye view of the contents will help in understanding the profound significance of the work for a meaningful life.

Ramana emphasizes that the purpose of all spiritual practice is to discover the natural state. What is this natural state? It is a state when the mind is silent, when bliss inundates, and consciousness shines in all its fullness. Why natural? It is termed natural because it is one's own, it is not given and therefore cannot be taken away. What hides it? The externalization of the mind prevents awareness of the natural state. By appropriate spiritual practice the mind must be made to turn within. This is one's paramount duty. The best method for turning the mind within is self-enquiry. What constitutes self-enquiry? It is an enquiry about the subject, about the "I." When

Ramana and Ganapati Muni

reflects it. If the mind consciously merges in the heart by vigilant self-enquiry a new way of life is thrown open. It is a heart-based life instead of a mind-centered life with all the limitations arising from attachments. Then it does not make any difference if one is in a jungle hermitage or in a London flat. For a steady river of bliss will flow through all actions.

"The 'A to Z' of such a free and joyous life has been set out by Ramana so simply and so directly in *Ramana Gita* that one regrets the wasted years of spiritual wandering at wrong doors."[9]

Verse 2 of chapter two of *Ramana Gita* is the first original Sanskrit composition of Ramana. Though Ramana was not familiar with Sanskrit at that time, because of his steady wisdom, words placed themselves automatically at the right place. It emphasizes the importance of Self-abidance by some appropriate practice, be it self-enquiry or breath regulation. The story behind its composition as narrated by Ramana is worth recording.

"In 1915, when we were staying in Virupaksha Cave during Chaturmasya (rainy season) an ardent devotee, Jagadeeswara Sastri, one day wrote down on a piece of paper the words 'hridaya kuhara madhye' (in the center of the heart's cavity), held it in his hand and sat down. When I asked him what it was, he said he wanted to write a sloka *(verse) but when he actually began it he could write only that much.*

"I asked him to complete the rest. He said that nothing was coming forth. Thereafter he just left the paper under my seat. Though I reminded him any number of times he pleaded his inability. One day he left for some place. Before his return, I completed the sloka, *wrote 'Jagadeesan' and showed it to him as soon as he returned. Those days he was very young. He said, 'Is it not Bhagavan who completed it? Why is it written Jagadeesan?' I said, 'I don't know that! Was it not Jagadeesan who completed it?' Then, saying, 'If it was written by Jagadeesan please give me the paper,' he took it away and preserved it."[10]*

Years later Kapali Sastri, one of the questioners in *Ramana Gita*, wrote in his commentary on it that he was filled with a sense of awe at the significance of this holy work. Writing in 1932 to a friend of his, Viswanatha Swami, he says, "My mind is given to the subject now. Waiting for the light to guide me aright so that I may not misuse the proud privilege of commenting upon the utterances of one the like of whom appears on earth once in a millennium or two."[11]

attention is so focused on the "I" it would be seen to be the center of the mind. Other thoughts exist only in relation to it. The "I"-thought and the mind are understood to be identical. Self-enquiry also reveals that what we call the mind is only a phenomenon of the waking state. It is non-existent in deep sleep. It rises on waking and sinks when sleep overtakes. Hence the necessity to search for its source. This search would lead one to the spiritual heart from which all thoughts spring. Ramana has explained, in great detail, the working of the spiritual heart and how its consciousness spreads to the mind and thereafter permeates the whole body. The analogy of the sun and the moon is given to bring out the essential relationship between the spiritual heart and the mind. The heart is the source of consciousness and the mind only

Some of the views expressed by Ramana in *Ramana Gita* are quite a departure from the traditional views held thus far. For instance he asserts that women too can practice the path of knowledge if they are ripe for it. He also states that the body of a woman illumni is a temple of God and consequently it should not be cremated but buried and worshipped. We also find that he places before the society as its goal the ideal of "brotherhood based on equality." Just imagine how radical these views would have been in 1917.

Ramana was in his mid-thirties at that time. But what wisdom flows from his lips! One wonders, "Is there anything which he does not know?" The image of the youthful, primal *guru* Dakshinamurti immediately comes to the mind.

Cast Your Burden on the Lord of the Universe

In May 1908, the Muni started to Tiruvottiyur for penance. He was in a great spiritual mood after staying with the Maharshi for several months at Pachaiamman Koil. His reason for deciding to leave for penance is best stated in his own words: "Even though seeking the Self resulting in the perception of one's own real nature is undoubtedly the best attainment, *siddhi*, I thought that it was not enough."[12] He also questioned the Maharshi, "Is seeking the source of 'I'-thought sufficient for accomplishing all my aims or is *mantra dhyana* needed?" The Maharshi replied, *"The former is enough."*[13] The Muni was convinced. Yet the idea of penance was so deeply ingrained that he sought Ramana's blessings. Out of the vastness of his compassion Ramana advised the whole world through the Muni how the goal of Self-attention is to be pursued.

"One should cast one's burden on the Lord of the Universe who is always victorious. He is the excellent doer of all actions. You should always concentrate your intellect on the heart, which is the seat of the Atman and abide there.

"This doer, the Lord, is powerful enough to fulfill your object in the future.

"The Lord of the Universe controlling the past and the future should be entrusted as the efficient actor.

"When the time comes, the excellent object would be fulfilled. Let there be no doubt in your mind, jewel of the learned. By steady abidance

in the heart, your welfare is sure. Let the work be surrendered to Siva."[14]

It is classic advice on par with the guidance to his mother Azhagammal in 1898, to Sivaprakasam Pillai in 1901, and to the Muni himself a year earlier when he had sought his counsel about the true meaning of *tapas*.

One might say that this statement is the distilled essence of both self-enquiry and surrender. One finds that in this statement Ramana is emphasizing one central point again and again that *"everything should be entrusted to the all powerful doer of actions, the Lord of the Universe."* Simultaneously one's attention is drawn to the fact that this enables one to shift the focus of attention to the source, the heart, and to abide there. Another angle of his advice is that this is the excellent object of all spiritual endeavor. At the same time one finds Ramana counseling patience. For while fulfilling the excellent object of Self-

knowledge is surely the Lord's burden, the best timing for it is known only to Him, because He is the all-knowing controller of the past and the future.

On reaching Tiruvottiyur, the Muni chose a temple of Lord Ganesa for his penance. While he was immersed in it, on the eighteenth day while meditating with attention, he saw the Maharshi sitting by his side. "Out of confusion, wonder, and devotion I got up and the *guru* placed his hand on my head and made me sit."[15] "A current of energy burst forth filling his entire body. The Muni was convinced that his *guru* the Maharshi, who was none other than Kartikeya, had covered the distance between Arunachala and Tiruvottiyur, miraculously, to bless him."[16]

Ramana never left Arunachala after September 1, 1896, when he arrived there *"in obedience to his Father's command and in search of him."* How then could his body have been in two places at the same time, both at Arunachala and at Tiruvottiyur? According to the Muni, "The Lord of the *yogis* in the world of Gods, flew by the path brightened by moonlight and having heard the word 'Tiruvottiyur' came down to the earth. Then he walked a long distance, turned west, saw the temple of Ganesa and entered it."[17] Perhaps the intensity of the disciple's penance and his desire to receive his *guru's*

blessings brought about this miracle. To complete the account Ramana himself stated many years later what happened then. When the Muni narrated this incident, Ramana explained, *"One day some years ago I lay down, but I was awake. I suddenly felt my body carried up higher and higher till all objects disappeared and all round me was one vast mass of white light. Then suddenly the body descended and objects began to appear and disappear. The idea occurred to me that I was at Tiruvottiyur. I was on a high road. On one side at some distance removed from it was a Ganapati temple. I went in and talked, but what I said or did, I do not recollect. Suddenly I woke up and found myself lying in Virupaksha Cave. I mentioned this immediately to Palaniswami who was always with me."*[18]

Ulladu Narpadu—Sat Darsanam

For many of Ramana's works Muruganar was a catalyst. In 1928, Muruganar felt that in the interest of genuine seekers of truth, Ramana should compose forty verses on Reality. Its purpose was to serve as a regular treatise on the subject by setting out, in logical order, the salient features of his teachings. Ramana would never say no to his earnest disciples and devotees. The forty verses were arranged in a proper order, according to the thoughts expressed in them, to make for the regular treatment of the subject. It was published under the title *Ulladu Narpadu.*[19] The world of seekers of truth, for all times to come, will remain indebted to Muruganar for it.

The Muni translated the work into Sanskrit in the mellifluous Upajati meter. The translation *Sat-Darsanam* has become a classic in spiritual literature. The reason is given by the Muni himself: "For it reflects the enchanting words of divine Ramana, which give the essence of truth easily, and is a delight to seekers."[20]

Sat-Darsanam is a compound word. *Sat* meaning Existence, the Real, the Truth, and *Darsanam* means its perception. It also means the experience of those abiding in *Sat* or Truth. In this case it refers to Ramana's experience. This work stresses that abidance in the spiritual heart is *Sat-Darsanam*. Ramana repeatedly said that the only infallible means to do so is to enquire into the source of the mind and he has given the necessary method for it. Hence this work is a practice-oriented scripture, in which we find that "the original and independent utterances of Ramana are like *Upanishads*, based on direct experience, and their message is for all."[21]

The Muni and the Maharshi—The Later Years

Whatever may be the other interests in his life, the Muni always gave top priority to spreading knowledge about

Ramana's unique stature. This was the constant undercurrent of the Muni's life along which he traveled with faith and devotion. His overwhelming devotion to Ramana is evident in his letters to his disciples, in his letters to Ramana from Sirsi in Karnataka, and in his compositions, particularly *Chatvarimsat—Forty Verses in Praise of Ramana*. When others tried to praise him he would not take the credit but say, "It is not I but the Maharshi who is doing all these things." To Ramana belonged the throne of the "Universal Teacher," a throne which had been vacant for centuries since Adi Sankara. He was the humble disciple seeking *sadguru* Ramana's blessings for a twofold purpose, for his own steady abidance in the natural state and even more than that for the glorification of Ramana himself.

Ramana held the Muni in the highest regard and used to call him Nayana, which is a term of endearment meaning child or disciple or father. Ramana started calling the Muni Nayana in the following circumstances. A devotee asked, "Why does Bhagavan call Ganapati Muni, Nayana?" *"There is a reason for it,"* he replied. *"It is my custom to address all people with respect. Moreover, he was older than me. I therefore always used to call him Ganapati Sastri Garu. That was very distressing to him. Hence he begged me several times not to do so, saying. 'Am I not your disciple? You should call me by a familiar name. This is very unfair.' I did not pay any heed to his protests. At last one day he insisted on my giving up the formal way of addressing him and adopting a familiar one. All his disciples call him Nayana. So I made it an excuse and said I too would call him Nayana like the others. He agreed to it because Nayana means a child and a disciple could be addressed as one's own child. I agreed because Nayana also means father and hence it would not matter so far as I was concerned. I was still addressing him in respectful terms. Whenever I asked him to come here or go there he was still uncomfortable because after all that he had done, I continued to talk to him with the respect due to elders."*[22]

When a telegram giving news of the Muni's *mahasamadhi* was received at Sri Ramanasramam, Ramana said in a voice choked with emotion, *"Where can we find another like him?"*[23] He also spoke at length very appreciatively about his humble conduct though he was so learned and capable. He referred to the great worth of the compositions of the Muni like *Uma Sahasram* and *Hara Sahasram*. Someone asked how the Muni had become an inspired poet, an *asu kavi*, Ramana mentioned that it is believed to be due to the *"milk or honey given to him by Lord Siva who appreciated his intense* tapas."[24]

Soon after the Muni's *mahasamadhi*, Ramana himself arranged the occasional stray verses in his praise composed by the Muni and titled the collection *Chatvarimsat*,

"Forty Verses in Praise." This was chanted before Ramana each morning before the Vedic chanting. Now it is being chanted in front of Ramana's shrine. This indicates the regard and love Ramana had for the Muni and also the Muni's stature. "Out of the tender store of the disciple and the *sadguru*, of Nayana and Ramana, something indefinable but extraordinarily beautiful and evergreen has been bequeathed to posterity."[25]

꧁꧂

F. H. Humphreys

Humphreys joined the Indian Police Service at Vellore, near Tiruvannamalai, in 1911. Due to his past spiritual practices he used to have visions which enabled him to

they performed miracles were they aware that they performed miracles?" Humphreys could readily see the logic of it, that they were only "the media through which God's power did its work." Another question related to helping the world to which Ramana advised him, *"Help yourself, you will help the world."*[3]

The main focus of Ramana's advice was to turn the attention of Humphreys to the supreme power responsible for everything. *"The phenomena we see are curious and surprising but the most marvelous thing of it all we do not realize and that is that one, illimitable force is responsible for:*

♦ *All the phenomena we see,*
♦ *The act of our seeing them.*

Do not fix your attention on all these changing things of life, death, and phenomena. Do not think of even the actual act of seeing them or perceiving them, but only of that, which sees all these things. That which is responsible for it all."[4]

The importance of Ramana's advice is further strengthened by the fact that it was given as a *guru* would to his disciple. Ramana told him, *"I have given you this teaching in the same words as the Masters give it to their intimate chelas."*[5]

Lesser Known Devotees of Ramana

Ramana Dasa Sadananda
(Seshagiri Iyer)

Seshagiri Iyer was a teacher in P.S. High School, Madras. On the suggestion of his brother-in-law, he visited Ramana for the first time on Tuesday, November 15, 1915 at Virupaksha Cave. The impact of this first meeting was so great that he was tongue-tied. He was filled with nectarine bliss in the joyous presence of Ramana.[1] On the following day he visited Ramana again because he had some doubts on the spiritual path which needed clarification. Some of these questions are as follows:

Q. How am I to ascertain who "I" am?
A. *By frequent, if not constant, questioning and searching within.*

foresee the coming events in the spiritual field. As soon as he landed in Bombay, he fell ill. While convalescing there in a hospital he had a clear vision of his Telugu teacher Narasimayya, who in turn was a disciple of Ganapati Muni, who regarded Ramana as his *guru*. One might say that the divine literally led him to Ramana.[1]

After joining at Vellore, he again fell sick and had to go to a cool hill station in April that year. On returning he drew a picture of a "mountain cave with a sage standing at its entrance and a stream gently flowing down the hill in front of the cave." The Telugu teacher identified this as Ramana and told him about his glorious state. He soon met the Muni and the three of them went to Virupaksha Cave in November. Shortly thereafter he paid a second visit on his own. He traveled all the way by his motorbike from Vellore in order to be able to do so. On the second visit A.S. Krishnawami Iyer, then a judicial officer, a District Munsiff, who happened to be present, acted as an interpreter.[2] Humphreys paid his third visit also in quick succession.

There is a contemporaneous record of the questions and answers on all the three occasions. We might say that this has ensured a permanent place for Humphreys in the minds of spiritual seeekers.

Humphreys was barely twenty-one years of age at that time and therefore we notice an uninhibited spontaneity in his interviews with Ramana and a special charm in the way Ramana clarified his doubts.

Because of his occult background some of his early questions related to miracles. He wished to know: "Master can I perform miracles as Sri Krishna and Jesus did?" Ramana countered it by another question: *"When*

Q. How to deal with the mind which stands in the way of such enquiry?

A. *The mind is nothing but thoughts and the root thought is "I" which is known as ego. When the question "Who am I?" preponderates it kills all other thoughts at first and it goes ultimately.*

Q. What displaces the disappearing ego?

A. *The all knowing feeling of bliss shining as "I" devoid of qualities will take its place.*[2]

Mastan

Mastan Sahib was a weaver from Desur. He, along with other devotees from that place, formed a group "Ramanananda Madalayam" for conducting programs connected with teachings of Ramana. He used to be a frequent visitor of Virupaksha Cave. From 1914 onwards he used to stay with Ramana for long stretches.

One day he requested Ramana to bestow his grace on him. Then the following conversation took place.

R.: *What do you like? Saguna upasana or nirguna upasana?*

M.: I would like to perform *nirguna upasana.*

R.: *If you observe wherefrom all the thoughts arise then they would all be dissolved in the heart. What Is only will remain.*

Even though he was thus instructed Mastan used to hear sounds during practice and sought the advice of Ramana. Ramana told him: *"Do not worry about the sound, but enquire wherefrom the sound arises. Everything arises from the Self. Therefore it will dissolve into the Self. What Is alone will remain."*[3]

Sacred Hands

On Monday the 31st August 1896, in most Indian homes the birth of Sri Krishna was being celebrated. Ramana was fatigued and hungry. After he left his home on the 29th of August he had not had any proper meal. So he walked to the house of one Muthukrishna Bhagavatar and begged for food. Being a happy and auspicious day he was given a sumptuous meal at noon. On the following day, the 1st September 1896, in the early morning hours he reached Tiruvannamalai. After reporting his arrival *"to his Father at Arunachaleswara temple"* he remained immersed in his own natural bliss. There was none to feed him and he was so intoxicated with inner bliss that he himself did not ask for food. It is then that on the following day, the Lord Himself made Ramana His concern. There were many mendicants in the temple. One of them who was a *mouna* Swami (a silent *sadhu*), who told his disciples through signs at noon, "I do not know who this boy is. But he appears to be tired. Please get some food and give it to him." With his photographic memory Ramana

recalls what they had brought. *"It was boiled rice. Each grain was sized. There was sour water under it and there was pickle in it. Taking it as the first* bhiksa *given to me by Arunachaleswara I ate the rice and drank the water given to me. That happiness can never be forgotten."*[1] The first sacred hands which fed Ramana were those of this anonymous *swami*. The hands which fed Ramana in those days were especially sacred. Because in his state then, the total inward absorption and outward silence as well, his body would have been lost to the world before the wonder of his liberating message could be revealed.

To escape from the mischief of urchins Ramana had entered into a dark underground shrine, Patalalingam, which was totally neglected, dingy, and full of insects and reptiles. There too the infinite took a hand by sending one Ratnammal who braved the darkness of the place, went into the underground cave, and gave food to Ramana. Hers too are sacred hands.

In B.V. Narasimha Swami's biography there is a reference to Ratnamma. When Ramana had gone into the dark Patalalinga area in the thousand-pillared hall of the Arunachaleswara temple, Ramana was not aware that his thighs and legs were full of sores from which blood and pus were flowing. This was because ants, mosquitoes, and worms were feasting on his thighs. Once Ratnammal, who went into the pit to give him food, pleaded with him about his pitiable condition and tried to persuade him to come to her house. To save him from the attacks of the pests she left a clean piece of cloth to sit on. Ramana did not respond. Such was the intensity of his inwardness that he noticed nothing.[2]

It appears that later, when Ramana shifted to the garden surrounding the temple, she had a more active role in providing food to him. A very graphic account is given by Ramana himself which is extracted in full: *"I was living under the madhuka tree; a twenty year old dancing girl, by name Ratnamma, saw me one day while going to and from the temple to dance. She grew devoted to me and got disgusted with her profession, and told her mother that she would not eat unless she consented to give food to me. So both of them brought food. But I was then in deep meditation and opened neither my eyes nor my mouth, even when they shouted. But they somehow woke me up by asking a passerby to pull me by the hand; they then gave me food and left. When Ratnamma insisted that she must feed me daily before she ate, her mother said, "You are young and so is the Swami, and he does not wake until somebody touches and pulls him. We can't do that: what can we do?" Ratnamma then asked a first cousin of hers for assistance and with his help used to give me food daily. After some time, however, relatives of the boy felt this work to be undignified and so stopped sending him. She, however, would not give up her resolve to feed me; so at last the old mother herself came regularly, and being elderly, and thinking that therefore there was no harm in it, used to wake me up by shaking me and then give me food. Shortly afterwards, the old mother passed away, and I too shifted from there to a distant place. Ratnamma could no longer go the long distance to feed me, and so gave up her attempts. What does it matter to what community she belonged, she was pure. She had great non-attachment and great devotion."*[3]

Ramana recalls the interlude with Ratnamma in every little detail nearly fifty years after the event. What compassion he had for this unknown dancer, who had lovingly insisted on his being fed properly when he had no thought of the body and its needs.

When Ramana was bodily lifted out of Patalalingam and brought to the Subrahmanya shrine the first Mouna Swami used to give him milk mixed with turmeric, sugar, plantains etc., which was poured on the Goddess Apeeta Kuchamba during *abhisheka*. The priest who noticed this one day said that pure milk poured over the Goddess should be collected immediately and given to him. This sustained him for a few more months.[4]

During November and December 1896 there was a big festival in the town, the Kartigai festival. During that time many *sadhus* used to come to the temple and one of them, Uddandi Nayanar, took up the responsibility of caring for Ramana's body. This privilege was later taken over by Annamalai Tambiran who passed it on to Palaniswami.

Echammal

After some devotees joined Ramana at Virupaksha Cave they went around the streets of the town every day collecting alms. This would be shared equally by all of them. It would serve as a single meal and often there would either be no food or only adequate food. Again the divine took a hand by bringing Echammal in 1906 to the Virupaksha Cave. Her name was Lakshmiammal but she was called Echammal. To this saintly person belongs the credit of serving food to Ramana and a few of his devotees for the next 38 years until she passed away in 1945. Before she was 25 she lost her husband, then her only son, and finally her only daughter in quick succession. The shock stunned her and she left her village Mundakolathur and went to various pilgrimage centers including Gokarnam. She met holy sages, yet her sorrow remained deep and inconsolable. When she returned to her village in 1906, she was told about Ramana and she immediately went to Virupaksha Cave. She stood for an hour in his presence and spoke nothing. No words were exchanged. Wonder of wonders! She stood transfixed and could not think of leaving the *asram*. Finally she somehow pulled herself away. By the grace of the Maharshi "the incubus of sorrow had been lifted from her heart."[5]

Noticing that there were no arrangements for Ramana's food she would prepare a meal every day for him and some of his devotees and carry it to him. Whatever was left over was to be her *prasadam*. This resolve she kept up even after mother Azhagammal came to stay with Ramana and after the kitchen came up in Skandasramam as well. When Ramanasramam grew very big everyone felt it was unnecessary for her to take the trouble anymore. But it was only for this purpose that she lived. She would not miss a single day. Even when she was sick she would arrange to send the food. Ramana in turn showed great compassion to her. Nagamma reports an incident when Ramana waited for her food. One day the cooks, forgetting to serve the food sent by Echammal, finished serving all the other items of food cooked in the *asram*. Bhagavan would usually signal to the others to start eating. But that time he sat silently with his left hand under his chin and his right hand over the leaf. All those waiting to dine began looking at one another. Those in the kitchen too began to enquire among themselves in whispers about the possible reason. Suddenly they remembered that the food sent by Echammal had not been served. They then served her food saying "Oh! We forgot to serve this." Only then did Bhagavan give the signal for eating and he commenced eating as well.[6] There is another incident relating to the compassion which Ramana had for Echammal. The *asram* management out of regard for her old age once decided that Echammal need not take the trouble of bringing the food all the way. For Echammal this was a great blow. Her very existence was for serving food to Bhagavan. Hearing this Bhagavan refused to enter the dining hall when the midday meal bell rang. He never gave any reason. The devotees soon understood that he was protesting on the ban on Echammal. By this time Echammal had gone back to town. On hearing about this she returned at once and requested Bhagavan to enter the dining hall and have his meal. Bhagavan did so.[7] After this every one knew the importance which Ramana attached to the great service which Echammal had been rendering from the time when he was comparatively unknown.

Ramana's Mother Azhagammal

Azhagammal was born at Pasalai, a village near Manamadurai, in Tamil Nadu. She was married to Sundaram Iyer of Tiruchuzhi at an early age. Sundaram Iyer was a very successful lawyer in the local court. Theirs was an open house in which guests were always welcome. Azhagammal would not hesitate to serve the guests even in the middle of night.

Azhagammal learnt hundreds of devotional songs, pregnant with Vedantic meaning, from the elder ladies

Ramana and Mother Azhagammal

at Tiruchuzhi. In those days, when formal school education of women was unknown, she learnt music and received spiritual instructions from these elders. They were only too ready to teach Azhagammal for she would serve them willingly and well. From one venerable old lady, Tulasamma, she also received *upadesa* of the sacred *mantra Aham Brahmasmi*.

Her first child, Nagaswami, was born in 1877. On December 30, 1879, on the Ardra Darsana day, sacred for Siva as Nataraja, her second son Venkataraman was born. During her pregnancy of Venkataraman, she had a tremendous burning sensation all over the body which did not respond to medical treatment. Only juice extracted from bilwa leaves, considered sacred for worship of Siva, could relieve her. After the child was as born Azhagammal had plenty of milk and Venkataraman fed on it even up to the age of five. Venkataraman and Azhagammal were so generous that in this feeding, a motherless child Meenakshi, from the neighboring house, would also partake.

Azhagammal would cast aside all distinctions when it came to the question of giving food. Her warm-heartedness in this regard stood out throughout her life. In those days there was a social taboo against the interdining of Muslims and Hindus, but Azhagammal would gladly provide many a meal for Venkataraman's Muslim friend, Sab Jaan.

In these happy years, a third son, Nagasundaram, and a daughter, Alamelu, were also born to her.

In 1892, Sundaram Iyer passed away. It was literally a bolt from the blue. Sundaram Iyer was in his mid-forties and was the head of the joint family. His prosperity as a lawyer was shared by everyone. His sudden death made a world of difference. Azhagammal and her younger children, Nagasundaram and Alamelu, went to Manamadurai and stayed with Nelliappa Iyer, a younger brother of Sundaram Iyer. Nagaswami and Venkataraman went to their younger paternal uncle, Subba Iyer, at Madurai.[1]

Mother's Anguish

The sudden departure of Venkataraman from Madurai on August 29, 1896, filled mother Azhagammal's heart with anguish. Being a helpless widow she could only entreat her brothers-in-law Nelliappa Iyer and Subba Iyer, to make an all out search, which they did. However, in the absence of any clue, they drew a blank.

Each passing day added to the agony of mother Azhagammal. Her dear son had left home on August 29. 1896. All leads and clues about his whereabouts were proving futile. Days were passing into months and months into years. Yet there was no trace of him. After two years she had reached the point of despair. Were all her prayers falling on deaf ears? Were all the great gods really cold and indifferent to human sorrow and suffering? True, her son had left a message of consolation, a message that he would be well taken care of wherever he was. He had told the truth, that he was leaving home at his Father's command. But can Azhagammal be blamed if she did not have this confidence? Could she be aware then of the certainty that no one can care more than God for his devotees? How could she know of a protection which would be greater than what even her motherly love could give? She was desperate and helpless. Therefore the mood of surrender was fully on her.

Though the laws of grace are mysterious, beyond the mind's comprehension, one thing is clear. When one realizes the utter futility of all human endeavors and recognizes that God alone is our true helper, then the support is very much there, unfailingly there. So here too we find the response. In one sense Ramana has no particular individual identity, he did not sign the note he had written before leaving for Arunachala. Yet, at this juncture he chose to reveal to his mother the necessary information by which she could find out where and how he was now. One government official insisted on his writing down his name. *"Venkataraman -Tiruchuzhi"* was what he wrote. What more definite data could be given? One is filled with won-

der at this act of grace. For Ramana never wrote his name after leaving his home, except on this solitary occasion. "For he knew the suffering of the heart separated from its dear one."[2] One might ask why he did not help earlier. The reason was that his mother and his relatives were making their efforts. They were confident of success. But when the dead-end situation came, when mother had no other recourse, Ramana responded to her prayers and revealed what perhaps could never have been discovered. He had allowed himself to be traced.

The identification happened at the Gurumurtam temple at Tiruvannamalai. How did this information reach mother and the family?

On May 1, 1898, Subba Iyer died at Madurai. Azhagammal, Nelliappa Iyer, the surviving uncle, and his family went there for the funeral. Before the ceremonies were over a young man from Tiruchuzhi, known to the

family, gave them the heart-warming message. He said "Venkataraman is a revered saint at Tiruvannamalai." This young man had visited some Mutt where he had heard Annamalai Tambiran describing with awe and utmost reverence the sanctity of a young saint at Tiruvannamalai who hailed from Tiruchuzhi. This young man had put two and two together and hastened to inform the family.[3]

At that time Ramana was staying in the mango grove adjacent to Gurumurtam. This sanctuary away from the crowd was facilitated by a devotee, the owner of the grove. He had given strict instructions to Rama Naicker, the watchman of the grove, not to allow anyone inside. In May 1898, Nelliappa Iyer came to the grove to meet his nephew but the watchman refused him permission to enter and would not budge despite all the persuasive skills of Nelliappa Iyer. Finally, however, the watchman agreed

to let him in if the Swami had no objection. He wanted to send him a note. But he had not brought any pen with him. He took out a neem twig, sharpened the end to a point, plucked a ripe prickly-pear from its stalk, cut it open, dipped the twig into the red juice of the pear, and wrote on a slip with it. It read, "Nelliappa Iyer, Pleader, Manamadurai, wishes to have your *darsan* (come into your august presence)."[4]

Ramana's observation was flawless. He noticed at once that on the backside of the slip there was the handwriting of his elder brother Nagaswami on a paper of the Registration Department, which meant that he had joined that department presumably as a clerk. Naturally the uncle was allowed to come in. He was in for a rude shock. Ramana's body was unwashed, dirt-laden, his hair matted, nails long and curled. He was deeply moved. After the death of Ramana's father he had mainly looked

Group photo with Ramana and his mother seated next to him

edge. Later Ramana recalled, *"He went away fully satisfied. Till then he was anxious about me. He passed away a few days later."*[5]

Ramana also added, *"If it had been Subba Iyer, he would never have gone back home leaving me here. For he was a man of great courage and pride. He would have bundled me up and carried me home. As I was destined to stay here, my whereabouts were not known as long as he was alive. Nelliappa Iyer being spiritually minded and mild in his ways, left me here thinking 'Why trouble him?'"*[6]

Nelliappa Iyer's trip to Tiruvannamalai in May 1898 and his attempts to persuade his nephew to return home proved futile. Naturally Azhagammal was sorely disappointed. Still, as a fond mother she was confident that if she went there personally, she would definitely succeed in persuading her son to return home. Even though she was eager to rush to Tiruvannamalai and bring him back she had to hold her impatience as she needed an escort. Her first son Nagaswami, who had joined Government service in the Registration Department, could get leave only during Christmas holidays. She was therefore forced to wait till then.

When Nagaswami and Azhagammal went to Tiruvannamalai, in December 1898, during Christmas vacation they learnt that Ramana had shifted to Pavazhakundru, a hillock adjoining Arunachala. Notwithstanding the exhausting climb, Azhagammal went there with eager anticipation. She was seeing Venkataraman after twenty-eight seemingly endless months. What she saw of his physical condition pained her to the core. Long nails, matted hair, a small cod piece, and a body covered with dust, presented a sight which she could not bear. Day after day she poured out her longing and loving concern. However, he did not break the silence which he had been observing since his arrival. On one occasion the mother enlisted the sympathy of other persons present and requested them to intercede on her behalf. One of them, Pachiappa Pillai, said, "Your mother is weeping and crying. Why should you not at least say 'Yes' or 'No.' You need not break your silence, but you can at least write—here is some paper and a pencil." Thereupon Ramana wrote thus: *"The Creator, remaining everywhere, makes each one play his role in life according to their karma. That which is not destined will not happen, despite every effort.*

after the family. In fact, initially he found it tough even to identify his nephew and could do so only with reference to a big light red mole on Ramana's right foot.

Nelliappa Iyer used all his argumentative skills as a lawyer to convince Ramana that he should return home. He assured him that the family members would in no way interfere with his inner or outer life. All that they were anxious about was that his body should be looked after properly when he was engaged in such severe penance. He could even continue his *tapas* at the temple at Manamadurai, undisturbed. These pleadings were obviously of no avail. Ramana had no longer any will of his own. He had come to Arunachala in *"obedience to his Father's command"* and had to stay there the rest of his bodily life to do his Father's work. Hence he continued to maintain silence. The uncle had no option except to return, sad and wondering how he could convey the disappointing news to Ramana's heartbroken mother Azhagammall.

To make matters worse, on the way he met a Swami who spoke disparagingly about Ramana's knowledge of Vedanta. This made his uncle wonder whether his nephew had lost on both counts, in the affairs of the world and "other-worldly" matters as well. Being a fond uncle he did come again, twice, to see Ramana when he was in the Virupaksha Cave. On the first occasion he sat quietly with the other devotees. However, on the second occasion Ramana was explaining the meaning of the *Dakshinamurti Stotra* when the uncle appeared suddenly. Ramana was caught in the act of explaining. Therefore he continued. It is only after hearing it that the uncle realized the stature of Ramana and his depth of scriptural knowl-

What is destined is bound to happen. This is certain. Therefore the best course is to remain silent."[7]

This was the first written message given by Ramana to anyone. Its beauty and appropriateness are enhanced by the fact that it was given to the mother.

This message has been interpreted to mean that in Ramana's view everything is pre-ordained. Such an interpretation would not be correct. This particular message needs to be understood in its context. Ramana had come to Arunachala in obedience to His command. There could be no question of his returning home. Therefore he did not wish to give the slightest hope or encouragement to his mother. She had to accept that the decision to leave home and to come to Arunachala was irrevocable. Again, Ramana's attitude should not be mistaken for harshness. On the contrary, it was his consideration which had enabled his mother to trace him, and to know that he would always be available to her at Tiruvannamalai. When the situation demanded there could be no better son, as would be seen later when he looked after his mother during her typhoid fever in 1914, and in the last years of her life from 1916 to 1922. It was Ramana's liberating touch which freed mother from the cycle of births and deaths at the time of her passing away in May 1922.

View of Skandasramam

Ramana and Mother at Virupaksha and Skandasramam

Mother had to return home with a deep sense of sorrow at the thought of complete neglect by Ramana of his body and the fear of its consequences. At that stage she was not ripe enough to accept the truth that her son belonged to the entire universe. He had come as the teacher of the age *"on his Father's business"* and could not be confined to the bonds of family life and home. Yet, deeply rooted as she was in the Vedantic tradition, she was not overwhelmed by the situation.

Unfortunately for her, much worldly sorrow lay ahead of her. Her first son Nagaswami died a couple of years later, leaving behind his young widow. Nelliappa Iyer, too, who had been a pillar of strength, passed away. She bore the brunt of the sorrow bravely. After an interval of fifteen years she again visited Ramana, in 1913, while returning from a pilgrimage to Varanasi. He was staying in the Virupaksha Cave at that time. Mother noticed two changes. He was held in the highest respect not only by Vedic scholars, but also the poor, the downtrodden, and even small children. He spoke very little but was no

Group photo with Ramana and his mother standing next to him

longer observing the silence which had baffled her in 1898. He had made himself more responsive to the needs of the devotees and seekers. For had not his universal role begun in 1907 when Ganapati Muni proclaimed him to be the world teacher? Be that as it may, she returned home after a short stay content that her worst fears had not materialized. Ramana was in reasonably good health though there was no cooking in Virupaksha and he and the inmates depended on whatever was offered by devotees or was procured as alms.

She had come with her daughter-in-law Mangalam, the wife of her youngest son Nagasundaram. Mother sought Ramana's blessings for her to beget a son. By his grace Mangalam conceived soon after and gave birth to a boy. The child was named Venkataraman in gratitude. He was to be the only lineal descendant of Sundaram Iyer's family, for Mangalam died young and Nagasundaram renounced family life.

In 1914, mother again came to her ascetic son, this time on her return from a pilgrimage to Tirupati. She stayed with Ramana for a longer spell during which time she fell seriously ill for two to three weeks. Once, when her condition became delirious, Ramana had no option except to pray to Arunachala at whose call he had left home, and who was his sole refuge. His composition "For Mother's Recovery," is most moving. In this we find Ramana's complete faith in Arunachala's powers, as the conqueror of death, to change the course of events. Every single line brims with love for his mother and faith in the supreme power of Arunachala.

> *Oh Lord in the form of hill,*
> *You are the remedy for the endless chain of births.*
> *For me your feet alone are the refuge.*
> *Your duty it is to remove my mother's suffering and*
> *governing her.*
> *O Conqueror of Time!*

> *Your lotus feet are my refuge,*
> *Let them protect my mother from death.*
> *What is death if scrutinized?*
> *Arunachala, blazing fire of knowledge,*
> *Burn away the dross.*
> *Absorb my sweet mother in you,*
> *What need would there be then for cremation?*
> *Arunachala, dispeller of Maya's veil,*
> *Why then the delay in curing my mother's delirium?*
> *O Mother of those who seek refuge in you,*
> *Is there a better shield than you from fate's blows?*[8]

In this prayer we find something unique. Bhagavan addressing Arunachala as "Mother" instead of as "Father" as he always used to. Lines like *"What is death if scrutinized?" "What need would there be then for cremation?"* take one to philosophical heights.

The prayer was answered. Azhagammal recovered and returned to Manamadurai.

Though mother recovered from her encounter with death she began to feel strongly that it was high time she stayed with Ramana in the last years of her life. Like all devout persons she wanted to bid goodbye to the endless death-birth cycle. Who could be a better guide than her own son to whom the world was turning for solace and an inward way of life? Having come to this firm conclusion, she shifted to Tiruvannamalai in 1916 to be in Ramana's close proximity and to visit him daily. In the beginning she stayed with Echammal, who would prepare food daily for Ramana and the inmates of Virupaksha Cave and take it to them. Mother would accompany her. Notwithstanding her resolve it was increasingly evident that the fatigue of climbing up to the cave was beyond her physical strength at her age. The lady devotees intervened on her behalf and pleaded that she should be permitted to stay with Ramana at the Virupaksha Cave itself. Not knowing Ramana's views and apprehensive that other lady devotees too would follow suit, the inmates flatly refused to hear their pleadings. The lady devotees persisted, saying that mother was mother, and therefore special. They also promised never to ask for such a privilege for themselves. Yet the inmates remained stubborn. The mother was about to return in deep sorrow.

Ramana, who was silent till then, was moved. He got up, held her hand and said, *"Come let us go, if not here we can stay somewhere else, come."* Alarmed, everyone regretted their negative stand and begged of him in one voice, "Please stay with us. Mother too is welcome."[9]

Ramana now had the opportunity to give the necessary guidance to his mother. Firstly, he had to wean her out of the kitchen-religion, out of her orthodoxy. He would make fun of it. For instance he would say, *"Amma, what are you going to eat? Today, they have brought drumsticks and onions. If you eat them, will you not encounter a forest of drumsticks and mountains of onions on the way to moksha?"*[10] Gradually she came to see that moderation in food was all that was required for *sadhana*.

Besides her ingrained orthodox habits there was an even more important hurdle. It was the understandable feeling of being special as Ramana's mother. Ramana would frequently tell her that all women were his mothers. There was undoubtedly a corrosion of her background because of these lessons from Ramana. Yet the real cause for the transformation in her was the way Ramana lived before her very eyes, day in and day out. How could mother's mental notions remain unchanged? She too felt like a mother to all those who had entrusted their lives to Ramana. Her heart began to blossom. This change would be seen in an illustration. Once a man carrying firewood fell down in front of the *asram* exhausted with fatigue and hunger. She led him unhesitatingly, ignoring caste restrictions. She would also refer to the many inmates of the *asram* as her sons.

All the same her motherly love kept alive her desire to provide Ramana with some items which he was fond of before he was lured away from his home by Arunachala. Ramana used to relish appalams as a boy. She want-

ed to make them without his knowledge, knowing that he would remonstrate and not accept any special treatment. She hoped to persuade him to accept her loving labor. Hence she secretly collected the necessary ingredients. What happened is best described in Ramana's own words: *"Leisurely she took out the wooden roller, wooden seat, loose flour, and the balls of paste and commenced making appalams. There were about two to three hundred to be made. She could not prepare them all single-handed. I knew the job. So she quietly began telling me, 'My boy, please help me with it.' I got the opportunity I was waiting for. If I were lenient in this, she would start something else. I wanted to put a timely stop to it. I said, 'You have renounced everything and have come here, haven't you? Why all this? You should rest content with whatever is available. I won't help you. I won't eat them if you prepare*

The *gopurams* over Sri Mathrubhuteshwara temple

them. Make them all yourself, and eat them yourself.' She was silent for a while and again started saying, 'What my dear son, please help me a little.' I was adamant. She continued to call me again and again. Feeling it was no use arguing anymore, I said, 'All right, you make these appalams. I will make another kind,' and I started composing the Appalam Song. She used to sing a rice song, soup song, and other such songs, all with Vedantic meanings. No one appears to have written an appalam song. So I felt that she could learn another song. By the time the preparation of the appalams was over, my song was also ready. 'I will eat this appalam (the song about appalams), and you eat those that you have made,' I told her."[11]

The meaning of the song runs thus: *"As the black gram is ground in the quern, mixed with Pirandai juice, flattened, rolled, fried, and eaten, so should the ego be crushed in the quern of self-enquiry, seasoned with good company, fried in the ghee of Brahman, with the fire of knowledge, and become food of the Self."*[12]

However, her love for Ramana would not be defeated. Slowly, at Skandasramam she started cooking, "first a vegetable, then a soup and so on. She used to wander all over the hill, gather something or the other, and say that he likes this vegetable, that fruit." She took no notice of Ramana's remonstration. In fact this was the beginning of the *asram* kitchen and the Ramana family of an ever widening circle of disciples and devotees.

Life on the hill was pretty tough for the mother. She was the very first woman to live on the hill with all the extremes of heat and cold, even lack of minimal comfort. She had renounced her home to be with her ascetic son and she roughed it bravely. Ramana did his best to help, particularly about her need for water to drink and bathe. In the Virupaksha Cave water was scarce most of the time. Hence Ramana would bring some water from higher up on the hill for her to bathe in. As he recalled later, *"We had at that time two big kamandalams with us. Each could hold a small potful of water. I used to bring water in both of them. She would sit wearing a small towel and I used to pour water on her head. This was how she used to have her bath."*[13]

In the last years of her life, mother completely surrendered herself to Ramana who had become her *sadguru*. Twice she had a glimpse of his divinity. "Once, even as she sat before him he disappeared and she cried thinking he had discarded the body. She saw him again in his usual form. On another occasion, she had a vision of him garlanded by serpents, a veritable Siva. These visions helped in infusing greater faith in him."[14] Above all it was life in Ramana's sanctifying presence, listening to his teachings, and observing his daily life, which transformed her. Such was her faith in Ramana that she used to tell him, "Even if you throw away my dead body in these thorny bushes, I do not mind. I must die in your arms." She flatly refused to attend the housewarming function in her daughter Alamelu's new house lest she should be unable to get back. The mother endeared herself to each and every inmate of the *asram* whom she served with single-minded devotion.

Mother's Liberation

Victory unto the Holy Mother of Maharshi
Victory unto the Mother's *Mahasamadhi*
Victory unto the *Linga* consecrated by
    Maharshi's hands!
Victory unto the Sacred Waters, new and all
    redeeming![15]

—Ganapati Muni

Mother's health started deteriorating from 1920. On the 19th of May 1922, her condition became critical. After his morning walk Ramana went to her room at about 8 a.m., and sat beside her. Throughout the day, he had his right hand on her spiritual heart, on the right side of the chest and his left hand on her head. Ramana took on the sacred assignment of liberating his mother from the travails of births. He had the power to bestow liberation. But he let her battle for it while at the same time he extended his gracious and invaluable support for it to fructify. What happened has been described by Ramana himself. *"The* vasanas *of the previous births and latent tendencies which are seeds of future births came out. She was observing one after another the scenes of experiences arising from remaining* vasanas. *As a result of a series of such experiences she was working them out."*[16] Later someone asked Ramana to explain the process, to which he replied, *"You see, birth experiences are mental. Thinking is also like that, depending on* samskaras *(tendencies). Mother was made to undergo all her future births in that comparatively short time."*[17] At 8 p.m., her mind was absorbed in the heart and she was liberated from all tendencies which give rise to future births. Even so Bhagavan waited for some time. For in the case of his faithful attendant of many years,

Palaniswami, he had done the same thing. But after the subsidence of the mind in the heart, Palaniswami had opened his eyes momentarily and the life force left the body through them. After a few minutes Ramana got up. When someone said that mother had passed away, Ramana immediately corrected and affirmed: *"She did not pass away. 'Adangi vittadu, addakam' ('absorbed')"* He added, *"There is no pollution, let us eat."*[18]

While Ramana was seated beside the mother, directing her mind to the heart, Ganapati Muni and a few others began to chant the *Vedas*. Some others started doing Rama *japa*. Yet others were reciting "Aksharamanamalai" (Marital Garland of Letters) composed by Ramana. The whole atmosphere was surcharged with holiness.

Mother's face was specially lustrous after liberation. It was like that of a *yogini* in meditation. The illumined Azhagammal was brought to the verandah and *vibhuti*, the sacred ash, was applied on her forehead.

Ganapati Muni ruled that mother's body should be buried and not cremated. He cited the authority of

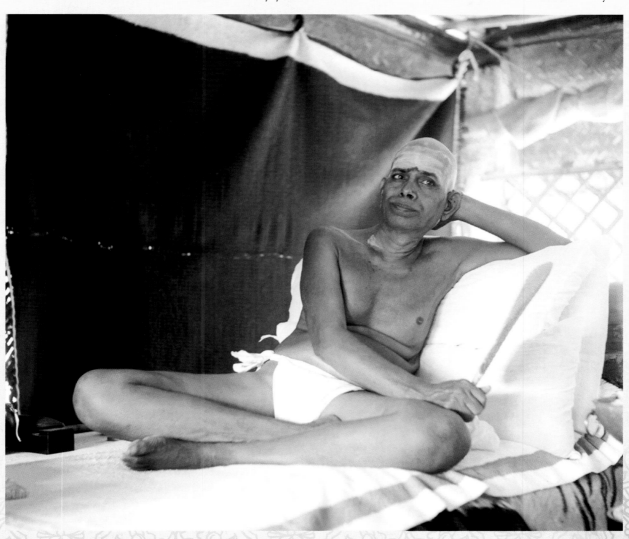

Ramana himself who had categorically stated in 1917 that *"liberated women are on a par with liberated men."* Since no burial was allowed on the Arunachala Hill it was decided to bury mother's body at the foot of the southern slopes of Arunachala, near Pali Tirtham.

Ramana sat beside his mother's body the whole night along with some devotees. Ramana also read the sacred text *Tiruvachagam* written by the saint Manikavachagar in praise of Lord Siva. Mother's body was brought down from Skandasramam to Pali Tirtham and the appropriate rites commenced. The *samadhi* was constructed according to the procedure laid down by the sage Tirumular in his famous book *Tirumandiram*. Elaborate *abhishekams* and *pujas* were performed. The mother's body was placed in a cloth bag in a yogic posture and lowered into the *samadhi*. Ramana showered a handful of sacred ash and camphor into the bag and others joined in.

Devotees decided that a *mandala puja* for forty-eight days should be performed. Water needed for worship used to be brought from the nearby Pali Tirtham. A

Above: View of Sri Matrubhuteswara temple
Left: Mother's *samadhi* at the Matrubhuteswara temple

72

miracle happened on the last day of the special worship. That day it was discovered that there was a small pit with clear water near the mother's shrine itself. Ramana inspected it and suggested that they should dig deeper and crystal clear water burst forth. Later on a well was dug on this spot and this has been a perennial source of water.

A thatched roof was put up over the *samadhi* and a hut constructed with mud walls. Niranjananda Swami decided to stay near the shrine to ensure proper and regular worship. In the following six months Ramana used to come every day in the morning and stay till noon before returning to Skandasramam. In December 1922, Ramana shifted permanently to the proximity of mother's shrine. The present Sri Ramanasramam grew around him. When asked as to why he shifted from Skandasramam, Ramana replied, *"The same power which brought me from Madurai to Arunachala brought me here."*

Mother's *Samadhi* and the Matrubhuteswara Temple

There are facts, which are not generally known, about the building which covered the mother's *samadhi*. Originally, the *lingam* had been covered with a small hut made out of coconut leaves.

"Some time in the mid-1920s a group of brickmakers tried to bake some bricks near the *asram*. When the bricks failed to fire properly, the brickmakers abandoned them. Bhagavan, unwilling to waste anything that was remotely useful, decided that the bricks could be used to build a wall around the mother's *samadhi*. A few days later, in the middle of the night, Bhagavan and all the resident devotees arranged themselves in a line between the brick kiln and the *samadhi*. By passing along the line they were able to transfer all of them to the *asram* during the night. The next day a wall was built around the *samadhi*. Bhagavan himself did all the work on the inside of the wall while a professional mason worked on the outside. The new building was completed by erecting a thatched roof on top of the wall."[19]

On September 1, 1939, the foundation was laid for the construction of a temple over mother's *samadhi*. It was to be a grand one on the lines of ancient temples built in accordance with scriptural principles (*Agama Sastras*). The date chosen has a special significance because it was on that date,

forty-three years earlier, on September 1, 1896, that Ramana had reached Arunachala.

The project had the full blessing of Ramana. It involved tremendous effort for fund-raising, which was very difficult in those pre-independence years. Besides, Ramana had clearly prohibited any fund collection in the name of the *asram*. On one occasion his permission was sought to seek funds for the construction of a lady's dormitory. He refused firmly, remarking, *"We are sadhus depending on God. Have you no shame? Must we stretch out our hands and ask like common beggars?"*[20] However, since the purpose of building mother's temple was laudable and had Ramana's approval the necessary funds were received, though at a slow pace. The construction had to be spread over a period of ten years and was completed only in 1949.

During this period between 1939 and 1949 while the temple was being constructed, Ramana took keen interest in every aspect of the same. "At night when no one was moving about, he would walk around the construction consecrating it. That he took such a demonstrative part in anything has deep significance. It was extremely rare and doubted by many. But I myself am an eyewitness and can vouch its truth."[21] He evinced keen interest

Ramana performing *puja* at mother's *samadhi*

Skandasramam

Room of Ramana's mother at Skandasramam where she spent her last hours of life in the arms of Bhagavan

ence of Ramana. "The resplendent face of Bhagavan, who was seated under the starry sky, was radiating cool luster around. People were spellbound at the sight."[22] "After the prescribed rites were over Ramana went straight to the new temple over mother's *samadhi*, touched with his hands the *linga* and Sri Chakra which was also to be installed and then went round the temple examining every detail."[23]

On the penultimate night he personally supervised the installation of the idols in the inner shrine. "It was an extremely hot night and with three charcoal rotators for melting the cement adding to the heat, it must have been intolerable inside the airless cave of the inner shrine. But for about an hour and a half, Bhagavan sat there telling the workmen what to do."[24] On the night before the consecration, Ramana stood inside the temple for five minutes with both his hands on the *linga* and Sri Chakra, charging them with his power.

Sadhu Arunachala (Major Chadwick) refers to the special significance of all this, "I do not think that anyone who has written about Bhagavan and the *asramam* has remarked on the extraordinary fact that here we have a temple dedicated by a *jnani*. I do not pretend myself to understand why he did so or what will be its consequences. But having been consecrated in this way, it must be a very sacred spot from which spiritual power must radiate."[25] We may not be able to completely comprehend the significance of Ramana's continued and intense interest in all the aspects of the temple over his mother's *samadhi*, and the Matrubhuteswara *linga* (the Lord who has become mother). Yet this is a clear indication that she has become the symbol of the universal mother. The daily worship offered here is a recognition of this fact.

Reflecting on Ramana's life and trying to identify certain landmarks, Kapali Sastri fixed a few of them.[26] These have been selected with reference to their significance from the point of view of being stimuli for drawing Ramana out and drawing people to him. The first was on November 18, 1907 when Ramana broke his silence of eleven years to explain the true import of penance to

in every aspect and gave appropriate instructions to the sculptors and workers.

The temple when completed was truly befitting a liberated illumni. The images in the temple had been carved under the direct supervision of an outstanding temple sculptor of the time, Vaidyanatha Sthapati.

The Kumbhabhisekam (the consecration ceremony which is to be performed when a temple is newly built or renovated) was fixed for March 17, 1949. Waters had been gathered from the Ganges and other sacred rivers for the purpose. The preliminary functions began on March 14 itself with the chanting of Vedic hymns and performance of purificatory rites by hundreds of priests in the pres-

Ganapati Muni. The next began in 1916 when mother came to live with Ramana at the Virupaksha Cave. For it was the beginning of the *asram* kitchen and the Ramana family and the ever widening circle of his disciples and devotees. The next is May 19, 1922, when Ramana liberated mother by his potent grace, which she was ripe enough to receive. Yet another significance of the year 1922 was that Ramana shifted from Skandasramam in December that year, to the place near mother's *samadhi*. It became the starting point of Sri Ramanasramam, which grew around him and mother's *samadhi*. It marked the steady growth of the awareness of his glorious life and message.

The significance of the temple is heightened by the fact that it is the best evidence of the great reverence given to the mother by Ramana. It also exemplifies Ramana's authoritative statement that a lady illumni is no different from a male *jnani*. Above all, the temple is a standing symbol of Ramana's grace which made mother's liberation possible.

Section IV: Skandasramam Years

Skandasramam Years: 1916-1922

There used to be a perpetual scarcity of water at the Virupaksha Cave. Hence Ramana and the devotees would shift to the Mango Tree Cave nearby during the summer months. The water problem became more acute after mother Azhagammal joined them. There was no water even for a proper bath. Ramana used to climb further up the hill every day and get the required water for mother's bath from a spring located higher up on the hill.[1]

One of the inmates, Kandaswami, noticed the trouble which Ramana had to undergo day in and day out. He felt that the best solution would be to construct a proper *asram* for Ramana at a place near the water spring. He also felt that there was need for a more spacious place in view of the growing number of devotees. When he made this request to Ramana, he did not object. Ramana had no plans of his own. For him everything happened according to the divine plan. One can therefore say that all the happenings in Ramana's life, including the construction of Skandasramam, were in accordance with the divine plan.

This view is further strengthened by the fact that Skandasramam was located on the eastern slope of the Arunachala hill which was traditionally the property of the Arunachaleswara temple. This point is made by Ramana himself, in the course of evidence, on commission, which he gave in 1938 in defense of the temple authorities.[2] Ramana stated, *"I am a devotee of Arunachaleswara. I have composed a poem in Tamil which says that Arunachala hill is Iswara swarupa.... I lived in the Virupaksha Cave for seventeen years. I lived in Skandasramam for six years. A building was constructed in Virupaksha Cave but no written permission was obtained for the same. Skandasramam was completed in 1916. Because it was built by a person known as Kandan, it came to be known as Skandasramam. No order was received from anyone for this* asram. *Because I was staying there no one objected. On the contrary they approved of it. These constructions were not done on my*

authority, but were treated by those who did it as their own work. I did not tell them to build nor did I prevent them. In this manner, Skandasram, Virupaksha Cave, and Sri Ramanasramam came into existence."[3]

It will be seen that though the temple authorities were the owners of the eastern slope, they did not object to the construction of Skandasramam because of the reverence in which Ramana was held by everyone as a *jnani*. The manner in which this construction took place clearly indicates that the implementation and construction of the new *asram* had come into existence not because of any individual volition but by the divine sanction.

Years later Ramana recalled the efforts of Kandaswami to construct Skandasramam. *"Kandaswami was keen to build a separate* asram *for me. He inspected various places on the hill and in the forest to select a site and finally selected the present site and sought my approval. Since I did not object, Kandaswami began converting what was a thick forest of prickly pear on the mountain slope. The result of his labor is the* asram, *we see now."* Ramana added, *"You cannot imagine the state of the site as it was originally. Kandaswami worked with almost superhuman effort and achieved with his own hands what even four people cannot do together. He removed all the prickly pear, reduced the stone and boulder to a level ground, created a garden, and raised the* asram. *Four coconut trees were planted. To plant them properly, Kandaswami dug huge square pits about 10ft deep. That would give you an idea about the labor he*

Skandasramam

put into the work. He was a strong, well-built man."⁴ This *asram* is situated next to a perennial water spring and is one of the most enchanting spots on the eastern slopes of Arunachala.

Ramana's stay at Skandasramam was studded with many happy events. It was the first *asram* of Ramana. It was here that mother Azhagammal started cooking regularly for the inmates, disciples, and the devotees. It is at this place that one of the most important scriptures of Ramana came to be recorded. In 1917, Ganapati Muni and seven of his disciples questioned Ramana on many aspects relating to the scriptures and spiritual practices. These questions and answers, recorded in Sanskrit

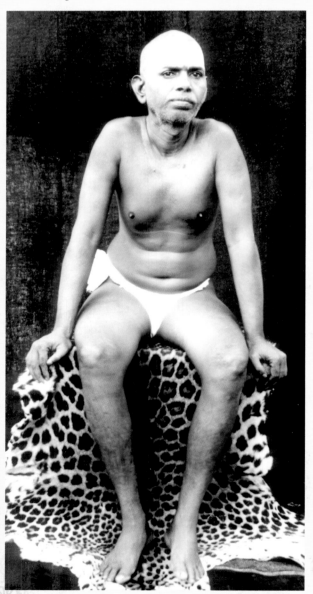

by Ganapati Muni, were published later as *Sri Ramana Gita*. Further it was at Skandasramam that many of Ramana's lifetime disciples joined him. This list includes Viswanatha Swami, Ramaswami Pillai, and Kunjuswami to mention a few.

While at Skandasramam, Ramana was in his best state of health. His golden-hued body was glowing and fascinating. It is said that his body was so bewitching that one would have to resist the temptation to hug him to one's bosom. Above all Skandasramam has been hallowed by the liberation of mother Azhagammal through Ramana's grace flowing from his hands. Small wonder that the place has a special and irresistible charm of its own.

Kunjuswami has given a clear report of the daily routine at Skandasramam. "Sri Bhagavan's mother would get up around four in the morning and sing devotional songs. Sri Bhagavan would be reclining. We would meditate. Sri Bhagavan would go out at five and be back in about an hour. We would begin to recite *Aksharamanamalai* verses and finish by six. Sri Bhagavan would go for his bath and we would also go out and finish our bath and be ready to eat with Sri Bhagavan at eight. Sama Iyer would get up at four in the morning, have his bath, and prepare rasam and rice. He and Ramanatha Brahmachari used to serve us. After the meal, Sri Bhagavan would sit out. Some devotees would meditate, some would read books like *Ribhu Gita*. The atmosphere was always very peaceful. Occasionally Sri Bhagavan would clarify the doubts of the devotees.

"In the evenings we would sit before Sri Bhagavan at 6.30 p.m. and we would recite *Aksharamanamalai* again. Sri Bhagavan used to close his eyes reclining on the pillow. We would finish the recitation exactly at 7.30 p.m., when we generally had our supper. Once in two or three days, during the *parayana*, Sri Bhagavan would go into deep meditation. Even at the end of the *parayana*, he would not open his eyes. We used to call him gently, but Sri Bhagavan would be completely oblivious of his surroundings. To wake him up, Perumalswami, Akhandananda, Mastanswami, and I would take out some conches at the *asram* and blow them. The sound of the conch used to penetrate into him and bring him back to the external world slowly. On such days, we would eat only at 9 p.m. This would happen frequently. Even after moving to his mother's *samadhi* at the foot of the hill, this used to happen once in a week or ten days. Dandapaniswami used to massage Sri Bhagavan's feet to wake him but in vain. He used to become aware of the external world only through our blowing of the conches. It is said in Vasishtam that Sri Krishna had to blow the conch to wake Prahlada from his *tapas*."⁵

A special incident relating to a golden-haired mongoose is also reported when Ramana was staying at Skandasramam. It appeared on a festival day when a crowd of people were climbing the hill. It was an extraordinary mongoose, golden-haired and without the usual black spot on its tail. It joined the party of pilgrims, went up first to the Virupaksha Cave, where Palaniswami was taking his bath in the spring. He stroked the animal, greeting it in the most friendly way. From there, the mongoose climbed up to Skandasramam. Narrating this incident, Ramana said: *"Everyone was struck by its attractive appearance and fearless movements. It came to me, climbed onto my lap, and rested there for some time. Then it raised itself up, looked about and moved down. It went around the whole place and I followed it lest it should be harmed by careless visitors or by the peacocks. Two of these did look at it inquisitively, but it moved calmly from place to place until finally it disappeared among the rocks to the south-east of the* asramam."[6]

Sadhu Natanananda

The story of Natesa Mudaliar, later known as Sadhu Natanananda, is one constantly yearning for the *guru*'s grace. One notices in his life dogged persistence for obtaining Ramana's grace.[1] Though it took many years for him to get replies from Ramana, this was more than made good in later years when all his doubts were cleared directly or through conversations which Ramana had with earnest devotees. His great contribution to Ramana literature was his work titled *Upadesa Manjari* or "Spiritual Instructions," covering a wide range of subjects relating to the practice of the Ramana Way. This work, considered as one of the important prose works, is included in the *Collected Works of Sri Ramana Maharshi*.

Sadhu Natanananda, who was then an elementary school teacher, read with avid interest the teachings of Swami Vivekananda on the path of *jnana*. He then proceeded to search for a suitable *guru* of the same caliber as Sri Ramakrishna who had inspired Swami Vivekananda. When he made enquiries everyone said in one voice that such a *guru*, Bhagavan Ramana, was living in Tiruvannamalai itself. However he was told that it was not his practice to give *upadesa* or instructions to any one. The following year, in 1918, Natanananda made his first attempt to get Ramana's instructions. He went to Skandasramam and sat in silence in front of Ramana for quite some time, Ramana remained silent. Disappointed, he went to other *gurus* but suddenly realized that none of them could compare with Ramana. Therefore, in 1920, he wrote a letter to Ramana requesting him "not to be selfishly indifferent to the fate of

Ramana's room at Skandasramam where he lived for many years before coming down the mountain after the death of his mother

longing souls."[2] When no reply came he wrote another letter, this time by registered post, conveying his resolve, "Whatever be the number of rebirths I have to endure, still I have resolved to get my *upadesa* from you and you alone. So for this purpose, if you fail to give me *upadesa*, considering me too immature to receive your instructions, you will have to be reborn I swear to this."[3] A few days later he had a dream in which Ramana appeared to him and told him, *"Do not constantly think of me.... First secure the favor of God Maheswara, the Lord of the bull. First meditate on him and secure his grace. My help will follow as a matter of course."*[4] He promptly put this advice to practice and a few days later he received a letter from the manager of Skandasramam to the effect that Ramana would not reply to letters, but it was open to Natanananda to come in person and seek his clarifications. Actually the difficulty of Natanananda was also the same as would be seen from the conversation which took place between him and Ramana a year later. At that first meeting he asked Ramana, "I wish to learn about and experience what your grace is, as people differ in their account of it." Ramana replied, *"I am always giving my grace. If you cannot experience it, what am I to do?"*[5] It is only then that Natanananda discovered that the *upadesa* of Sri Ramana was on the lines of the ancient *guru* Dakshinamurti who taught in silence.

Still unable to grasp the impact of Ramana's silence, Natanananda was very worried when he had another dream in which Ramana said, *"Let your vision be unified and withdrawn from objects, external or internal. Make your outlook equal and practice it."*[6] After following this *upadesa* he had another dream in which Bhagavan gave him what he had been eagerly waiting for. In this dream Ramana drew him near, placed his palm on his head and then on the right side of his chest. Though received in a dream, this was the traditional form of a *guru*'s initiation. He was delighted.

Not being a scholar in scriptures, Natanananda would sometimes doubt if this would make him ineligible for Self-knowledge. Noticing his depression Ramana told him, *"Why are you anxious? What you seek is that which is already at hand, ever existent."*[7] Once he also assured, *"Grace is always flowing. It is not an occasional thing. It is causeless and flows forever. It can be experienced by those who meditate."*[8]

About 1926, Natanananda approached Ramana with the intention of renouncing his home. Ramana advised him against it. He told him, *"There is no difference between domestic life and that of hermits. Just as you avoid the cares of home when you are here, go home and try to be equally unconcerned and unaffected at the circumstances amidst home life."*[9] Notwithstanding this advice

Natanananda renounced home only to regret it later and return to lead a householder's life.

Subsequently he put down the conversations that took place between himself and Ramana. Some of his devotees arranged and expanded his notes and showed them to Ramana who expressed his appreciation. There are seventy questions and answers covered in this extremely useful book set out in four chapters.[10]

Q.1. What are the marks of a real teacher, *sadguru*?

A. *Steady abidance in the Self, looking at all with an equal eye, unshakable courage at all times, in all places and circumstances, etc.*

Q.2. What are the marks of an earnest disciple?

A. *An intense longing for the removal of sorrow and attainment of joy.*

Q.3. What are the marks of the *guru*'s grace?

A. *It is beyond words or thoughts.*

View of Arunachaleswara temple from Skandasramam

Q.4. Is the state of "being still" a state involving effort or is it effortless?

A. *It is not an effortless state. All mundane activities which are ordinarily called effort are performed with the aid of a portion of the mind and with frequent breaks. But the act of communion with the Self, or remaining still inwardly, is intense activity which is performed with the entire mind and without break.*

Q.5. What is meditation?

A. *It is abiding as one's Self without swerving in any way from one's real nature and without feeling that one is meditating.*

Q.6. What are the rules of conduct which an aspirant (*sadhaka*) should follow?

A. *Moderation in food, moderation in sleep, and moderation in speech.*

Q.7. How long should one practice?

A. *Until the mind attains, effortlessly, its natural state of freedom from concepts. That is, till the sense of "I" and "mine" no longer exist.*

Q.8. If everything happens according to *karma*, how is one to overcome the obstacles to meditation?

A. *Karma concerns only the out-turned mind and not the in-turned mind.*

Sadhu Natanananda continued to stay opposite Sri Ramanasramam for many years after Ramana's *mahanirvana*. No genuine seeker was denied his advice about the practical aspects of self-enquiry. He wrote a commentary in Tamil on the *Five Hymns to Arunachala*. He also wrote a collection of incidents from Ramana's life titled *Ramana Darsanam*.

Section V: Sri Ramanasramam Years

The Liberty Hall

Ramana had come to Arunachala *"in obedience to his Father's command"* as he had stated in the letter before leaving his uncle's home in Madurai. At that time he had no further need for any spiritual practice for he had become enlightened on July 17, 1896. The confrontation with death, leading to his discovery of his identity with the Self, firmly established him in steady wisdom. The body too had served its purpose. But the irresistible call of Arunachala pulled him. His first act was to report, *"Father I have come."* There his body could well have perished in the early months when he was in *samadhi*, immersed in the infinite, oblivious of the body. Though he was unaware of the difference between night and day in his state, the divine protected his body through some sacred hands, because his role of universal *guru* was divinely ordained. Universal because his teachings could be practiced by all seekers of truth regardless of their religious affiliations, regardless of geographical locations, regardless of any circumstances.

This role began in November 1907 when Ganapati Muni proclaimed it and christened him as Bhagavan Sri Ramana Maharshi. In this role Ramana's uniqueness, his incomparable universal love, stands out.

The next overt act of compassion was his remaining at one place, Tiruvannamalai, during this entire period. The logic and importance of it can be seen in his explanation to a young girl who asked him to accompany her to Madras. *"If I left this place, would not the visitors who came expecting me here be disappointed? You have come here with your parents to see me. If I were not here would you not be disappointed? And even if I leave this place what certainty... is there that I will reach your house? There would be so many calls and so many places to visit, that I might never see your house at all."*[1]

Ramana stayed for nearly twenty years from 1927-1928 to 1949 in what is now called "Old Hall." He used to sit, stretch, and sleep on the couch in a corner of this hall. Above his couch the sparrows would continuously build nests. The squirrels would run all over and freely move on Ramana's body. Monkeys would be on the lookout for an opportunity to snatch the fruit offerings kept on the stool near the couch. Cow Lakshmi would take over the place whenever she wanted to. There was no stopping her. She knew this only too well and chose her own timings to be consoled, petted, or fed by Ramana. People would

be coming in and going out continuously at all times of the day. No one needed any permission to see Ramana, no appointments, no preferences, no fixed timings. One would seize the best opportunity to clear his doubts, no matter whether it was immediately after the midday meal or after dinner. For they were aware of his compassion, his willingness to help earnest seekers.

Let us look at some descriptions about the scenes which used to prevail. "One comes and praises him in Sanskrit verse, another in Tamil prose, a third in Telugu or Malayalam. Several go to pour out their woes into his ears and seek solace in their heart-broken condition. Another wants the Maharshi's blessings to win a lawsuit."[2] A few ask for guidance on the path of *vichara*. A vast variety of people, each living in his own world, with their own set of problems, but united in their love for Ramana and confident in his love for them.

There is yet another graphic description which highlights this "open to all" situation that existed. "Day by day brings fresh indications of the greatness of the man. I am learning to see the Maharshi's way of helping others, an unobtrusive way, silent and a steady outpouring of healing vibrations into troubled souls."[3] How else can one explain the simultaneous presence of an illiterate peasant and the most erudite scholar? "An illiterate peasant and his family stay for a few hours hardly speaking, all of them gazing in reverence, a prosperous judge is there for it is vacation for the courts, and a general group of meditators."[4] Each is happy and in tune with the atmosphere thick with the aroma of Ramana's presence. It was only at twilight time that Ramana would slip into his powerful and potent silence. His eyes would be wide open and he would have a far away look as if he was gazing out of the window. Nothing could disturb those hours of intense peace. Every entrant into the hall would also be drawn into that dynamic silence. Their minds too would become quiet, their questions would lose their relevance and they would not mind whether these were asked or not. Why disturb that spellbinding peace? Why not get immersed in it? So they would feel.

While this time would almost certainly be the true hour of inwardness, during the daytime also quite often Ramana would just not be there except perhaps as a physical form. The silence could be baffling to those who were used to question and answer sessions or discussions on various spiritual subjects. One newcomer, puzzled by Ramana's equipoise, questioned it. "Swamiji, many men and women are now sitting before you in order to get some instruction. You do not speak even a word. They too do not put any questions to you. They are all silently sitting to learn something. What are you teaching them? What are they learning from you? Please explain this secret." Ramana remained silent. After some time, losing his patience, the visitor repeated the question. Smiling gently Ramana told him, *"The question must be put 'there.' Why are you putting that question 'here'?"*[5]

Many would seek and get counsel from Ramana for his equality was patent, his consideration obvious. There would be no looking down on the questioner, no condescension. The answer would depend upon the background, earnestness, and open-mindedness of the questioner. For he would not accelerate the pace nor disturb one's faith. But invariably there would be one common stream. The doubter's attention would be turned to the core question of one's identity and the source of "I"-consciousness.

For many years, one might say up to the mid-thirties, the inmates were only few though there was a regular stream of seekers of truth and visitors who wished to have Ramana's *darsan*, having heard of his glory. This was because there was no infrastructure worth the name. There were only two huts from 1922 to 1928. One was used as the living quarters and the other was used as kitchen-cum-dining hall. Then the "Old Hall" was constructed and gradually other buildings. Though few in numbers, each one of the inmates of those early years was great in their own right and has contributed in a rich measure to the understanding of his life and teachings. Ganapati Muni, Muruganar, Viswanatha Swami, Kapali Sastri, Yogi Suddhananda Bharati, Sundaresa Iyer, Ramaswami Pillai, B.V. Narasimha Swami were the first group of what one may term as the "Inner Circle" of devotees. After the visitors departed and also before breakfast in the early hours of the morning they could literally plunder Ramana for themselves. "On the first Sivaratri that I was with him in 1923, Bhagavan did not start out to walk around the mountain, as was his usual custom. Everyone else went around the hill. Only four of us: Dandapani, Viswanathan, myself, and one other devotee sat with him all through the night. We were all awake in a blissful state, which it is impossible to express in words."[6]

Narasimha Swami has recorded a couple of scenes which would help to recall those years. "The evening was calm but cloudy and somewhat cool. Mr. A.S.K,[7] Sub-Judge of Cuddalore, had come to see the Maharshi accompanied by two elderly ladies, his aunt, his cousin, and Raghupati Sastri, Pleader. He started the discussion by asking, 'Has enquiring into the Real and unreal the efficacy, *per se*, to lead us to the realization of the one

imperishable?' Ramana clarified, *'As propounded by all and realized by all seekers after truth, abidance in the Self alone can make us know and realize it.'*[8] Srinivasa Gopala Iyenger, an auditor, plies Ramana with questions. 'How is it possible to attend to one's business if he is to simultaneously be meditative also?' *'No, business will be all the easier for you when your mind is strengthened and steadied by meditation…. Your viewpoint will change.'*[9] A visitor from Andhra queries, 'Should I not get away from wife and family?' *'What harm did they do? First find out who you are,'* was Ramana's quick reply. Narasimha Swami has many lengthy interviews with Ramana. He was a lawyer skilled in cross-examination, not ready to accept without arguing till the end.[10] Ramana convinces him that happiness is inherent, one's own, and capable of being universally experienced. Ramana gives the reason for his failure to grasp this truth. *'It is because it has long been your habit to think of and identify yourself with other objects that you have never faced your "I." You have always been exercising your intellect and never your intuition.'*[11]

An anonymous devotee has described the atmosphere which was then prevalent. "I had the good fortune and opportunity of watching him many times when he was sitting with his eyes fixed like a statue for two or three hours at a time. Only the persons who have enjoyed this calm and holy atmosphere can know about its immense value…. Verily Maharshi who is always in *sahaja* state is God…. Though he is silent yet he teaches volumes through his look, casual talk, and by his example. One glance of his is enough to cross the ocean of *samsara*."[12]

The thirties saw the growth of buildings in the *asram*, the cowshed, Vedic school, storeroom, and dining hall and later the *asram* dispensary. But for the devotees there was only the "Gents Common Guest Room." Hence there would be a rush of seekers in the weekends and vacations, when they would make their own arrangements for their stay. In the *asram* itself, permission to construct had been given to Yogi Ramiah, Swami Rajeswarananda, Major Chadwick, and Devaraja Mudaliar. Muruganar lived in the nearby grove Palakottu. The magnetism of Ramana drew everyone notwithstanding the outward hardships. To be in the presence of Ramana, to listen to his soft divine voice, to imbibe his firm and simple guidance was enough compensation to face these problems. In this they were encouraged by the certainty of Ramana's accessibility, day in and day out, at all times of the day and one might say at night as well in those years. Hence Narasimha Swami termed the Old Hall as the "Liberty Hall." Everyone has the liberty to enter. And once they entered its portals their liberty from bondage to the mind and its attachments would also be assured.

Robbers Worship Ramana

They are blinded by ignorance. But let us note what is right and stick to it. Sometimes your teeth suddenly bite your own tongue; do you break them out in consequence?

—*Bhagavan Ramana*

Ramana had shifted from Skandasramam to his mother's *samadhi* in December 1922. By then he had spent twenty-three years on the hill, first at the Virupaksha Cave and later at Skandasramam. Both these places were uninhabited except for the inmates and devotees of Ramana and a few other ascetics also living on the hill. In spite of it there was no incident of even any petty theft while Ramana was staying there.

Hardly a couple of years after he had shifted to the *asram*, a robbery took place. It happened on June 26, 1924. Though the incident took place about seventy five years ago, full particulars of the event are available because of an authentic record of it in the proceedings in the Criminal Court in Tiruvannamalai in Crime No. 52/1924.

It is difficult to understand why the robbers committed this offence at all. At that time there were only two huts at Ramanasramam. One was in the front of the *samadhi* shrine and the other to the north of it. There was hardly any sign of affluence. The author of *Self-Realization* ventures a guess. He refers to the fact that even in those years the doors of the *asram* were open to everyone. If any visitors arrived at the meal-time they were sure to be fed. Besides there was also the practice of feeding the poor. Possibly this could have given the impression that the *asram* was wealthy. The onlookers could not have been aware that the feeding took place only because of Ramana's unswerving principle of sharing equally whatever was available.

Whatever be the reason, three persons chose to strike a little before midnight of that date.

Their attempt was to effect an entry by breaking open the window on the southern side of the *samadhi* hut. The relevant facts have been clearly narrated by Ramakrishna Swami in his First Information Report to the police. Ramana, Kunjuswami, Mastan, Thangavelu Pillai, Muniswami Iyer were sleeping there. In the northern hut a few others including the complainant were sleeping.

While attempting to break the window the robbers persisted in shouting various threats. They also burst crackers to give the impression that they had firearms. At this stage Kunjuswami opened the door and brought Ramakrishna Swami into the *samadhi* hut for help and they latched the door. Ramana dissuaded the other persons from facing the thieves saying, *"let these robbers play their role; we shall stick to ours. Let them do what they like; it is for us to bear and forebear. Let us not interfere with them."*[1]

Both of them pleaded with the robbers to come in by the door which they were ready to open provided no needless harm was done to the inmates. No request was made not to cause any property loss for there was none. These repeated exhortations went unheeded. Hence Ramana and those in the *samadhi* hut opened the door for moving out to the northern hut leaving the *samadhi* hut free to the robbers to do what they liked. Before doing so Ramana ensured that the weak dog Karuppan which was with them would remain unhurt. Kunjuswami was sent to the town to report the matter to the local government authorities and also to get some help.

When Ramana and others were crossing over to the northern hut one of the robbers cruelly beat each one of them with his stick and Ramana also received a blow on his left thigh. He told them, *"If you are not satisfied yet you may strike the other leg also."*[2] Even though stone-hearted the robbers did not cause any further bodily harm.

Having gained entry into the *samadhi* hut the robbers ransacked everything in their disappointment at not finding anything worthwhile. They asked for a hurricane lantern which was provided. They broke open the almirah. All that they could get was a few strips of silver that adorned the images, a little rice, mangoes, and about Rs.10 in cash which too belonged to a visitor. They continued their threats and wished to know where the money was secreted. Ramana told them, *"We are poor* sadhus, *living on alms and never have cash."*[3] They had no alternative except to accept the statement for the stark reality was before them.

In the meantime Ramakrishna Swami saw the swollen left thigh of Ramana, who humorously remarked that he too had received adequate *poosai*, which means in Tamil both beating and worship. Unable to bear the sight of the physical harm done to his *guru*, Ramakrishna Swami seized an iron instrument nearby and sought permission to go after them. Ramana held him back advising, *"We are* sadhus. *We should not give up our* dharma. *If you go and strike them some may die. That will be a matter for which the world will justly blame us and not the thieves. They are only misguided men."*[4] The following day many police officials came to enquire and recorded the details. Ramana did not even mention about his injury. Only the others reported what had happened. Later the robbers were apprehended and tried for offences falling under the Indian Penal Code. One of them was additionally charged for causing hurt. The offence was committing robbery and hurt. The sad part was that the three accused, Ayya Kannu, Kuppan, and Subbarayan were all only twenty-five years of age. The first two were sentenced to one-year rigorous imprisonment and the third to two years as he had hurt them physically as well.

At the request of the devotees Ramana would recall and explain in graphic detail many incidents in his life. However, we find that there has been no reference to this incident by him. For all purposes it was a non-event for him, which was over once and for all. By this example Ramana had demonstrated the need for strict adherence by renunciates to the principle of *ahimsa*, non-injury. Its importance also springs from the fact that Ramana accepted everyone as they were without any judgment. Hence he did not attach any importance to the cruelty of the robbers. To him they were merely ignorant and misguided men. Hence to them also his heart flowed in love in equal measure.

Ramana in the Kitchen

When Ramana was staying in the Virupaksha Cave there was no regular cooking. The alms gathered by devotees would be shared by Ramana and those present. Subsequently, when he shifted to Skandasramam, mother began to cook regularly for Ramana and the devotees. The fire lit by her is continuing with even greater vigor since then.

In May 1922, after mother's liberation, a hut was constructed over her *samadhi* around which Sri Ramanasramam has grown since then. Ramana's younger brother Nagasundaram, who had joined him at Skandasramam, shifted to the *samadhi* where he would cook the required offerings. He was known as Chinnaswami or the younger swami. He was an expert cook. Later, in December 1922, Ramana also shifted to mother's *samadhi* site and regular cooking had to commence. This was in the hands of Chinnaswami, Dandapani Swami, and a few others. It would appear that gradually the cooking was taken over by Ramana himself. He commenced the work with a team of regular assistants, also supported by a few devotees who were present at that time. Under his guidance the kitchen became a regular school for teaching the inner way of life and strong sense of equality. As a rule the kitchen staff would ripen in wisdom.

Ramana would be in the kitchen between 2.30 a.m. and 4 a.m. He would begin by cutting vegetables along with the kitchen staff and devotees. Then he would prepare sambar and chutney for breakfast and occasionally some extra dishes also. He would not permit any special attention being bestowed on him. The work included grinding and other manual jobs. When the dishes were ready he would taste a little of each and give the co-workers a sample to ensure that the dishes were tasty. After

finishing his work Ramana would return to the hall to be in time for Vedic chanting.

It may be mentioned that Ramana was a strict disciplinarian. For he would not tolerate the least sloppiness. The allotted duties had to be performed by understanding the requirements. One of the volunteers, Subbaramayya, who was in charge of spicing the dishes with salt, was late one day. Ramana gently told him, *"Since you were absent, I thought of you at the moment of adding some salt and that is the reason for this excess."*[1] The reprimand for unpunctuality went home. Ramana once explained to one of the kitchen staff the need for care. *"All this trouble is for you people. When I sit for lunch, Echammal will bring one dish, Mudaliar Patti another, some other devotee a third preparation specially for me. I just mix what they all bring with what you prepare and eat."*[2]

The touch of Ramana's gracious hands would make the dishes nectarine. Sampoornamma, one of the kitchen staff, recalls, "He would patiently guide me in every detail about what to cook and how to cook. He used to lay stress on proper grinding, the need to put a lid on vegetables to make them tasty, and so on.… He was quite strict and would not countenance any deviation from the instructions.… Because of his care for us even the toughest jobs would seem light. In his com-

pany we would always be energetic and ready to take on any amount of work."[3]

Santamma was from Ramanathapuram and had been attracted to Ramana thanks to Muruganar, who hailed from the same place and gave her a photograph of Ramana. She had a strong spiritual bent of mind. At her very first meeting she prayed to Ramana to destroy her mind. Ramana told Muruganar, *"Ask her if there is such a thing as mind! If so, what is its form? Does it have a moustache and a beard?"*[4] She would leave the *asram* reluctantly. She told Ramana, "Here I am filled with peace. At home my mind is constantly disturbed." Ramana advised her to stay till her mind became steady. He added, *"Thereafter wherever you go your mind would be peaceful."*[5] She mentions how once a devotee complained that he had to stay elsewhere whereas the inmates of the *asram* could receive Ramana's grace in full measure. Ramana assured him, *"The Lord always remains close extending his protection to those who have surrendered to him. The frog stays near the lotus. But it is only the bees which suck the honey of the flowers however far they may come from."*[6]

Another kitchen mate, Subbalakshmi Amma, was keen on meditation and would ply Ramana with questions. Once she asked him about the nature of the Self. Ramana advised, *"Abide in the Self, free from thoughts instead of enquiring about the nature of the Self."*[7] She would fret and fume about the absence of time to meditate because of excessive kitchen work. Ramana told her, *"If you identify yourself with the body, you are bound to dualities. Work will appear difficult. Even if we free ourselves from work, would the mind cease to wander? It does not let us sleep in peace. It keeps wandering as in dreams."*[8]

The *asram* dining hall as it is today; food is being served on banana leaves on the floor in the traditional Indian way

All the kitchen staff would feel privileged to be able to work with Ramana. One of them remarks, "The privilege of companionship of Lord Krishna was given to *gopis* of Brindavan. The same fraternity with God was our blessing in the Ramanasramam kitchen."[9] Was he not compassionately compensating them for their inability to join the other devotees in the Old Hall?

Ramana stopped working in the kitchen in the late thirties. Thereafter also he would spend some time with the kitchen staff by chatting with them after his meal, teaching them new verses and songs, and generally making them happy.[10]

Equality in the Dining Hall

The equality which Ramana insisted upon in the dining hall is an aspect of his universal love. He was fully aware that the kitchen staff and the devotees would show him preferential treatment if given the slightest opportunity. So, he was always hawk-eyed about any attempt at such preferential treatment. Share and share alike was the golden rule which he observed to the last day. A few instances would be illustrative.

Bhagavan suddenly stopped drinking buttermilk. Devaraja Mudaliar, who used to sit near Bhagavan, noticed this and asked: "Bhagavan, we eat all the items sumptuously. But you keep giving up one item or the other. How can we bear this?" Bhagavan replied, *"They are only too ready to give me extra helpings. But when it comes to the devotees their hands are paralyzed."* On enquiry Devaraja Mudaliar learnt that Bhagavan was provoked into making this remark because a young girl from Bangalore had been refused extra quantity of sambar which she had asked for. The kitchen workers had their human weakness too. They looked after the old devotees and those sitting near Bhagavan well. Yet, newcomers and those seated farther away were sometimes neglected. Repeated statements of Ramana that service to his devotees was the best form of service to him would be of no avail. Hence he would stop eating or drinking some item

to draw the pointed attention of the kitchen-staff to impartiality.[1]

One of the nephews of Suri Nagamma, Tilak, had come from London. While leaving he brought an offering to the dining hall. Bhagavan was served first and then the others. Bhagavan noticed the attendants cutting the bananas into small bits to the last few persons. Bhagavan said in disgust, *"This is what I don't like. Why do you serve me when you cannot give the same quantity to all people? That is why I am telling you. If you serve Bhagavan after you serve all others, there will be equal distribution. If by chance nothing remains, it does not matter if I do not get anything; if all eat, I am satisfied even if I do not get my share."*[2]

The ladies who were serving in the kitchen had to be particularly careful because to them Bhagavan was the embodiment of God and their *sadguru*. They would

therefore unwittingly transgress the rule of equality only to be pulled up by Ramana. In the beginning of her stay at the *asram*, one such kitchen-helper, Santamma, served an extra helping on Bhagavan's leaf-plate. That night Ramana called her and asked, *"Why do you serve me more of the curry than the rest? Have you come all the way here to learn this. If you serve more to others and less to me, I would be happy. If you show the devotees the same love as you are showing to me, then your love for me too will grow."*[3]

Another lady helper, Subbalakshmamma, also was given a similar lesson by Ramana. She noticed that Ramana used to add a little quantity of sweet buttermilk to his rasam rice. For a few days at a stretch however, there was only sour buttermilk available in the *asram*. Then, one day someone brought a little quantity of sweet buttermilk. Thinking that Bhagavan ate so sparsely and therefore it would not be wrong to give him this item even though it was not equally available to others, she served him. *"All are equal here,"* he said. She reports another incident. Ramana used to take an extra helping of rasam by cupping his hands. One day he refused. When asked by her, he said, *"In order to give me a little more rasam, you are keeping others waiting."*[4] On one occasion Sri Sundaram, a kitchen helper, noticed that the vegetables in the sambar had not been cooked properly. When he served Ramana he carefully avoided the pieces in the sambar. However, nothing could escape Ramana's observation. He told Sundaram, *"If something is considered unpalatable for me, it should be considered the same for others also."*[5]

In the later years when Bhagavan's health deteriorated, many devotees would press him to take healthier food for their sake. They would argue that the others could eat any number of dishes whereas Ramana ate very little even though he was in need of nourishing food. He would invariably refuse such requests. A humorous incident took place once in regard to this. A devotee suggested that Ramana should regularly drink some orange juice, to which he replied, *"How could we afford to have such a luxurious diet? For us there can only be a poor man's rations."*[6] That devotee told him that the cost was not much for one glass to be given to Ramana.

Ramana said, *"No, no, we require about two hundred tumblers of juice. Do you want me to gulp down the drink alone when all of you are waiting empty handed? Moreover how can poor people like us provide two hundred tumblers of this juice daily?"*[7] Similar overtures by even longstanding devotees would be instantly scorched because what was not equally shared was like poison to Ramana.

Sometimes dosas would be prepared for breakfast. When Bhagavan was doing kitchen work he would be given one for tasting and another would be tasted by others. At breakfast Ramana would insist on taking only one dosa since he had one earlier in the morning. For him the rule of sharing equally was never to be broken under any circumstances.[8]

Kinder You Are Than One's Own Mother

Ramana's love for all creation was natural and spontaneous and was not a cultivated quality of mind. A common misconception is that when one attains Self-knowledge, since there is a total absence of difference in perception, individual love is not possible. Ramana has often pointed out the mistake in this. The *jnani* is aware of individual differences whether one is short, fair complexioned, a woman or man and so on. Besides he is fully aware of the shortcomings of persons who come within his ambit. At the same time he is conscious of the underlying essential quality of life as the one Self. His life is therefore not based on give and take. It is only "human love which requires human meriting." Expectations and attachments would not be there. His love would be total and unqualified in respect of each and every person. Therefore some devotees used to feel that "Ramana alone knows what it is to love." Others would say, "It is hard to describe the wonder of how Bhagavan bound us all with his love." Words would never pass between him and some of the long-standing devotees. Nevertheless they knew that Bhagavan loved them and that his grace was showered on them. "We lived together like a huge family with Bhagavan at the center guiding us and shedding his grace on all."[1]

One Ramanatha Brahmachari had come to Bhagavan when he was very young and was deeply attached to him from his Virupaksha days. In the early twenties, there was a severe outbreak of plague in Tiruvannamalai. Some of the inmates of Skandasramam, where Ramana was staying, died from plague. Ramanatha Brahmachari also developed plague boils and was in a miserable condition when some of them burst. Some of the devotees thought of a ruse to protect Ramana from contamination of plague. They suggested circumambulation of the hill. On the way they told Ramana not to return to Skandasramam. They said that they would look after Ramanatha Brahmachari while Ramana could stay elsewhere. When Ramana heard this he retorted, *"What a wonderful idea! He came to me as a boy with complete faith in me. Is it proper for me to stay here leaving him there? If you are so afraid of plague, you may all stay here. I will go and stay with him. When you bring food for him, you can bring some for me also."*[2]

Once Chadwick, an inmate of the *asram*, was down with fever. Bhagavan asked one of the devotees, *"How is Chadwick now?"* The devotee replied, "I do not know; I have not seen him today." Ramana replied, *"Please go and see him at once. He has left his country and traveled thousands of miles making us his own. Should we not take care of him and look after his needs?"*[3]

Strange paradox that the spiritual colossus totally unconcerned about his own body should concern himself with very small details of his devotees' lives. "Kunjuswami had to go to his native place and did not have money to buy himself some food on his journey. Ramana packed puris for him for the journey. Narayana Iyer was returning home. The cooks were tired and asleep. Ramana roasted almonds for him."[4]

Long after Annamalai Swami had left the service of the *asram*, one night at 8 p.m., he was walking at the back of the *asram*. When Bhagavan saw him, he told an attendant, *"When Annamalai Swami was here he used to enjoy*

the avial. Go to the kitchen and bring some on a plate." When it was brought Ramana stood next to him while he was eating throwing light from his torch till the last morsel had been consumed.[5]

Ramana's classmate Rangan, while proceeding to Madras in search of a job, halted at Skandasramam. Ramana told him, *"Men go here and there and somehow manage. What arrangements have you made for your wife and children at home?"* On being assured that this was done, he left it at that. Later it transpired that this provision had been inadequate. When Rangan returned Ramana expressed his concern about it.[6] Soon, by Ramana's grace Rangan got a good job and the family problems were solved. During a certain period astrologers had predicted the worst for Rangan. At that time Ramana kept him with himself and would always caution him to return at night. He would remark, *"Come back straight without loitering anywhere or spending the night in town."*

At the time when the *asram* hall was being construct-ed, the attendants also used to carry stones to the site. One day an attendant Rangaswami's finger was crushed when a stone fell on it. Till the finger was fully healed, Ramana himself took over the work of carrying stones.[7]

Identification With the Poor, Humble, and Meek

Though there was no sense of difference for Ramana one often wonders whether he had a special soft corner for the poor, humble, and meek. There are many heart-warming instances where he would so completely be one with them. Then one sees the all-embracing nature of his love.

When Ramana was in Virupaksha Cave the sum-mer months used to be very hot and there would be no water. Therefore he would shift to the Mango Tree Cave. In those days the caste system was severely enforced. Women of lower caste with heavy loads used to be thirsty and hungry by the time they had collected grass. This is what Ramana once said in a reminiscent mood about them. *"Poor people, they start from their homes early in the morning after taking a little gruel (kanji), go up the hill and secure a head load of grass. As soon as they come to the cave they throw down their bundles, bend down and say, 'Swami, Swami, first throw a vesselful of water down our spines.' I used to stand on the verandah there and when I threw water on them as desired, they used to recover from their exhaustion, saying, 'Oh, how good this is!' Then, cup-ping their palms they used to drink water until their thirst was satisfied, wash their faces, take some rest in the shade of the trees, and then depart. They alone could experience*

the happiness of it all. It is only when one experiences the oppressiveness of the heat that one knows the relief of the coolness of water.

"I knew they would be coming at that hour and so would sit there with the water ready. What could they do? They should not touch the water in the Mulaipal Tirtham (holy tank) and there is no water anywhere else on the hill. The heat is unbearable. They cannot have food unless they sell the grass and get some money. They have children at home. They must reach home quick to look after them. What can they do, poor people! They used to come to the cave with the hope that the Swami would supply water. We were not cooking at that time. If any day we did cook, I poured a lot of water into the rice while cooking, took out the gruel, poured it into the pot, mixed water with it liberally, and added salt. If dry ginger was available I would mix it in also. By the time they came, the gruel water would be quite cool. When a tumblerful of it was poured into their hands, they used to drink it like nectar and go away. The taste of that gruel and the happiness of drinking that water they alone could know."[1]

In 1943, the Old Hall used to be overcrowded with visitors and devotees. The children who came with the women dirtied the place and there were no proper arrangements for cleaning. The attendants, in a mood of disgust, suggested that the women could sit outside the hall. Bhagavan queried, *"If ladies are to sit outside, why not the men too? When there is no work in the hall even for Bhagavan, it will be alright if I sit under the tree which is opposite the hall. Then there will be no trouble or worry for anybody for whatever the children may do."*[2] Consequently the attempt to separate the women was given up. A separate door was opened to ease the overcrowding of people.

On special occasions like *jayanti* and *mahapuja* originally only after the poor people were fed, would eating in the dining hall commence. Later it was changed such that when the poor started to eat their food it could be served in the hall also. One day Bhagavan noticed that a poor man had not got any share of food. Next day when the gong was struck, Bhagavan got up and went to the tree where the poor people were gathered and said, *"If you will not give them food first, I will not come to the dining hall at all. I will stand under the tree and stretch out my hands for food like them and when I am given a bowl of food I will eat it, go straight to the hall, and sit.*"[3] Then the old practice was revived.

This happened in 1948. The hall was full of visitors. When the lunch bell rang, everyone went to the dining hall. Bhagavan got up slowly because of the pain in his knees. Near the door he noticed a shepherd standing with an earthen pot on his shoulders. He said *"Oh! It is you Chinnappa. If you have come to see me, you must have brought koozhu. Why do you hesitate? Pour some into my hands."* Then he cupped his hands and began drinking it slowly as if it were nectar. "In the meantime one of the devotees came from the dining hall and protested, 'Oh! Bhagavan you are feasting here and there we are waiting for you.' Ramana told him, *'Who looked after me when I was on the hill? It is only the shepherds.'*"[4]

It was 3 a.m., Ramana and a few other devotees were working in the kitchen. A group of women and children wished to see Ramana and were told that it was not possible at that hour. On hearing this Ramana intervened remarking, *"Poor people! Why should they go away disappointed? Tell, them to come to the back door and I will meet them there."* Ramana stood at the doorstep and the party bathed his feet with their tears of joy.[5]

One afternoon the attendants brought a large quantity of sweets given by devotees for distribution. Just then an old lady also came with a packet of dosais (pancakes) enclosed in a banyan leaf. She went straight to Ramana, overruling the objections of the attendants, and gave those dosais to him saying, "Swami take these dosais. I am sorry I have nothing better to bring." Noticing the fact that she was upset Ramana told her gently, *"Grandma, they are little children. They do not know what is what. Please do not mistake their remarks. With what flour did you prepare these dosais? Are none of your brother's sons looking after you properly? Did you come walking, or in a cart?"* As he made these affectionate remarks, he started eating what was given to him. He ate all the dosais without even leaving a bit. Some attendants protested remarking, *"Instead of eating those dosais, which are not properly roasted, why not give them to us and eat the sweets?"* Ramana told them, *"Oh! those sweets you think will be much more tasty than these dosais? If you want, you eat all the sweets. These dosais are enough for me."*[6]

While attempting to save a squirrel from a dog, Ramana accidentally broke his collarbone. It took some time for the collarbone to heal. This accident also weakened him considerably. It had hardly healed, yet Ramana wanted to join a staunch devotee, T.P.R, and his friend, when they informed him that they were going to Skandasramam. It was immediately after lunch. Naturally the two devotees were afraid that the hot sun and Ramana's frail health would make such a trip in-

advisable. Thinking that they had persuaded him out of it, the two friends set out on their own only to find Ramana trailing behind them, slowly, along with his attendant Rangaswami. Somehow Ramana managed to reach Skandasramam, with their help, after three grueling hours in the hot sun. Why he should have done so was a mystery to them.

Soon they discovered the reason. A solitary mason was doing some odd jobs there. Ramana told him, *"I came for your sake. Your prayers dragged me here."* Ramana himself explained what his prayer was. *"As you know, four days ago, in connection with the raising of pillars for the New Hall they had a special worship. With*

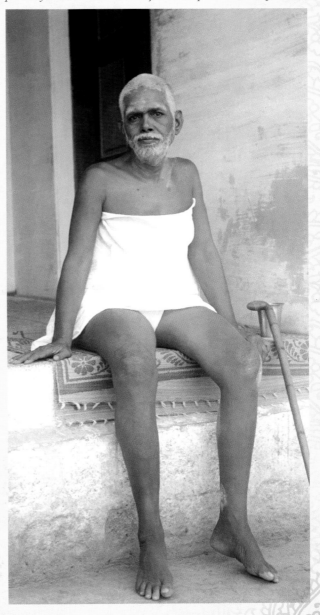

the doctor's permission the sthapati *had taken me for this function. Many had come. One of them was this mason. He thought, 'How lucky are these people who are constructing this hall! To see their work Bhagavan himself has come. How will Bhagavan come and see the work, which I am doing at Skandasramam, with such patient care? It is a year since he has come to Skandasramam. It would be too much to hope that he would do so now. How wonderful would it be if he did'*[7]

Ramana then personally inspected the work. Understandably the mason was in the seventh heaven.

One Consciousness

Monkeys

D: Does one who has realized the Self lose the sense of "I"?
R: Absolutely.

D: Then there is no difference between yourself and myself, that man over there, my servant. Are all the same?
R: All are the same, including those monkeys.
D: But the monkeys are not people? Are they not different?
R: They are exactly the same as people. All are the same in One Consciousness.

—*Mercedes de Acosta*

Ramana's identity with all creation, with all life, was total. There were no "others" for him. While he was fully aware of the differences in forms, he would at all times be simultaneously aware that behind each form there was only one power, the power of Consciousness. As he had explained to Uma Devi the Polish devotee, the *jnani* sees the basis of all as the screen is to the movement of pictures on it, the paper to the print on it, the cotton behind the cotton cloth. To Ramana the objects were only consciousness and forms. He would never miss out on the essential unity of life notwithstanding the difference in appearances. As a result Ramana was a loving friend of all life, human, animal, plant, and other. His compassionate heart would make him plead on their behalf whenever he noticed or felt any kind of discrimination or harm to them.

Between 1899 and 1922, Ramana was staying in the various caves of the Arunachala hill but mainly at Virupaksha and Skandasramam. The hill abounded in monkeys. Ramana would refer to it as their kingdom and to humans as intruders. Even after he shifted to Ramanasramam on the southern slope of Arunachala, his jungle hermitage was also the monkeys' home. Ramana was very observant. His love of all life made him study the general behavior and attitude of the monkeys who were daily visitors in large numbers to Virupaksha Cave and Skandasramam. As a result he knew about their way of life, their sports, their system of government, their attitudes and priorities. Often two monkey groups would come to him to arbitrate and his decision would be readily accepted.

Generally monkeys are looked down upon and one refers to their restlessness and mischief when talking about the mind. The mind is referred to as a "monkey." However, Ramana would always talk about their strengths, as would be seen from his remarks, *"I have known something about their organization, kings, laws etc. Everything is so perfect, so much intelligence behind it all."* He would say, *"I even know that* tapas *is not unknown to monkeys. A monkey whom we used to call Mottaipaiyan was once oppressed and ill-treated by a gang. He went away into the forest for a few days, did tapas, acquired strength, and returned. When he came and sat on a bough and shook it, all the rest of the monkeys, who had previously ill-treated him and of whom he was previously afraid, were now quaking before him. Yes, I am clear that* tapas *is well known to monkeys."*[1]

On one occasion, when some of the big monkeys snatched away the fruits brought by a devotee, Bhagavan said, *"They take their share of the fruit, why be angry with them? That is the concentrated look or the* lakshya drishti. *Some of them will find out where the fruit is kept and in the twinkling of an eye, all of them would come and take away their share. Their attention is always on the fruit. That is why in Vedantic parlance, monkey's look is given as an illustration of the concentrated look."*[2]

Once a devotee brought a big basket of mangoes from his garden for being offered to Bhagavan and said, "The monkeys are plucking the mangoes one by one. So we hurriedly plucked all of them and brought them here." Bhagavan said smilingly, *"Oh! Is that so? The monkeys take the fruit one by one, while the people take them in one lot. What the monkeys do is petty theft but what we do is regular looting."*[3]

The story of a lame monkey which was looked after by Ramana is interesting. An elder member of his tribe bit him so badly that he became lame. He was left near Skandasramam to let him die gradually. But Ramana nursed him back to health. He enjoyed many privileges. He would be given a plate right next to Ramana. He was a scrupulously clean eater. *"He was very sensitive though,"* says Ramana. *"One day for some reason he threw out some food, and I chided him saying, 'What! Why are you scattering food?' He at once hit me over the eye and slightly hurt me. As a punishment he was not allowed for some days to approach me. But he cringed and begged hard, and regained his blissful seat. That was his second offence. On the first occasion Nondi felt irritated at his own cup of hot milk being taken near my lips to be cooled when he struck me over the eye, but as there was no serious hurt and he at once affectionately re-occupied my lap and cringed as much as to say, 'Forget and forgive: let bygones be bygones,' he was excused."*[4]

Over the years we have a number of interesting stories relating to the monkeys and also stories which show the great compassion which Ramana had for monkeys. One day a male monkey snatched some fruits and ran away. However a female monkey with her babe on her breast came near the fruits and was immediately shouted away.

Ramana said, *"It is a mother with a child. Why not give her something and send her away?"* But he was not sufficiently audible, and so the monkey got frightened, went off, and hid herself in a tree. "Bhagavan, full of concern said, *'Is this fair? We call ourselves* sannyasins, *but when a real* sannyasi *comes we drive him away without giving*

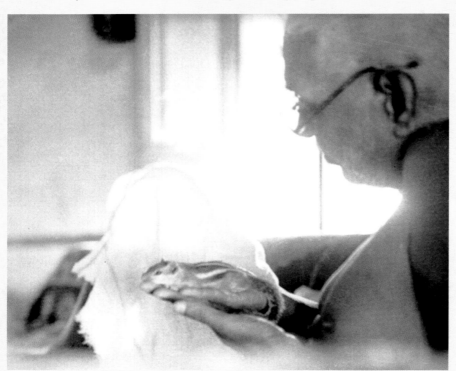

him anything. How unfair! We want to eat for years and live. We store things in a room, lock it and keep the keys with us. Has the monkey got a house? Can it put anything by for the morrow? It eats whatever it can get and sleeps on whatever tree available. It carries the child under the belly wherever it goes until the child is also able to walk about when it leaves the child to itself. Who is a real sannyasi, *the monkey or ourselves? That is why the male monkey took its share on the way itself. That was a male and could do it with impunity. This is a female. What can she do?'* So saying Bhagavan began calling that monkey cajolingly. The monkey came on to the side of the couch and stood there. In an endearing manner Bhagavan gave her all the fruits she wanted and sent her away."[5]

Once a monkey tried to bring her newborn baby through a window near Ramana's couch. The attendants were preventing her. Ramana chided them as follows, *"Don't all of you bring your newborn babes to me? She also wants to do so. Why should you prevent her?"*[6]

One day as usual someone complained to Ramana about the nuisance created by the monkeys and added

that "at this rate nobody would be able to remain in the *asram*." Ramana laughingly remarked, *"In that case the monkeys would have Bhagavan all to themselves."*[7]

Squirrels

Ramana was so fond of squirrels, peacocks, monkeys, and other animals that when he was shifted to the New Hall to accommodate the growing number of devotees, he found it hard to accept the change. He was concerned that it practically meant the denial of entry to these animal friends. He told his attendant Sivananadam, *"Do you see this? How can they, the squirrels, come here?"* When the attendant pointed out that it was for Bhagavan's comfort that the change had been made, he remarked, *"That's alright. If we look to our comforts is it not at the expense of the sufferings of others? Squirrels, monkeys, peacocks, and cows have no chance of coming here."* As soon as it was evening, he sent some of his attendants to feed the squirrels, monkeys, and peacocks who came to the *asram*. He remarked, *"They may perhaps think that the Swami has given them a slip and gone elsewhere. Please go. What a pity! Go, at least give them some food and come back."*[8] After the attendant came back, he once again enquired, *"Have you fed them all? They will think that the Swami has deserted them and has gone to a better place to sit there so that he alone can be happy. Perhaps they thought I had forgotten them. There is no room for them here."*[9]

Peacocks

In April 1947, the Rani of Bhavanagar presented a white peacock to the *asram*. Initially Ramana did not accept the gift because he felt that there might be quarrels between the white peacock and the colored peacocks which were already in the *asram*. Besides it had to be protected from the attacks of cats. As it usually happened, the donors never took back their gifts to the *asram*. Hence the white peacock stayed. It would move about freely in the presence of Ramana enjoying the feed given by him. Sometimes, however, the peacock would run away somewhere else and it had to be brought back by the attendants. Then Ramana would place his hand on its neck, and stroking it up to the heart with his other hand, would say, *"You naughty chap, where did you go? How can we manage to look after you, if you go away? Please don't. There will be cruel animals elsewhere. Why not stay on here?"*[10] Thus he cajoled it. Sometimes this white peacock would listen intently to music on the radio. When someone remarked, "See how carefully it is listening!" Bhagavan would point out, *"Peacocks are fond of music, especially if it is from the flute."*[11]

Once referring to this white peacock someone said, "Though this peacock is white, it is the other peacocks that are really beautiful."[12] Pointing to the peacock Bhagavan said, *"If it is like this, it has a beauty of its own. Those peacocks have many beautiful colors. This is pure white without any mixture of other colors. That means it is* suddha sattva *(pure Self), without the mixture of other gunas (attributes). See, in Vedantic language, the peacock also can be taken as an example. Even the other peacocks*

do not have so many colors at birth. They have only one color. As they grow up, they get many colors. When their tails grow, they have any number of eyes. See how many colors and how many eyes! Our mind also is like that. At birth there are no perversities. Subsequently, there will be many activities and ideas, like the colors of the peacock."[13]

Sometimes the conversation would revolve around the past when he would recall some of his experiences with peacocks. Referring to one particular peacock, which used to be with him at Skandasramam, he said, *"When I was in the Melasramam (Skandasramam), there was one peacock which would come to me daily from the town and remain there for prolonged periods. The owner used to come and take him home. One day the owner came as usual and tried to take the peacock, but in vain. The peacock persisted in coming often and remaining with me. The owner, perhaps, lost his patience and suddenly one day he burst out rather humorously, 'Swami! Give me money and take this peacock. Of what use is it to*

me when it does not stay with me but is always found only in your presence?' I told him, 'Why should I do so? Where am I to go for the money? I am a penniless samiar with a piece of koupinam. You can take your peacock away. I did not call it here.' But the peacock continued to come as usual and none succeeded in stopping it from coming to me.

"*Once when Palaniswami was laid up with fever, I used to visit him daily at Virupaksha Cave. This peacock also would follow me during such occasions and after some time, if I overstayed, he would remind and call me by signs to return to the usual abode, Melasramam. One day I just tried to play with the peacock by simply proceeding some distance towards Melasramam from the Virupaksha Cave and returning again slowly. Knowing this clearly, the peacock also followed me hurriedly, came in front of me and actually waylaid me, beckoning me to return without proceeding further. He did not leave me till I reached the Melasramam. He used to give some strokes on my head at times, which would sound—Pottu-pottu—if I did not yield to his wishes.*"[14]

Wild Animals

Ramana had no fear of wild animals nor did they have any fear of him. There is a graphic account of a happening in the days when Ramana was staying in Pachaiamman Koil in 1906. It is extracted in full as it shows how Ramana treated wild animals and humans alike. "One day a devo-

tee, Rangaswami Iyengar, arrived there at 1 o'clock in the blazing sun. Bhagavan received him with his usual beaming face, his smile, and kindness. Sri Iyengar was asked by the devotees around to have his bath in the pond nearby. He left Sri Bhagavan's presence to bathe there in front of the temple.

"The spot was very lonely. Sri Iyengar was bathing at the eastern ghat. All of a sudden Sri Bhagavan, who was

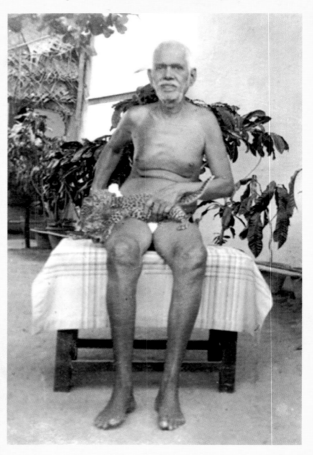

seated inside the temple, left that place. Those around thought he was walking out for some bodily need of his own. When he came to the tank he saw a leopard which had come to quench its thirst at the northern edge.

"Bhagavan quietly told the animal: *'Go now, and come later; he would be afraid,'* referring to the man bathing nearby. At these words of Bhagavan the animal went away.

"Sri Bhagavan went to the bather, who had by then finished his bath, and said to him, *'We should not come here at this time of the day; wild animals come at these hours to quench their thirst.'* He did not add that a wild animal had actually come there, lest the man be frightened."[15]

Some devotees are familiar with the picture of Ramana holding small cheetah cubs with his hands. It happened in 1946. Some person who had reared two baby cheetahs brought them to Ramana's presence. There they were fondled and given milk after which they moved freely with Ramana, slept with him soundly for some time. Some devotee took a photograph on the occasion after they had woken up.

The wonder of it was that while they were there, squirrels came and ate nuts and sparrows came and ate broken rice as usual. In olden days when animals and birds of all sorts moved about together without any enmity, people used to think that the place was a *rishi*'s *asram*. These are stories related in the *Puranas*, says Suri Nagamma, "But here we see the same things before our very eyes."[16]

Snakes

Dr. Srinivasa Rao, the *asram* doctor, asked Ramana whether a snake had once crept over his body. Ramana said, *"Yes. Snakes raise their hoods and look into our eyes. They seem to know when they need not be afraid and then pass over us. It did not strike me either that I should do anything to it."*[17]

When another devotee asked how he felt, Ramana replied, *"Cool and soft."*[18]

One devotee wished to know from Ramana whether it was true that he was friendly with snakes while living on the mountain. Ramana replied, *"Yes, it is true. One particular snake used to be friendly and would crawl over my legs. At its touch my body used to feel as if it was tickled. The snake used to come and go of its own accord."*[19]

While at Skandasramam a peacock would follow Ramana everywhere. One day a huge black cobra appeared at the *asram* and this peacock attacked it fiercely. The two natural enemies were poised to fight to the death. Then Ramana went near the cobra and said, *"Why do you come here? The peacock will kill you. Better go away at once."*[20] The cobra immediately lowered its hood and slithered away.

On noticing a snake near Ramana's hall, there was shouting outside. "What kind of snake is it. Beat it! Beat it! Ramana's protest was not heard and the snake was killed. Then Bhagavan remarked, *"If these people are beaten like that, then they will know what it means."*[21]

One night, a sleeping snake fell down from the roof of the *asram* hall. Ramana ordered the men to take a lantern to light its path to the door and told them not to harm it. Regarding the snakes which infested the place he said, *"We have come to their abode as guests and so we have no right to molest them. Let us leave them in peace."*[22]

Liberation of Cow Lakshmi

On Saturday, the fifth of Ani in the year Sarvadhari, the twelfth day of the waxing moon under the asterism Visakha, the cow Lakshmi attained mukti.[1]

—*Bhagavan Ramana*

Liberation means freedom from the death-birth cycle. Unless one's mind, with its tendencies, subsides in the spiritual heart, the pre-existing tendencies will cause rebirths, the rebirth being in accordance with one's ethical balance sheet. A person who becomes Self-aware while in the body is called a *jivan mukta*, one who is liberated while alive. When the mind force merges in the heart at the time of death, it is called *videha mukti*, liberation at the point of death. It is generally believed that liberation is attainable only by human beings and it is not open to animals, who do not have a discriminative mind, by reason of which one can discover the truth. However, this general rule has very rare exceptions. One such exception recorded in the Hindu epics is that of Gajendra, king of

elephants, who got liberated by the grace of God Vishnu. The divine power of Ramana's grace, flowing through his hands, has been responsible for liberating his mother Azhagammal, Cow Lakshmi, the deer Valli, and the dog Jack.

The story of Cow Lakshmi is particularly moving as we have the full details of it, stretching from the time when she came to the *asram* as a calf in 1926 till her *mukti* in June 1948.

Sometime in 1926, four years after Ramana settled down near the *samadhi* of his mother, one of his devotees

brought a cow and a calf as a gift to Ramana. The calf was the now famous Lakshmi.

When she was young and frisky, occasionally she would damage the vegetable garden. However, when she was blamed for it Ramana would immediately defend her, saying, *"She is not to be blamed. She went where she found good food. If you didn't want her to go there you ought to have fenced the garden properly to keep her out."*[2]

When the number of cows increased in the *asram*, a special *gosala* (cowshed) was built and it was decided that Lakshmi would be the first one to enter it. For this purpose, she was bathed and decorated to enter her new abode. But she slipped away and went to Ramana and sat down there refusing to budge until he came and stepped into her house first. She stepped in behind him.

Many of Lakshmi's calves were born on Ramana's *jayanti* or birthday. Whenever she came to the hall Ramana would pay attention to her, pat her, feed her with plantains, or rice cakes. To every onlooker it was evident that there was some special bond between them although Lakshmi was a cow.

In her book, Pascaline Mallet records, "Maharshi's favorite cow Lakshmi is a most beautiful creature with deli-

too overflowed as he looked at her with great love. How could those standing nearby hold back their emotions? He asked her tenderly, *"Amma, do you want me to be near you? I must go now as people are waiting for me in the hall. But wherever I may be, I am always with you."*[4] Then he "placed his hand on her head as though giving *diksha*. He put his hand over her heart also and then caressed her, placing his cheek against her face. When he had convinced himself that her heart was pure, free from all *vasanas* entailing rebirth and centered solely on him, he took leave of her and returned to the hall.... Her eyes were calm and peaceful. She was conscious up to the end and left the body at 11.30 a.m. quite peacefully."[5]

A stone tomb was built over her grave, surmounted by a likeness of her. On her tomb was engraved an epitaph by Ramana which makes it quite clear that she attained liberation.

Later Ramana was asked by some devotees whether he had used the term euphemistically. Ramana said that he literally meant that Lakshmi had in fact been liberated.

Though Ramana was compassion incarnate, he would do his best not to show any outward signs of it, possibly

cate horns and almond shaped eyes. The love she showed for Maharshi was very touching. As we were sitting in the *asram* hall we heard a noise outside and to our amazement up the steps came Lakshmi, as if it were the most natural thing. She went straight up to Maharshi's couch and he at once greeted her most affectionately and ordered that she should be given some plantains to eat. Lakshmi, quite satisfied, turned away and went down. Needless to say people seated on the floor gave way to her amidst general laughter.... Maharshi sees the same life in all although he recognizes differences in outer forms. His vision of equality is based on the realization of the one behind the many."[3]

On June 17, 1948, Lakshmi fell ill. The following morning, June 18, it looked as if her end was near. At about 10 o'clock in the morning Ramana went to her. He found her breathing hard and she was lying prostrate. Taking her head into his arms, stroking her neck, Ramana fixed his gaze on her eyes. Her breathing became steady immediately. Tears began to trickle from her eyes. Ramana's eyes

because it might lead to jealousies among the devotees or the feeling "I am a favorite of his." However, there are two notable exceptions to this. The first relates to his mother Azhagammal in whose case we have the only known prayer by Ramana for her recovery from fever and also from the delirium of illusion. The other instance is that of Cow Lakshmi where we find that he unhesitatingly and at all times showed his love towards her. Even during the construction of the *gosala* he took special interest. "Again a few minutes after Lakshmi's liberation, Ramana came to the *gosala*, squatted by her side, took her face in both his hands as though she were a little child, lifted it and said, *'Oh Lakshmi! Lakshmi!'* Then controlling his tears, he said, *'Because of her our family has grown to this extent.'"*[6]

It is the total surrender of mother and Lakshmi which must have evoked such obvious gestures of love from Ramana.

Some Western Devotees

Paul Brunton

O, sage of Aruna Hill, I bow at your feet with
    thankfulness
You have conferred spiritual riches on me, a
    foreigner living in the West.
Your grace you showered on me and made me a
    divine man.
I am happy through your grace. No earthly
    affliction can now disturb my peace.
I have dedicated this book to you as my humble
    tribute.
You belong to the ancient line of Maharshis of
    India.
If I can impart to others what you are pleased to
    teach me, my life's purpose would be fulfilled.
I salute you over and over again.[1]

           —Paul Brunton

Paul Brunton's *Search in Secret India*, published in 1934 has remained a bestseller since. From then onwards and even now, sixty-five years later, more and more seekers, particularly in the West, have been drawn to Ramana through this book. Its fascination has been and is such that there can be little doubt about its being inspired by Ramana. Paul Brunton had a powerful pen, being a journalist from London. But it is Ramana's grace which has made his book a mighty instrument for spreading Ramana's message.

Surprisingly, though Brunton had come to India specifically for finding out the secrets of sacred India, his list of holy personages did not include Ramana Maharshi. Brunton firmly refused to meet him, not knowing the divine scheme of things which started working. Venkataramani, a journalist friend of his, took him to H.H. Chandrasekhara Saraswati Swami of Kanchi. The sage not merely suggested but insisted that Brunton should go to Ramana. He said, "He is called Maharshi. I have not met him but I know him to be a high master. Shall I provide you with full instructions, so that you may discover him?" In his negative frame of mind Brunton demurred saying, "All arrangements are made for my departure from the South tomorrow." Then out of compassion the sage insisted on Brunton meeting the Maharshi before leaving South India.[2]

The memorable first meeting was totally unexpected for Brunton. The atmosphere was saturated with an uncommon, silent, and magnetic peace. Ramana's eyes were wide open and he seemed to be looking out into space. Brunton too was drawn into this pervasive peace. In the steady river of peace which was flowing, his thought-tortured mind rested. After the midday meal Brunton found the opportunity for his first question and answer session with Ramana.

Q: I wish to have the experience of enlightenment. Can you assist me to experience enlightenment? Or is the search itself a mere delusion?

A: You say "I." "I" want to know. Tell me, who is that "I"? Know first that "I" and then you shall know the truth. There is only one thing to be done. Look into your own self. Do this in the right way and you shall find the answer to all your problems.

Q: How long will it take to get some enlightenment with a master's help?

A: It all depends on the maturity of the seeker's mind. The gunpowder catches fire in an instant, while much time is needed to set fire to the coal.[3]

The Maharshi had given the core of his teachings but Brunton was not yet ready to comprehend it, let alone accept it.

Brunton kept extending his stay, first to a week and later to a fortnight, with growing impatience. His stay was a "tantalizing mixture of sublime moods and disappointing failures to effect any worthwhile personal contact with the Maharshi." On the last day of his stay he managed to interview Maharshi again, this time about combining work and wisdom. Ramana told him, *"The life of action need not be renounced. If you meditate in the right manner, then the current of mind induced will continue to flow even in the midst of your work. It is as though there were two ways of expressing the same idea; the same*

line which you take in meditation will be expressed in your activities. As you go on you will find that your attitude towards people, events, and objects will gradually change. Your actions will tend to follow your meditations of their own accord."[4]

What Brunton had received was an epoch-making message of universal usefulness. For, Ramana's teachings enable an inner renunciation, which ends conflict between activity and meditation. One need not renounce home or activities in order to discover the ultimate truth behind all life. The inbuilt equipoise, resulting from well-directed self-enquiry, would be the undercurrent in one's busiest hours. The joy, which is one's inherent nature, would not be affected by the changing flow of circumstances in the dynamics of life.

Unfortunately for Brunton, he did not realize that he had arrived at the journey's end. He was on the threshold of discovering the truth for himself but let go his chance. Much suffering and heart searching was still in store for him. He had to wander round different parts of India in

a vain, physically exhausting, and depressing hunt before returning to Ramana a second time.

At that eleventh hour, after he had booked his passage to return to England, he responded to a compelling "Inner Voice," which forced him to return from Bombay to the Maharshi.

This time he was open to receive the truth from the Maharshi. He had come as a disciple would to the *guru*, in a mood of humble surrender. He settled down near the *asram*, built a small cottage for himself and adjusted himself to the unhurried pace of life at the *asram*. Each day would seemingly be no different from the earlier one. But the steady grace flowing from Ramana was effecting an inner metamorphosis. To Brunton "day after day brought its fresh indication of the greatness of this man." He could see for himself the daily occurrences in Ramana's presence. His absolute equality and firm wisdom became evident to Brunton. At last his constant judgment of the Maharshi, his comparison of him with others, and his own preconceived ideas ended, thanks to Ramana's overflowing grace.

Brunton learnt "to submit to the enigma of his personality, and to accept him as he found him." As a result spiritual inwardness started peaking. He began to understand that Ramana's immense silence was even more potent than his replies. "The realization forces itself through my wonderment that all my questions are moves in an endless game, the play of thoughts which possess no limit to their extent; that somewhere within me there is a well of certitude which can provide me with all the waters of truth I require."[5] Then he was ready to receive the Maharshi's grace in full measure. One night in the Maharshi's hall it happened. "His sense of awareness was drawn out of the narrow confines of a separate personality. It had turned into something sublime and all-embracing."[6]

Later an old devotee tells him, "You have been in a spiritual trance for nearly two hours. The Maharshi watched you closely all the time. I believe he guided you."[7]

The onset of fever forced him to take a reluctant farewell. This too was to be only in the physical sense. For Ramana was always with him, particularly during his meditations.

M.A. Pigot

After the publication of Paul Brunton's *Search in Secret India*, serious seekers in the west started coming to Sri Ramanasramam for guidance and clarification on the spiritual path. Though several hundreds of such seekers had come, only some of them have left useful records which throw light either on the personality of Ramana or on his teachings. The clarifications sought by a few of them and the replies given by Ramana have been recorded in *Talks with Sri Ramana Maharshi*. However, we find that the recording in the *Talks* is often very brief.

Whereas they themselves have given elsewhere a complete account of what happened in their meetings with Ramana. The first western lady devotee to come to Sri Ramanasramam was M.A. Pigot, an English lady, who had read *A Search in Secret India* and had come to India to see the Maharshi.

Often she would be desperate because there would always be a crowd and Ramana was never alone. His hall was open to one and all at all times. But early one morning when she came into the hall she found him unattended, "emanating a wonderful stillness and peace." With his permission she put him some questions and got his clarifications.

P: What are the hindrances to the realization of the true Self?

R: *Memory chiefly, habits of thoughts, accumulated tendencies.*

P: How does one get rid of these hindrances?

R: *Seek for the Self through meditation in this manner, trace every thought back to its origin which is only the mind. Never allow thought to run on. If you do, it will be unend-*

ing. Take it back to its starting place—the mind—again and again, and it and the mind will both die of inaction. The mind exists only by reason of thought. Stop thought and there is no mind. As each doubt and depression arises, ask yourself, "Who is it that doubts? What is it that is depressed?" Go back constantly until there is nothing but the source of all left. And then, live always in the present and only in it. There is no past or future, save in the mind.[8]

P: What meditation will help me?

R: *You must learn to realize the subject and object as one. In meditating on an object, whether concrete or abstract, you are destroying the sense of oneness and creating duality. Meditate on what you are in Reality. Try to realize that the body is not you, the emotions are not you, the intellect is not you. When all these are still you will find….*

P: What?

R: *You will discover, it is not for me to say what any individual experience will be. It will reveal itself. Hold on to that.*[9]

It will be seen that Ramana is emphasizing the necessity for holistic meditation. Ramana traces the malaise of objective meditation to non-existent division between subject and object. The object is only for the subject and exists only when the attention of the subject or the individual is there. If this is forgotten and the fact that the Self is one, whole, is forgotten, no meditation can result in sustained, inherent, peace of mind.

At the time of the farewell his talk was most touching. He was so gentle and humane. He discussed the difficulties of everyday life and mundane problems. Ramana's parting message was, *"Do what is right at a given moment and leave it behind."*

Mercedes de Acosta

A Spanish American devotee, Mercedes de Acosta, was at Sri Ramanasramam in November 1938. At that time she was a Hollywood socialite and scriptwriter for films. Twenty-four years later she wrote a book titled *Here Lies the Heart.* Notwithstanding this long time gap her account is at once gripping and full of devotion to Ramana to whom it has been dedicated.

Once in Ramana's presence she felt that questions were needless. Doubts were getting dissolved by themselves. Out of her planned long list she needed to ask a couple of questions only.

M.A.: Should I follow my inner-self?

B.R : *I do not know anything about your inner self. You should follow the Self. There is nothing or no one else to follow.*

M.A: What about religions, teachers, and *gurus*?

B.R.: *It is only by diving deep into the spiritual heart that one can find the Self.*

"Placing his hand on the right side of his chest Ramana continued. *'Here lies the heart, the dynamic spiritual heart. It is called* Hrdaya *and is clearly visible to the inner eye of an adept in the spiritual path. Through meditation you can learn to find the Self in the cave of this heart.'"*[10]

At her first meeting as she was meditating, sitting at the feet of Ramana and facing him, he looked directly down at her, his eyes looking into hers. She says, "It would be impossible to describe this moment. I can only say that at this second I felt my inner being raised to a new level. Then Bhagavan smiled at me. It seemed to me that I had never before known what a smile was."[11]

"The transformation which took place in her by merely being in his presence was sufficient nourishment for a lifetime. How could it have been otherwise?"[12]

After returning to America she sent a few questions to Ramana for clarifications. These questions are about reincarnation, the past, and the future.

Q: Is reincarnation a fact?

A: *You are incarnated now, aren't you? Then you will be so again.*

Q: What is death? What is birth?

A: *Only the body has death and birth.*

Q: How much time may elapse between death and rebirth?

A: *Perhaps one is reborn within a year, three years, or thousands of years. Who can say? Anyway what is Time? Time does not exist.*

Q: Why have we no memory of past lives?

A: *Why do you want to remember other lives that are also illusions? If you abide within the Self, there is no past or future and not even a present since the Self is out of time. It is timeless.*

Q: Then when we leave this body, will the ego immediately grasp another body?

A: *Oh, yes it must. It cannot exist without a body.*

Q: What sort of body will it grasp?

A: *Either a physical body or a subtle-mental body.*

Q: Do you call this present physical body the gross body?

A: *Only to distinguish it, to set it apart in conversation.*

Q: What causes us to be reborn?

A: *Desires. Unfulfilled desires bring you back. And in each case—in each body as your desires are fulfilled, you create new ones.*[13]

Having answered all the questions Ramana gave her a most important piece of advice which is universally applicable. "*These questions are good, but tell de Acosta she must not become too intellectual about these things. It is better just to meditate and have no thought. Let the mind rest quietly in the Self, in the cave of the spiritual heart. Soon this will become natural and then there will be no*

need for questions. Do not imagine that this means being inactive. Silence is the only real activity."[14]

Uma Devi

Uma Devi, a Polish lady converted to Hinduism, was one of the staunch devotees of Ramana. She has written a book *The Teaching of Ramana Maharshi* which has attracted many seekers from Poland to Ramana. She has also translated *Bhagavad Gita* into Polish.

Uma Devi was a frequent visitor to Sri Ramanasramam. During one of her visits in February 1938, she put some questions to Ramana, whose replies are a lucid exposition of the all-pervasiveness of Consciousness. She

Group photo with Ramana; Uma Devi is seated in the second row, first from the right

wished to have a continuous vision of Siva, who meant everything to her. Ramana clarified to her the importance of direct perception of the Self through self-enquiry. "*A vision depends on the subject. It would appear and disappear. It is not inherent, not first hand.*" Bhagavan continued, "*Therefore enquire 'Who am I?' Sink deep within and abide as the Self....*"

Q: Yes, But how shall I effect it as quickly as possible?

A: *This is the obstacle for realization. There is no question of time. Surrender to Him and abide by His will whether He appears or vanishes, await His pleasure. If you ask Him to do as you please it is not surrender but a command to Him. You cannot have Him obey you and yet think that you have surrendered. He knows what is best and when and how to do it. Leave everything entirely to Him. His is the burden, no longer do you have any cares. All your cares are His. Such is surrender....*

Or enquire to whom these questions arise. Dive deep in the Heart and remain as the Self. One of these two ways is open to the aspirant now. Think of the man who sees only the cloth and not the cotton of which it is made, or the man who sees the pictures moving on the screen in a cinema show and not the screen itself as the background; or again the man who sees the letters which he reads but not the paper on which they are written. The objects are the consciousness and forms. The ordinary person sees the objects in the universe but not the consciousness in these forms.[15]

Arthur Osborne

Such have I known,
Him of the Lustrous eyes,
Him whose sole look
Pierced to the Heart,
Of wisdom deeper than in the holy book,
Of truth alone.[16]

—Arthur Osborne

Ramana and Adam Osborne

When one thinks of Arthur Osborne, a tall, saintly figure comes to one's mind. From his youth he was attracted to the inner way of life thanks to the influence of René Guénon, the French philosopher. Guénon had expounded the view "that all beings manifest the one Self or pure Being and that I, in my essence, am identical with the Self."

The first meeting was only towards the end of 1945. Osborne had gone to Tiruvannamalai, more because his family was staying near Ramanasramam rather than to meet the Maharshi. This is surprising because Osborne was to be a vital instrument of Ramana. A large number of Western seekers were to be drawn to the direct path of Ramana through Osborne's books and his editorials in the quarterly magazine *The Mountain Path*. This only indicates that the divine has its own timings.

Osborne was not much impressed by Ramana when they met first. He says, "During the weeks that followed he was constantly gracious to me and the strain of nerves and mind gradually released, but there was no dynamic contact."[17] All this changed suddenly when on a festival day, in the evening the "revelation occurred." Osborne was sitting facing Ramana whose eyes pierced him intensely. "It was as though he said, 'You have been told, why have you not realized?' And then quietness, a depth of peace, and an indescribable lightness and happiness."[18] Osborne was convinced that Ramana had accepted him as his disciple and taken over the responsibility of guiding him as a *guru* on the universally acceptable path of self-enquiry. Osborne quickly learnt that Ramana's path, far from being impractical, was entirely oriented towards practice and experience. Osborne began to feel the vital presence of Ramana in the heart and the support of his "outpouring grace" in his *sadhana*. He felt that Ramana was the inner *guru*, available always to seekers who relied on him. This enabled him to face the long illness of Ramana's body for fourteen months, and his *mahanirvana* in 1950, with fortitude and courage. He had firm faith in Ramana's statement *Where can I go? I am here.*

The Thirties and Forties

The publication of *Self Realization* in 1931 by B.V. Narasimha Swami, the first biography of Ramana, followed by Paul Brunton's *Search in Secret India* soon thereafter, helped in making Ramana's life and teachings well known in India and abroad. There was therefore a regular stream of seekers, devotees, and visitors. In the scheme of providence practically the entire recorded talks and conversations with them has been contemporaneously preserved, through *Talks, Conscious Immortality, Guru Ramana, Day by Day with Bhagavan, Living by the Words of Ramana* and *More Talks*. Between them they cover more than a thousand pages, a standing testimony of Ramana's grace and compassion for all who had sought his guidance for the inner journey.[1] This makes the position of Ramana as a universal *guru* very special. "Maharshi is unique in the history of world seers." "To have lived for full fifty-four years after Realization, to have influenced so many from his seat in one place, to have been accessible to all at all hours, to have stemmed the tide of skepticism as he did, is something truly unprecedented."[2]

In 1938 Rajendra Prasad spent three days at the *asram* as a messenger of Mahatma Gandhi. He was accompanied by Jamnalal Bajaj. During this visit Bajaj put some interesting questions.

Q: If Swaraj is gained by intense struggle is not a person justified in being overwhelmed with joy?

A: *In this sacrifice one should have surrendered himself to the higher power, which alone has brought about the result. He should not forget it. Then where is the cause for elation? One would have done his duty without caring for the result. This is* nishkama karma.

Q: Is there no suitable power on earth which would bestow grace on the devotees, so that they may work efficiently and gain Swaraj?

After a pause J.B. continued:

Is not the *tapasya* of the ancient *mahatmas* still valid? Will it not benefit the present generation?

A: *Yes, of course it will. But it should be remembered that no single person is a claimant of it. It is only that grace which has aroused awakening among the people.*[3]

However, Rajendra Prasad remained silent throughout. At the time of their departure, he asked; "Mahatma Gandhi has sent me to the Maharshi. Is there any message that I can take to him?" to which the Maharshi replied,

"What message is needed when heart speaks to heart? It is the same sakti *which is working there also."*[4]

The great event of the post-war years was the celebration of the Golden Jubilee of Ramana's advent at Arunachala, on September 1, 1946.

The first intimation of the special event was hinted to Subbaramayya by Ramana when he visited the *asram* in June 1946. While going up the hill Ramana informed him, *"Venkatachalam Chetty had a brain wave. The idea of such a celebration first occurred to him and since he made the proposal, it seems to have caught everyone's*

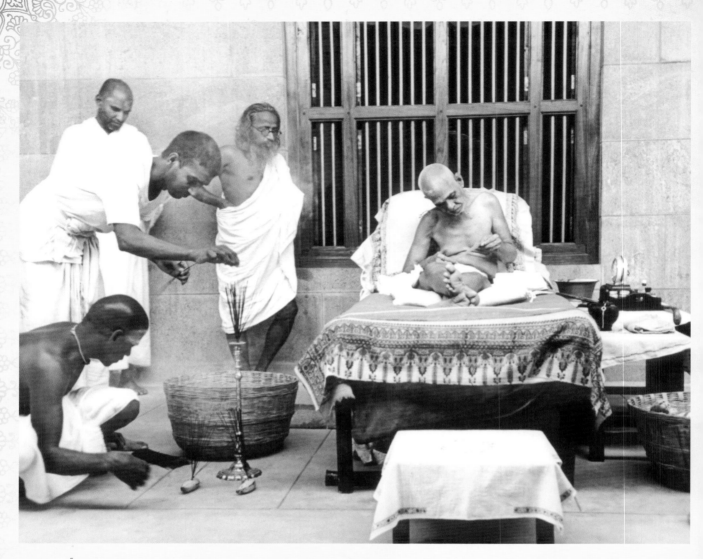

fancy."[5] All were geared to its befitting celebration thereafter. A few days prior to the event the *asram* was crowded with devotees from different parts of the country. They had come by buses and lorries braving the railway strike from August 23, 1946. Compositions in praise of Ramana were read both in the mornings and evenings from August 30, for many were keen on expressing their gratitude and reverence. Suri Nagamma echoes their feelings when she says, "When he who is omnipresent, who is omniscient, and incomprehensible comes in human form what can you give him"? How can we worship him?"[6] A special, spacious thatched shed was erected to the north of and adjacent to the Old Hall, which came to be known as the Jubilee Hall. The floor was cemented and the hall was tastefully decorated.

The event of events was the consecration of the Matrubhuteswara temple on March 17, 1949. Ramana participated fully in all the ceremonies connected with it. It is the only temple for an enlightened woman anywhere in the world. That it should be in honor of Ramana's mother is in the fitness of things, for it was he who had declared in 1917 that in enlightenment, and the efforts to discover it, men and women are equal.[7]

Vicarious Penance

He who was crucified and rose again
Has taught the noble *dharma*
That for the sins of others too
We should do penance
And redeem them.
May this *dharma* of compassion

Taught by the true *brahmin*, Venkata,
Flourish ever, this *dharma* of the cross
The *dharma* of vicarious penance.[1]

　　　　　　　　　　　—Muruganar

Jesus Christ was crucified on the cross. Sri Ramakrishna suffered from throat cancer. Sri Ramana's body suffered from sarcoma for many long months from early February 1949 to April 14, 1950. Four operations had to be performed on his body and the pain was excruciating. The world is unable to understand the suffering of the bodies of the saviors of humanity like them. "Why should the pure, spotless ones suffer?" is the question which arises in the minds of many.

The reason for this is given in the above verses of Muruganar. The crucifixion of the bodies of world teachers is a logical corollary of their universal love and compassion. They suffered for the sins of others. Theirs is vicarious penance.

Early in February 1949, the *asram* doctor, Dr. Shankar Rao, assisted by Dr. Srinivasa Rao, removed a very small growth on the left elbow of Ramana. They duly bandaged it and the bandage was removed on February 22, since it was presumed to have healed.[2] This comparatively innocuous, minor operation, was to be the beginning of the end of Ramana's sacred body.

The lump which had been removed early in February 1949, and which was thought to have healed satisfactorily, subsequently started to grow again. So the services of an eminent surgeon from Madras, Dr. Raghavachari, were availed of. On March 27, he came from Madras with surgical instruments and assistants to remove the growth.[3]

We may regard this as the second operation. Earlier, a report had come from the analysts about the small growth removed in February 1949 and the growth had been diagnosed as malignant sarcoma.[4] Dr. Raghavachari and his panel of doctors came to the *asram* again on May 1, and

after thorough examination they came to the conclusion that the only solution lay in the amputation of Ramana's left arm. Ramana told him, *"As I let you look after your body, you will please let me look after mine."* Ramana had expressively negated the only hope of saving his body. The devotees felt that he had literally pronounced the death sentence on his body. Ramana was totally unconcerned and walked back to the Old Hall.[5]

Even though Ramana had rejected the only possible cure Dr.Raghavachari kept trying his best to prevent the growth of sarcoma. On August 8, the third operation started.[6]

The fourth and final operation took place on December 19. The fourth operation too was not success-

ful because the lump appeared again higher up. "The surgeon came both on February 15, and March 17, and gave his report which was not released. Presumably it was to indicate that no further operation was possible."[7]

We have to be thankful to S.S. Cohen for maintaining a diary for the entire period from June 16, 1948 to April 16, 1950. Consequently we have an authentic record of

the long ailment of Ramana's body and the manner in which he faced it. The dreaded disease racking his body was taken by him in the stride. He remained calm, peaceful, and steadfastly rooted in the Self.

⁂

Devotees Panic—Ramana's Response

For devotees who were deeply attached to the physical form of Ramana, this long suffering was unbearable. All said and done they looked upon his body not the way he would look upon it, but the way they would look upon their own body. One's identification with the perishable body would be transposed on to the *sadguru's* body as well. The very purpose of the *guru* is to remove the illusion caused by this identification and though he is constantly drawing one's attention to one's nature, yet the identification, being deep-rooted, is difficult to erase.

Small wonder that the devotees panicked after the fourth operation. Each came forward with his pet theory as to what would be the best course of treatment.

Earlier some of the poets, among them Muruganar and Subbaramayya, tried to persuade Ramana to cure himself. Muruganar handed Ramana a poem praying that he should live up to a hundred years in perfect health. A devotee read it aloud. Hearing it Ramana said, *"There is a story of a Vaishnava saint, in whose centenary celebrations his disciples prayed that he should live for nearly a hundred years. You want me to live up to hundred years so that you may at the end of it pray for another hundred years!"*[1]

Subbaramayya indirectly hinted that Bhagavan should cure himself by exercising his will power. He read out a passage in a journal, which stated that if will-power is strong it would be effective in curing any disease. After hearing this Ramana told TPR, *"Subbaramayya wants me to cure myself with will-power. He indicated as much by showing me an article today. But the jnani has no will of* his own. Nor is he identified with the body and the ills to which it is heir."[2]

Ramana's reaction against this suggestion was continued even the next day, *"Yesterday Prof. Subbaramayya spoke to me of curing disease by will-power, implying that I should cure my arm by my own will. Did I ask the tumor to come so that I may tell it to go? It came of its own accord. What then has my will got to do with it?"*[3]

Another lady devotee said to him with tears, "Bhagavan, you, who are curing others must cure yourself and must spare your life for us, your devotees." Ramana replied with great tenderness, *"Why are you so attached to this body? Let it go."*[4]

These remarks of Ramana clearly indicate that so far as he was concerned he was aware that the disease had come to claim his body. It should be allowed to run its course. This reminds one of the advice Ramana had given to Sunderesa Iyer in 1930. Sunderasan was attempting to learn to make leaf plates. Ramana, who was also making them, told him, *"Look at these leaf plates. With considerable trouble you prepare these leaf plates. And then we use it once to eat our food; thereafter it is thrown away. Such is the case with this body of ours. We must attend to it with care till its purpose is served."*[5]

After the fourth operation, devotees more or less took the course of treatment into their own hands by their collective strength. Their fears gave them the required resolve. "The pent-up feelings of the devotees has run so high yesterday, it found expression in the cry 'Homeopathy, Homeopathy' from many of them."[6] At their insistent demand, a veteran homeopath T.S. Iyer was requested to take up the case. He started his course of treatment on December 24th. When his treatment also failed some devotees questioned him. Ramana intervened and said, *"Why do you cross-examine him like Alladi (a famous lawyer of the times). Ask me. I will tell you. I am feeling better after he began the treatment."*[7]

Lastly, devotees from Bengal took a hand and suggested that the case should be handed over to Khaviraj from Calcutta who was in their opinion the best Ayurvedic doctor. He was rushed in and started his treatment on March 29, 1950. His strong application and medicines were totally unsuited to Ramana in that state of health. Ramana told his attendants, *"I do not want to eat or drink. If I take more than two ounces, I feel as if I*

have taken a big meal." Again he also remarked, *"Why all this kanji? Give me buttermilk."*[8]

In spite of the contra-indications of its obvious failure, his treatment was continued till April 10. As usual Ramana's attitude of cooperation with what was decided for him, out of the love for devotees, made him go through the treatment without any kind of protest.

Ramana's own attitude towards the varied treatments to his body is well summarized by Viswanatha Swami. "Whenever a course of treatment was decided upon by the *asram*, he abided by it, rather to please the devotees than to get cured. He has often said, *"It is for us to witness all that happens,"* and his behavior was a perfect illustration of this."[9]

In December 1949, when the devotees were at a loss as to what treatment should be tried next, one of them approached to ask Ramana. He replied with a smile, *"Have I ever asked for any treatment? It is you who want this and that for me. So it is you who must decide. If I were asked, I would always say, as I said from the beginning, that no treatment is necessary. Let things take their course."*[10]

Did Ramana Suffer?
His Attitude to Darsan

In June 1938, Cohen questioned Ramana on the issue whether a *jnani* has pain. In the context of Ramana's sarcoma, this question and Ramana's answer are relevant.

Cohen: Does a *jnani* who is in *sahaja samadhi* feel any physical pain, say a sting or cut?

Ramana: *All pains, even physical, are in the mind. Everybody feels the pain of a cut or a sting, but a jnani whose mind is sunk in bliss feels it as in a dream. His re-*sembles the case of two lovers in the story who were tortured together, but did not feel the pain because their minds were in ecstasy gazing at each other's face."[1]

Ramana's constant mood of bliss, his concern for the devotees, his gracious look and smile might have misled one about the response of his body to the extreme physical pain caused by the deadly disease sarcoma. Once he remarked to a devotee R. Narayana Iyer, *"Appa! Who could conceive that such a disease as this could be in this world? When a hiccough comes the whole body splits like flashes of lightning in a cloud!"*[2]

Another devotee notes Ramana's remarks to his attendants, *"There is not a spot which has not been painful to touch."*[3] This too was said not in an attitude of complaint about the pain but as a hint to his attendants to take greater care when they lifted or touched in the painful spot. According to the surgeons who operated on him, the way he bore the post-operational pain was exemplary. In this context one might remember that Ramana underwent four operations for his sarcoma.

The suffering must have been quite intense. When one of his attendants asked whether there was a need for a commode, Ramana told him, *"I do not want to eat or drink, so that I may not need the use of the commode. If I take only a little nourishment, it will dry up inside and I will not need to rise every now and then. Besides, if I take more than two ounces, I feel as if I have taken a big meal."*

In the context of this great pain the compassion and love of Ramana for the devotees assumes great significance.

The devotees were extremely anxious about Ramana's condition. But he, compassion personified, did not want to break even his common dining with the devotees in the dining hall! This meant he had to climb some steep steps for entry. But he took care to instruct his attendant Satyananda, not to disturb the dinner schedule.

Having regard to the condition of his body, the management decided to limit the hours of *darsan* by closing the doors of his hall for a couple of hours in the afternoon, but Ramana had it opened immediately arguing, *"Many people come from great distances for the* darsan *and cannot wait till evening; they must not be disappointed.... If you pin the devotees to only these hours, the time may not suit some of them who will be greatly inconvenienced."*[4] The devotees had to be requested not to disturb him during these hours. But quite often new visitors who were not aware of this request would be barging in.

A day after his third operation, against the doctors advice for rest, Maharshi left the dispensary where the operation had taken place and went to the hall for *darsan*. As always what he cared for was not to inconvenience the devotees. Both in the morning and evening, though for an hour at each time, there was *darsan* till his *mahanirvana*.

In this context one could refer to two verses from *Yoga Vasishtam*, which he had translated, reading, "A *jnani* who has found himself as formless pure awareness is unaffected though his body be cleft with a sword. Sugar-candy does not lose its sweetness though broken or crushed."[5]

Two days before *mahanirvana*, in the morning, a relative of his came to have his *darsan*. Ramana remembered that it was the day of the relative's father's death anniversary and asked him, *"Have you performed shraddha ceremony today? Did so and so (naming the person) attend it?"*[6]

Mahanirvana

Darsan had been limited to a few hours in the morning and a few hours in the evening after January 1950. Ramana was too weak to go to the hall. There was a narrow little verandah outside the room where his *mahanirvana* was to take place, where his couch was put right up to a few days before April 14, 1950. Devotees would file past. They again did so in the evening. Many of them had received in the "last few days a direct luminous penetrating look of recognition which they felt was a parting infusion of grace."[1]

Swami Satyananda, the attendant who was looking after Ramana's body at that time, has given an account of what happened. He reports, "On the evening of 14th April 1950, we were massaging Sri Ramana's body. At about 5 o'clock, he asked us to help him to sit up. Precisely at that moment devotees started chanting 'Arunachala Siva,' 'Arunachala Siva.' When Sri Bhagavan heard this his face lit up with radiant joy. Tears began to flow from his eyes and continued to flow for a long time. I was wiping them

from time to time. I was also giving him spoonfuls of water boiled with ginger. The doctor wanted to administer artificial respiration but Sri Bhagavan waved it away.... Sri Bhagavan's breathing became gradually slower and slower and at 8.47 p.m, it subsided quietly."[2]

We also have the first-hand account of what happened precisely at this moment in the heavens. "Suddenly, a bright and luminous body arose from the southern horizon, slowly went up and descended in the north somewhere on the Arunachala hill. It was not a meteor as it was bigger than what Venus looks to our vision and its movement was slow. It was so lustrous that when it was at the zenith the light shed by its trail stretched as far as the horizon like an arc in the sky."[3]

This luminous body in the sky was witnessed at Chennai, Bombay, and all over India. Witnessing it at Chennai, immediately K.K. Nambiar, who guessed the

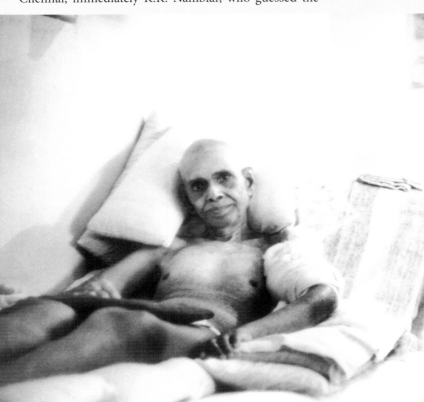

reason, hastened to Tiruvannamalai. Similarly, one Kaikobod, a Parsee devotee, who happened to be on the terrace of his house, immediately hired a taxi and came over. Ms. H.P. Petit who was sitting on the balcony of her house in Bombay about 1000 miles away also saw this phenomenon at this fateful moment. At Tiruvannamalai itself, the famous French photographer Monsieur Cartier

Above and opposite: the final photographs taken of the Maharshi

Brassen witnessed the event and rushed to check the exact time.

Samadhi Function and Significance of the Samadhi

After *mahanirvana*, the body of Ramana was duly garlanded and put up on a couch in the hall in order to enable the large crowd to pay their last homage. The news had spread like wildfire and thousands of persons from the town and nearby villages started gathering to pay the last homage. "A proper queue was formed seven to ten broad and they filed past the dear body at a quick march pace till about midnight."

A large congregation of devotees kept vigil the whole night singing and chanting the *Vedas* and Ramana's compositions.

"Next morning the body was shifted to the south verandah for worship. The *samadhi* pit was dug 10 ½ x 10 ½ feet and seven feet deep. In its center the masons isolated a small area of 4 ½ x 4 ½ feet and surrounded it by a wall of granite stones, lime, and cement. The remaining portion they filled with many cartloads of sand said to have been brought from the sacred Ganges and Narmada valleys.

"At 6.30 p.m., the body, which by then had received the homage of not less than about 40,000 persons, was carried in a decorated palanquin reserved for the Deity of the temple to the *samadhi*. Here it was placed in the same *yogasana* into a bag made of the finest *khaddar*, which was then filled with pure camphor and lowered into the small area reserved for it. Then the pit was filled to the brim with camphor, salt, and sacred ashes to protect the body from worms and rapid disintegration, and closed with masonry work."[1]

Section VI: Timeless in Time

The Post-Nirvana Scene

Absence

Lonely they go, with heavy heart,
The simple folk whose sunlight was His smile,
Who loved His laughter and deep silences
And gracious ways,
Hungry they go, who fed on Grace,
As Ramana,
Whose only doctrine was their love of Him.
Life holds henceforth an endless emptiness,
Though filled with Grace.
Silent they sit before His tomb,
Or pace around.
Bereaved they go in a sad life;
And well l know
The heart-ache for the living graciousness
The outer world will never hold again
For eyes of ours.[1]

—Arthur Osborne

This poem by Arthur Osborne reflects the state of mind of the devotees immediately after the ceremonies connected with the *samadhi* shrine of Ramana were over. They just could not accept the reality as it was. They loved him too dearly and could not envisage a situation in which his bodily presence would be absent. So when the *mahanirvana* happened each and every one of them was plunged in deep gloom and despair. Life had lost its meaning. He was not there, nothing else mattered.

Writing in his diary, on April 12, 1950, Cohen says, "It looks as if we are on the eve of the Doomsday, the eve of a day on which we are destined to be deprived of everything we hold worth living for…. Our refuge, our hopes, our greatest treasure, the precious life of the master."[2]

Osborne reports, "The crowds dispersed and the *asram* seemed an abandoned place, like a grate with the fire gone out. And yet there was not the wild grief and despair that so often followed the departure of a Spiritual Master from earth. The normality that had been so pronounced still continued. It began to be apparent with what care and compassion Sri Bhagavan had prepared his devotees for this. Nevertheless, during those first days and weeks of bereavement few cared to remain at Tiruvannamalai, and some who would have cared to could not."[3]

The Continuing Story

There was no emptiness, no cause for tears,
When I went back to Arunachala
And trod the ways that for these many years
Shone with God's Grace in the form of Ramana.
And then, I sat in silence, as of old,
Before Him. Like a sudden wave
His mighty Peace surged through me to enfold
In Knowledge-Being beyond birth and grave.
Ineffable, beyond the range of thought,
The timeless Peace that from His Presence flows:
Even vaster now the wealth of Grace He brought
Through human form and formless now bestows.[1]

—Arthur Osborne

The inside of the Old Hall, where Ramana spent most of his life after moving down from Arunachala

The *samadhi* of Bhagavan Sri Ramana

Today daily *pujas* take place at Ramana' shrine

The impact of Ramana on those who had seen him when he was in the body and even those who had merely heard about him ever remains with them throughout their lifetime. That silence, that piercing look, that long glance sideways would establish a continuing relationship which lasted even after the *mahanirvana*. They would do the work of the *guru* in turning the person inward, heartward. This is so be it a student on a casual visit to the *asram* or a seeker searching the secrets of India or even

those who heard about Ramana from the disciples. In this sense all those thousands of seekers who had either been in Ramana's presence, read his works, or heard about his reminiscences continued to be the channels of his grace and focal points of imparting the same to others.

Paul Brunton, writing in 1970, forty years after his sessions with Ramana at Sri Ramanasramam, emphatically notes the continued impact of Maharshi's presence: "Forty years have passed since I walked into his abode and saw the Maharshi…. I can truthfully declare that his face, expression, figure, and surroundings are as vivid now as they were then. What is even more important to me is that during my daily periods of meditation, the feeling of his radiant presence is as actual and as immediate today as it was on that first day."[2] Thinking of the reason for this he concludes that this was because Ramana was a pure channel of a "Higher Power."

Like Osborne, many old devotees found for themselves the truth of Ramana's affirmation, "Where am I to go? I am here." Denied the outer sight and its extraordinary beauty, they learnt to discover his inner presence more keenly than before. This faith was confirmed for them by continual experience. Duncan Greenlees refers to the *gopi*-devotees of Vrindavan to whose adoring eyes Krishna had to deny his form, only to awaken in them more keenly the awareness of his dancing presence in their hearts. Greenlees says that Ramana too had veiled the form they loved so well, "that its beauty might no longer draw our gaze away from the everlasting presence enthroned in our heart."[3]

Similarly Ramana revealed his continued presence to Cohen who writes, "When Bhagavan used to say that the *guru* is not the body many failed to grasp its meaning; but as time passed and as he continued to show them his grace and support in their meditation the significance of these words gradually became clear."[4]

What of those who did not have this blessing of a physical contact with Ramana in some way during the time when he was in the body? The answer to this question is that it has made no difference to the power of his presence. Many have recorded the experiences they have had at his *samadhi* at Sri Ramanasramam, by reading his books, or by merely looking at a photograph of his.

Teachings

The raindrops showered down by the clouds, risen from the sea, cannot rest until they reach, despite all hindrance, once again their ocean-home. A bird may hover here and there and cannot in mid-heaven stay. It must come back the way it went to find at last on earth alone its resting-place. Even so the individual must turn to you, O Aruna Hill, and merge again in you alone, Ocean of bliss.[1]

—*Bhagavan Ramana*

Ever as "I" in the heart you dance,
Hence you are called the Heart.[2]

—*Bhagavan Ramana*

To his first disciple Gambhiram Seshier, Ramana termed his teaching as "Intuitive Knowledge of the Heart"—*dahara vidya*.[3] Experientially it is the feeling of bliss brimming over in the heart. It takes the form of a ceaseless throb, "I," "I," which is expressive of the fullness of consciousness. It is natural and inherent and therefore accessible to all. It is ever there. Only, awareness of it is obstructed by the illusory superimposition of a separate mind apart from this heart. Once the illusion, the false knowledge, is dispelled by the searchlight of truth, and steadily at that, one is back in one's true home, one's natural state, in the heart. All search on the spiritual path must end in this discovery, in this revelation. When this happens the mind is rid of its limitation caused by identification, by

concepts, by thoughts. It will be pure like ether, reflective of the bliss of the Self.

Ramana's path is straight, one travels from illusion to knowledge by a proper understanding of the mind. This implies understanding its nature and its source. Source! One has to proceed step by step. Was there a mind in

The Vedapatasala at Ramanasramam, where the young *brahmin* boys are taught to chant the *Vedas*

sleep? No. Is there a mind on waking? Yes. It must have a source, must it not? Otherwise where can it subside and wherefrom can it rise again? Surely it must be from within oneself. For there is no break in the identity, in the continuity between the two states. The source must,

If "I" is only a phenomenon of the waking state, can it be the "I"-consciousness? Is it self-conscious? Or is its consciousness, its strength, its energy derived from its source into which it had subsided unconsciously in sleep?

This would give rise to an attitude of doubt about its nature. What then is the mind? If one observes it would be seen that the mind is a movement of thoughts, coming and going, but built around a core, center, the "I" thought. Though thoughts are beguiling in their numbers and variety, they are essentially disparate. When the individual's attention is on them, they surface on the mental horizon and disappear when there is a shift in that attention to another thought. Therefore, Ramana states that it would be logical to regard the mind as only the "I" thought, the thinker, the individual. Further enquiry into the nature of this center would be possible only to the extent one can isolate it or separate it from its association with innumerable thoughts. Otherwise attention cannot be focused on it. For this, Ramana suggests a weapon in the form of a question, *"Who am 'I'?"* This has the instant effect of refocusing attention on the center, away from other thoughts. The main advantage would be to disentangle oneself from a jungle of thoughts.

The thinker is so deeply mixed up with his thoughts, so nostalgic about some, so anticipatory about others, that their grip is quite powerful. They would not let go their suzerainty, let go their power to be obsessive, to be resilient. Shifting attention from them, from their ceaseless chattering, is rendered all the more difficult due to addiction to thoughts. We cling to thoughts thanks to the idea that when one is not having thoughts, heaven knows that we have cartloads of them, we would be life-

inferentially, be said to be an energizing source, for one wakes up refreshed, and recalls the repose enjoyed during sleep. One would not like to miss sleep even for a single day. The second point therefore is that the source must be fullness of consciousness, responsible for this daily rejuvenation.

less. The truth is that the mind which is spacious alone can be supple, sharp, and fully responsive. This situation has been brought about by our being choosy regarding thoughts, being selective, wishing to retain some and discard others, instead of throwing them all, lock, stock, and barrel, into the dustbin where they belong. Hence, in his instructions given in 1900, Ramana says, *"Immediately, a thought arises, it must be annihilated at its source. If entertained for a little while, it would hurl one down headlong like a treacherous friend."*[4]

This requires "patience and more patience" for the enemy is long entrenched. The habitual way is to be focused on the mind's center, on the "I" thought. As Ramana once remarked, the malaise arises because *"one has never faced the 'I.'"* The mind's searchlight has not been on itself but on the movement of thoughts, away from itself.

But self-enquiry, taught by Ramana, is a sure means, an infallible way to get to the source. Thoughts will become weakened, enervated, and reduced in number by the simple act of ignoring them. They die from inattention. Ramana has given the analogy of capturing a fort by starving its inmates, by a siege which cuts off food and water supply to the soldiers within it.[5]

Self-enquiry would have the effect of silencing the mind by warding off one's association with thoughts. The intermingling would end. The mind's energies can and need to be focused on the mind itself. It must be kept active in pursuit of itself, in paying attention to its source. This may be termed as Self-attention. Self-enquiry has acted as the initial thrust, enabling one to cut oneself off from the mental movement. Self-attention completes the job for one is now on the threshold of Self-knowledge. For this, the second weapon in Ramana's armory,

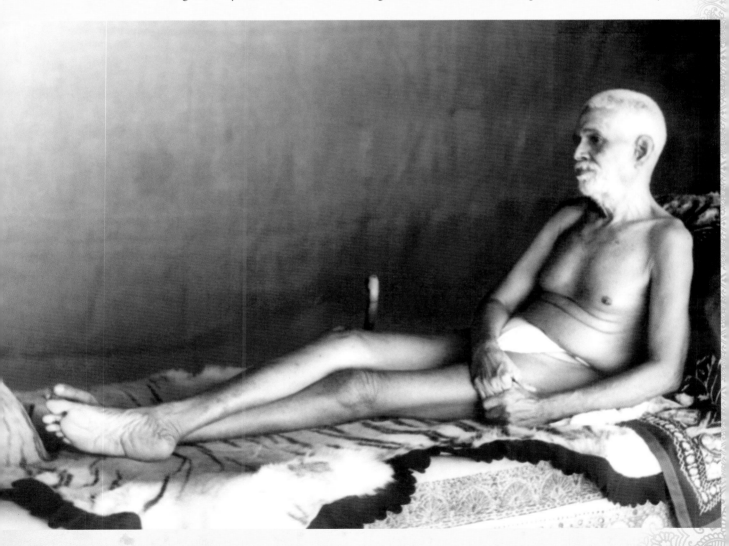

"Whence am 'I'?" has to be pressed into service. It is the other blade in a pair of scissors. Having actively warded off thoughts one has to be passively alert and let the power within take over. Ramana assures that this will happen naturally. He has explained, *"The Self is like a powerful magnet hidden within us. It draws us gradually to itself.... The truth is that we are like iron filings. The process of finding the Self is a kind of divine magnetism."*[6] Cleansed of the rusting caused by thoughts the mind is drawn irresistibly within to its source, to the divine current, to the heart.

In one of his compositions Ramana has explained his method with utmost clarity: *"When there is no 'I' thought there can be no other thought. When other thoughts arise, ask, 'To whom? To me? Where from does this "I" arise?' Thus diving inwards, if one traces the source of the mind and reaches the Heart, one becomes the Sovereign Lord of the Universe. There is no more dreaming of such as in and out, right and wrong, birth and death, pleasure and pain, light and darkness, O boundless ocean of Grace and Light, Arunachala, dancing the dance of stillness in the dancing Hall of the Heart."*[7]

Practicing the direct path of Ramana one has to remember that Ramana was sharing his own experience, of the day of enlightenment, and stressing that it can be experienced by everyone with an indrawn mind in search of its source. A look once again on that epoch-making date July 17, 1896 would throw much light on the path. Facing the overwhelming fear of death Ramana passionately enquired into his true identity, into the question of the nature of "I"-consciousness. He himself has termed this enquiry as *"Who am 'I'?"* enquiry. Reality was given to the enquiry by putting aside the body as if it were a corpse. Immediately, there was an upsurge of the feeling of "I," distinct and apart from the dead body. Enquiring further he discovered that the "I" was a current, a force or center. Though it existed in connection with the body it was independent of the rigidity or activity of the body.[8]

Based on this experience he later explained to his disciples and seekers that the physical location of this current is on the right hand side of the chest, two digits from the center. He termed it the "spiritual heart" to distinguish it from the physical heart on the left side. Just as the physical heart pumps blood through arteries, the energy of the "I"-consciousness of the divine current is channeled through *nadis*, first to the mind and from there to the body.

We find Ramana laying great stress on the search within in his original work *Ulladu Narpadu*. This is also the case in most of his conversations with the disciples up to the mid-thirties when the *guru*-disciple relationship, practically on a one to one basis, was possible.

To enquire, silently and deeply, as to the source
Of the mind, the "I,"
Alone is self-enquiry.
Ideas like "I am that," or "I am not this" are but
*   aids.*[9]
The ego falls, crestfallen, when one enquires
"Who am I?" and enters the Heart.
Then another "I"-"I," throbs unceasingly, by itself,
It is not the ego but the Self itself, the whole.[10]

The importance of diving within, seeking the source of the mind, of the "I," is stressed by Ramana in his *Upadesa Saram*: *"Sinking the mind in the Heart, its source, is karma, bhakti, yoga, and knowledge."*[11]

In self-enquiry also Ramana stresses this point to Gambhiram Seshier. *"Do not even for a moment lose sight of the Self. Fixing the mind on the Self or the 'I' and abiding in the Heart is the perfection of yoga, meditation, wisdom, devotion, and worship. Since the Supreme Being abides as the Self, constant surrender of the mind by absorption in the Self is said to comprise all forms of worship."*[12]

This path is termed the direct path or the straight path because it is based on the truth that Self alone is, the One, the Whole. Other methods of meditation are based on the acceptance of the reality of the mind as an entity apart from the Self. They are essentially dualistic. The assumption of duality would be found to be illusory, for this false notion ends when enquiry leads one back to the mind's source, the heart, where it merges. It is called meditation on the heart because one is seeking one's conscious source, the heart, which is the seat of consciousness.

The invaluable advantage of self-enquiry is that it makes living in the present possible. Presently, in the mental firmament there are many thoughts which are carried forward based on memories of the experiences of past action. There is also a heavy load of thoughts about the future rewound into the present. The past and future thoughts, which are brought into the present by the individual's attention, destroy the present, in which alone all experience can take place. Self-enquiry, by cutting off all thoughts, enables one to escape from the time frame. One would live in the "now" experiencing fully each moment with thought-free exhilaration.

The common doubt is whether a meditative, reflective life where the mind is immersed in its source is conducive to an active life in the world. Or is it open only to those who withdraw from the life current in a single-minded pursuit of inwardness? As early as 1911, Ramana has clarified to Humphreys about the benefits of self-enquiry done even for a short time. He told him, *"Give yourself a quarter of an hour a day.... The results will show themselves in four or five months time—in all sorts of unconscious clairvoyance, in peace of mind, in power to deal with troubles, in power all round, always unconscious power."*[13]

One Venkatarama Iyer questioned Ramana, in Skandasramam days, whether combining activities and Self-attention is possible.

Q: Whichever way one turns, one finds that the mind has to be subdued. We are told it has to be controlled. Can this really be done when on the one hand the mind is an entity not easily grasped and on the other one continues to have worldly worries?

A: *A person who has never seen an ocean must take a trip to it to know about it. Standing there before the huge expanse of water, this person may wish to bathe in the sea. Of what use is it if, seeing the roaring and rolling of the waves, he were to just stand there thinking, "I shall wait for all this to subside. When it does, I shall enter it for a quiet bath just as in the pond back home"? He has to realize either by himself or by being told that the ocean is restless and that it has been so from the moment of creation and will continue likewise till* pralaya *(destruction). He will then resolve to learn to bathe in it, as it is. He may wade into it and learn to duck under a wave and let it pass over*

ways to be aware of the Self. Everything is achieved if one succeeds in this."[16]

During the practice of the Ramana Way one would be in and out of the experience of the natural state and its bliss. Knowledge and ignorance would be intermittent, and co-exist in this transition stage. But as the experience of the power of the Self grows, the mind's capacity to lure one away would weaken. Ramana's purpose would have been done when all straying ceases, when the mind is merged in its source firmly, without a break. Who can describe the joy of such a life?

A traveler on the spiritual journey may wander

him. He would naturally hold his breath while doing so. Soon he would be skilled enough to duck at a stretch, wave after wave, and thus achieve the purpose of bathing without coming to grief. The ocean may go on with its waves and though in it, he is free from its grip. So too here.[14]

Paul Brunton has also plied Ramana with questions on this point.

Q: How is it possible to become selfless while leading a life of worldly activities?

A: *There is no conflict between work and wisdom.*

Q: Do you mean to say that one can continue all old activities, in one's profession for instance, and at the same time get enlightenment?

A: *Why not? But in that case one will be centered on That, which is beyond the little self.*[15]

The busiest hours will not be different from those earmarked for meditation. The current generated by association with the energy source in the heart would be the continuous substratum with its overflowing peace and joy.

The habit of externalization of the mind is long ingrained. Till the experience of an inward way of life with its beauty and bliss grows upon one there is need for steadfast practice. To use Ramana's words: *"Long cultivated tendencies can indeed be eradicated by long continued meditation."* He asks, *"Can a man become a high officer by merely seeing such an officer once?... Can a beggar become a king by merely visiting a king and declaring himself one?... Gradually one should, by all possible means, try al-*

around on indirect paths, may take detours, but in the end he has to come to self-enquiry and the way of the heart. The individual separated from his roots, from his moorings, from his source, must inevitably get back to this true home as surely as the restless raindrops rejoin their source, the ocean, or the birds return to earth from which they have risen and hovered for a while in the sky.

Sadguru

The Truth and the Way

O Aruna Hill, embodied love, loveless I was
And yet you chose to claim me as your own....
If now you fail to fill me with love and if you let
Me perish in a loveless state, would it be fair?
O joy which is my refuge, your will is mine. Here in
This surrender, is pure Joy, Lord of my Life.[1]
  —*Bhagavan Ramana*

If I died while yet clinging
To your feet, it would be a standing pillar of
Disgrace for you, O blazing light of Aruna Hill,
    expanse
Of grace more subtle than ether.[2]
  —*Bhagavan Ramana*

Most of Ramana's compositions on Arunachala are auto-biographical. The dominant mood of all the eleven verses of "Decad" from which these verses have been taken is one of love which brooks no barriers, which readily accepts the *guru*'s will, in the spirit of "Thy will be done." These verses, as also the *Eight Verses* seem to have a special significance, for the words appeared before Ramana's eyes and compelled him to put them down. The words arising in his pure mind were literally written down by the Maharshi, seer of seers. The moods alternate between gratitude for the love showered and plaintive requests to fulfill the longing for overflowing oneness in the heart.

Sadhu Natanananda has elicited clear answers on two important questions:

Q: What are the marks of a *sadguru*?

A: *Steady abidance in the Self, looking at all with an equal eye, unshakable courage at all times, in all places, circumstances etc.*

Q: What are the marks of an earnest disciple?

A: *An intense longing for the removal of sorrow and attainment of joy.*[3]

To this we may add, earnestness in making the teachings of *sadguru* Ramana integral to one's life. From the day of his enlightenment on July 17, 1896, Ramana was steadily abiding in the Self. As for his equal treatment and courage his life itself is the testimony.

What of us, disciples and devotees? Do we fit the bill? Is our longing for a new birth in the heart, for becoming aware and remaining in the natural state strong enough to sustain the momentum on a long-term basis? Do we have the kind of passion which Ramana had for his *guru* Arunachala

and which is so evident in his "Five Hymns"? Do we have the intensity to discover the truth, to discover the source of "I"-consciousness, which Ramana had on that memorable day?

Each person must pose these questions for himself and find the answers. To begin with, the mood of surrender to Ramana's guidance and the certainty of his being the helmsman is not strong enough due to the enervation caused by the externalized mind. Therefore the attitude

of surrender needs to be nurtured and developed in order that one's faith in the omnipotence of *guru* Ramana grows. His advice that, *"it is the indefinable power of the lord that ordains, sustains, and controls everything,"*[4] must be watered to take root. Unfortunately the embattled ego keeps showing its head in a negative form. The disciples start judging their progress and, thinking it to be tardy, are inclined to find fault with Ramana for it. Sometimes they wonder why Ramana should not quicken the pace and make the spiritual practice easier, is the feeling which overcomes them sometimes. One starts praying to Ramana to correct the situation and help out.[5] We find Ramana pointing out that surrender would only be a word which is lipped unless one is ready to give a general power of attorney to him. To quote, *"Whether I do or don't do anything you have to simply surrender and keep quiet."*[6] This is because Ramana is doing his job like a mother who feeds her child when the child is asleep. The feeding has taken place but the child on waking up says that it did not take anything the previous night. The extraordinary, more than mother-like compassion of

Ramana is there. Why doubt it? As long as the source of the "I" is not discovered the mind does not give up so easily and it keeps doubting. One may refer to the conversation which Cohen had with Ramana. Cohen had resigned his job in Bombay and built himself a cottage next to the *asram*. However, on the day of housewarming he prayed to Ramana that he should ensure his reaching the goal. Ramana gazed silently on the calm waters of the pond nearby and replied, *"Your firm conviction brought you here, where is the room for doubt?"*[7] What an assurance to him and to all disciples and devotees!

Ramana's core teaching is that for the subsidence of the mind there is no means more effective and adequate than self-enquiry. Otherwise even though the mind subsides, that is only apparently so, for it will rise again.[8] Ramana would also frequently remind the inmates and attendants about the need for self-enquiry. He once told Kunjuswami, his attendant for many years, *"There is no use saying, I am serving Sri Bhagavan.… The greatest service to the* guru *is to be engaged in self-enquiry and meditation in all sincerity."*[9] Ramana would also stress the

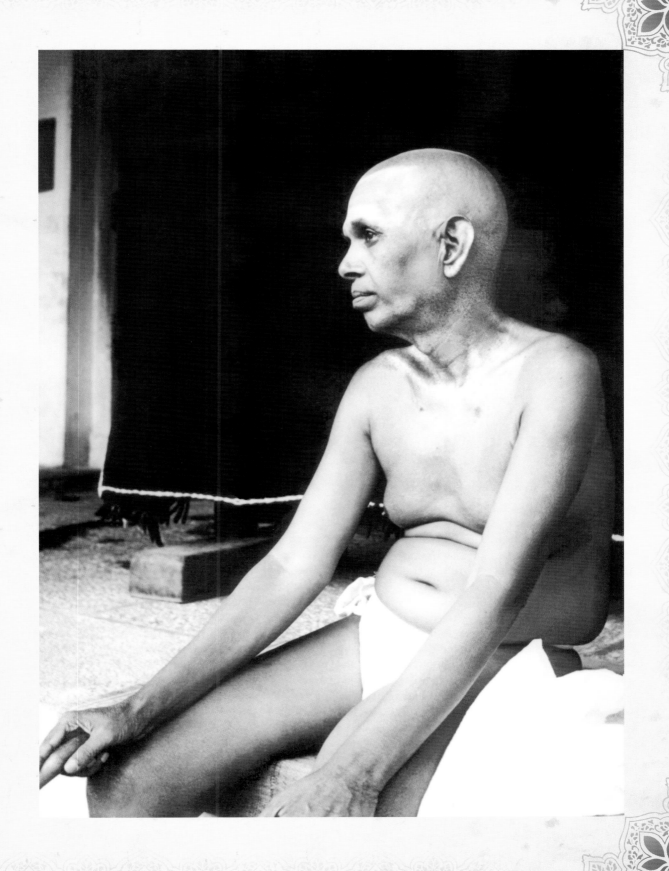

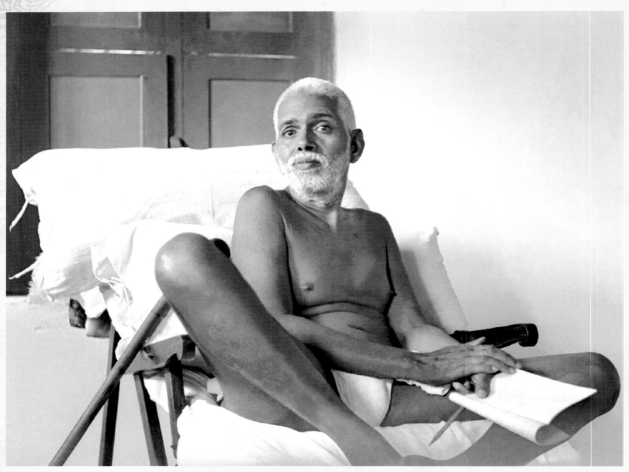

need for interweaving self-enquiry into all waking hours. The idle time while traveling, waiting, and so on, can be turned into self-enquiry time. If this is done it would result in the *guru*'s grace being felt as an undercurrent all the time, bringing him closer and strengthening inwardness.

The devotees however, do not seem to attach due significance to self-enquiry. Attachment to past practices and the fear of dropping them seem to come in the way. Actually, as Ramana has told some disciples, the past practices have served their purpose in so far as they had prepared one for self-enquiry, which if diligently pursued opens up the vast space of the mind and heart. This point comes out clearly in a conversation which Ramana had with Poonjaji. He had taken to repeating Lord Krishna's name thousands of times, seeking joy through conversations with the Lord and visions of Him. Then one day all this came to a dead-stop. It ended with abrupt suddenness. Though Poonjaji had earlier rejected Ramana's counsel, on this occasion, when there was a spiritual crisis in his life, he turned to him and made a beeline to the *asram*. There he narrated what had happened. Ramana

put him wise by asking, *"Where is your ticket? Is your conveyance waiting for you?"* The ticket had been surrendered at the station while exiting, the fare had been paid for the conveyance which had left. Ramana then pointed out that the railway ticket was useful till the journey was over, so too the conveyance. Similarly when the past *sadhanas* have outlived their purpose they should be allowed to drop off as naturally as a ripe fruit from a tree.

Lack of implicit faith in Ramana's guidance has a debilitating effect. For in the direct path one recognizes that the goal is already there, that there are no intermediate steps and that the practice itself is the experience. Dependence on Ramana's guidance is a must. For all their problems in *sadhana* everyone is sure that the entry of Ramana into their lives has made a world of difference. Its like sunshine breaking the darkness of one's life for he is "the light shining within, without, and everywhere."[10] Each individual alone can be aware of the bounty Ramana is showering but there it is. It would appear that Ramana plays the game of hide-and-seek with his devotees, sometimes so close, closer than the closest. Often one plays the eye-meeting game with Ramana when he looks out of the corner of his eyes, with his sidelong glance. And at other times he is distant, far away, almost like his far away look, at twilight time when he is gazing into space.

What is Ramana doing when we are seemingly toiling on the path on the strength of our own might?

A rare, unlooked-for guest he came,
Right in he came, of his own accord,
This Venkata, Lord of my own self,
And ate up the whole of my fond mind
As if it were uncloying nectar.[11]

Ramana will not leave his task unfinished, or abandon one midway, half-baked and still tormented by the wily tricks of the mind. His feet stand guard "abolishing the dark night of ignorance with their pure radiance."[12]

Ramana is ever ready, in fact one should say eager, to bestow on his true disciples and devotees, holding steadfastly to a life dependent on his grace, his own state of natural bliss. As one soaks more and more in his grace, one joins in singing with Muruganar:

What extravagance of grace! What extravagance!
To hold me in this bliss, both mine and his
Together and apart.[13]

Ramana's Daily Miracles

You asked me, did you not, to come to you? Very well, I have come. Now you have to assume the burden of maintaining me. Go on suffering thus. It is your fate to look after me, O Arunachala.[1]
—Bhagavan Ramana

On his devoted head he carries
As if they were His own, all burdens
That His devotees should bear.
He tells me "Fear Not" and protects me,
Ramana, the Lord of Aruna.[2]

—Muruganar

The best known adjective of Ramana is "Bhagavan." This was given to him by Ganapati Muni in 1907 and it means God. The Muni thought it to be a fit attribute to his *guru* Ramana, because he was not only an abode of tranquility, of peace, but also the storehouse of power in an equal measure. The scriptures attribute six-fold powers to God which are plenitude, courage, renown, beauty, knowledge, and dispassion. Ramana had all these in their fullness. For he was firmly rooted in the Self. It may also be mentioned that in response to a specific query, Ramana has said that *"for granting boons the* jnani's *powers are the same as Iswara's or God's."*[3]

When one is omnipotent like Ramana, and at the same time filled with love which has no boundaries, it is only natural for a large cross-section of devotees to pray to him for fulfillment of some desire or the other. A regular observer of what happens when shrine-goers visit Ramana's shrines of grace, is bound to notice a varied scene. "A lady comes, bows her head, and proceeds straight for the tray containing the sacred 'ashes' and *kumkum*. She reverentially applies the *kumkum* on her *mangalasutra* lost in deep prayer. Perhaps her husband is ill. Ramana's protection is needed. A young couple in love walk in, hand in hand, chatting. Suddenly a great silence comes over them too. They kneel lost in prayer. Ramana has to unite them in marriage. A small boy rushes in followed by his parents, garland in hand, to offer to Ramana for the well being of the boy. It is the boy's birthday. A middle-aged devotee enters, circumambulates the picture of Ramana, places a cover on the plate as his contribution. It is his mother's death anniversary. Maybe Ramana's motherly care is on his mind. Another comes, places the plan of a building in front of Ramana and stands for a few minutes. He is apparently about to invest his whole fortune in his residential building. Ramana's blessing is needed for its completion without a hitch. Three or four boys drop in with books. They are making last minute preparations for writing the forthcoming examination and hoping to graduate with flying colors. They study for a couple of minutes, gaze into the eyes of Ramana, and leave."[4]

However, fate does not always give a forewarning. Its blows are often swift and sudden. Therefore they cannot be anticipated or warded off by a prayer to Ramana in advance or even at the time of their happening. For instance, a heart attack may happen with the speed of lightning. But Ramana is there as the family doctor giving him the necessary presence of mind, in the intensive care unit, making the doctors there take the right decision, and also ensuring that the medicines prescribed are effective. His job does not stop there. It is not a temporary reprieve which is provided, but a long term saving act. One can well understand why Ramana's fame, as a giver of boons unasked, remains bright and shining.

Like a tree which on a scorching day
Offers cool shade to every comer,
By nature, not by choice,
Even so He stands,
Calm, immutable, impartial,
But saving all who reach his feet.[5]

Ramana had blessed Muruganar with the gift of Self-awareness. Since Ramana is such a munificent giver of gifts, Muruganar suggests, "Why not pray for the biggest prize, Self-knowledge? Why settle for less?" Of course it is left to each one to pray according to his need. For to whom else can one turn in the hour of one's need than to Ramana?

Ramana's miracles are daily occurrences like the sunrise. Many who have experienced this would like to keep it a secret between themselves and Ramana. Fortunately some of them have shared their experiences by giving a first hand account of what happened.

There is a need for clarifying Ramana's theoretical position. Miracles fall into two broad categories. One is the miracle performed using mental power called *siddhis*. The exercise of such powers would deflect one from the goal of Self-knowledge by leading to a desire for name and fame, adulation and so on. More important is the fact that the enemy, the uncontrolled mind tossed about by innumerable thoughts, would remain to be understood. The other category of miracles is non-mental. It does not involve the exercise of the mind at all. For in the pure mind there are no desires. Ramana's miracles are of this type. The question is, how do they happen? All powers are vested in a *jnani*. They are manifest automatically, for saving all, "by nature not by choice." Because that is God's way. Small wonder that Ramana is extolled as golden-handed for his "generous gifts fail not, even though the seasons fail."[6]

Timeless in Time

Can there be space, can there be time, except for
*   me?*
Space and time bind me, only if I am the body,
I am nowhere, I am timeless
I exist everywhere and always.[1]
                              —*Bhagavan Ramana*

Ramana was born on December 30, 1879, in Tiruchuzhi, got enlightened at Madurai on July 17, 1896, arrived at Arunachala on September 1, 1896, and remained there till his *mahanirvana* on April 14, 1950. If one looks at the chronology, Ramana's molten-gold body had a beginning in time and an ending in time.

Those who were too close to these events could hardly be blamed if they could not visualize what was in store even fifty years later, the beginning of the new millennium, the year 2000. The growing presence of Ramana the world over is indicative of the shape of things to come and his timelessness.

One could view the phenomenon of Ramana's timelessness in many ways. Firstly let us have a look at his human form, his tall handsome figure, his gentle smile, his grace-filled lustrous eyes. It is evident that the imprint of these are very much there in the minds and hearts of the people as much as, if not more intensely than, when he was physically in the body.

There are over one thousand photographs of Ramana taken over fifty years, mostly by non-professionals, out

View of Arunachala from Ramanasramam

ticular photo might vary, their appeal is universal. One person expresses "their charm that every photograph is ever new, yet always familiar.... It is every face and all faces.... It is love at first sight at every sight."[3] Be it the large luminous eyes of his first photo in 1900 when he was in Virupaksha Cave or the powerful and penetrating eyes in Mani's bust taken while at Skandasramam in the early twenties or those compellingly beautiful eyes in the Welling photograph taken in 1948, it is the same story of an irresistible magnetism.

When you look into his eyes like a shy bride lifting her head to see the bridegroom or when you exchange furtive glances, his response is terrific. Such abundance of grace pours forth from those eyes floating one's mind in bliss. Is not the secret of this perennial charm of Ramana's photographs and particularly those eyes to be found in his timelessness?

of which five hundred of them are in good condition or have been restored to their original condition. This gallery of Ramana's photographs, spanning fifty years, has infinite variety and one keeps "falling in love" with them. They have been taken most naturally while he was "walking, sitting, eating, wiping his feet and so on. He has been snapped smiling, laughing, silent, or even in *samadhi*."[2] The attraction of a particular photo is of course different for different individuals. But while the choice of a par-

For, after his enlightenment, Ramana's body radiated the power of God, of the Self, of Consciousness. The body of a Self-realized person becomes the "tabernacle of the spirit" and the power of God shines in the body of such a person in all its majestic splendor. Though every

pore of his body is filled with radiance it is best expressed through the eyes.

While his body has a human form in one sense, it ceases to be perishable. It is for this reason that Ramana's body was not cremated or buried in the usual way but enshrined in a special structure in accordance with the time-honored prescribed rites for the *samadhi* of a Self-realized person. The *samadhi* is a temple of God where one offers worship and derives worldly and spiritual gains.

Whether one accepts this explanation or not the fact remains that thousands of persons all over the world, cutting across all the geographical barriers, regard Ramana as the worshipful one. They offer the flowers of love at his altar where some photograph of his has been reverentially placed.

What about his name? The name always goes with the form. It is ordinarily identified with a particular body. Not so Ramana's. He was named Venkataraman by his parents in 1879. Ganapati Muni to Ramana changed his name in an expression of his gratitude as a *guru* who revealed the truth to him. He re-christened him as Bhagavan Ramana Maharshi. *Bhagavan* is an adjective to indicate that the person has in him all the six-fold powers of God.[4] *Maharshi* means a pre-eminent one among seers of truth. The name itself was changed from Venkataraman to Ramana. This was in 1907. The new name has different shades of meaning, "dear darling," "one who revels in the Self," "one who is the Self." It has been a magical name for devotees and seekers. Just three syllables "Ra," "Ma," "Na." What power to draw within and fix one in the Self! The very name fills the heart with delight. The power of the name is such that though to begin with it may be integral only to meditation time, gradually the remembrance of the name goes on amidst all activities of life as well. For the beauty of the name grows on one. It becomes not just a name but a name amongst names. "The

Name, It will be doing its job of ripening one to be rid of the dross, so that the inner pull of the Self would be felt strongly. Nurturing and protecting, it watches over loving devotees, whose delusion is immolated in the vast fullness of final realization."[5]

While being aware of Ramana's timeless presence, one has to remember his role as *sadguru*, as a guide on the path, as an unfailing friend in the inner journey to the heart. According to the scriptures the relationship with the *guru* may not be confined to a lifetime only. The *guru*'s grip on the ego-based, externalized life, is firm. One can compare it to the hold of the tiger's jaw on its prey. The *guru* will not leave his job half finished. Even as the

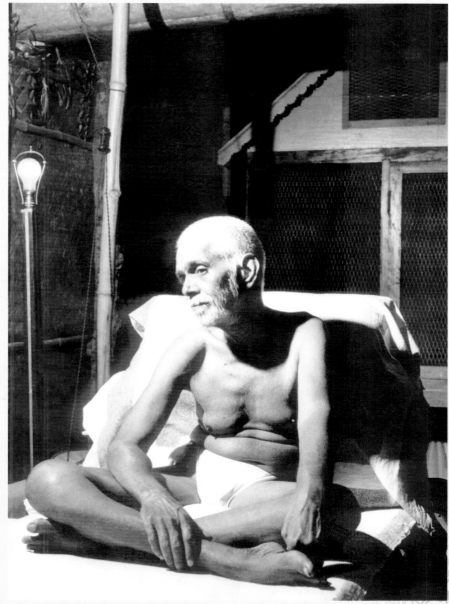

devotee stands on the "threshold of the womb," Ramana would pull him out. He would not let go until the disciple too abides steadily in the natural state. He determines the right pace of the spiritual evolution and checks the pulse of the disciple's progress. It cannot be accelerated for the devotee must be able to receive the grace. Therefore the *guru*'s job may extend over the entire life or many lives.

Ramana being the deathless Self, the changes in the disciple's bodies, and the consequent changes in identification which occurs from life to life, would make no difference. The disciple or devotee's faith in reincarnation or absence of it makes no difference to it. None will be left stranded midway to be lost among the teeming millions of the world.

The Self is the repository of all powers. For it is the totality of consciousness. Nothing exists apart from it. Hence if one becomes steadily Self-aware, then without any kind of seeking on his part—all powers of God are naturally in him. Hence such a person is "miraculously strong to save."

Ramana's daily miracles are happening because the automatic divine action is set in motion as soon as the

matter is referred to him for protection and help. The power of granting boons being an inherent power in the *jnani*, there would be quite a spate of appeals and prayers to him for a multiplicity of boons. All those facing a dead-end situation in which they feel utterly helpless take recourse in Ramana, in the faith that he is omnipotent and can grant their prayers. And he does grant, not by wishing to do so but because it is the divine law. He has become a channel for the divine's grace. Any number of seekers have been recipients of Ramana's secret or overt help in response to prayers. Here it has to be mentioned that Ramana's rescue acts do not even require any awareness on the part of the recipient or request from the person. For, coming events need not always cast their shadows. The act of grace often precedes faith.

In the post-*nirvana* period these miracles continue unabated and are on the increase, they are happening day in and day out. It would quite obviously be an error to think that there may be a full stop at any point of time in the future for the manifestation of Ramana's power under varied and impossible circumstances. It is universally known that problems in life turn up unexpectedly every now and then. The devotees of Ramana cannot therefore be blamed if they too join the bandwagon of boon seekers, confirmed as they are in Ramana's capacity to grant them. The greatest miracle which Ramana

continously performs, of course, is revealing the glory of Self-Knowledge.

One could always turn to the original works and to any of the recorded talks as one would to the teachings of Mahavira, Gautama Buddha, or the sacred Bible, Quran, Collected Works of Adi Sankara, Granth Sahib, and the Gospel of Sri Ramakrishna, which have been providing courage and strength to millions. The simple and direct teaching of Ramana, which opens up the floodgates of joy, is perhaps the most important reason for Ramana's timelessness. Truth has been made so easily accessible, so unbelievably close, so experientially possible for each and every one that the fascination of Ramana's teachings is irresistible. More and more, in ever increasing numbers, are drawn to him and his teachings. This is bound to be so for centuries to come.[6]

The growing universal presence of Ramana because of his attraction to human beings, irrespective of geographical, racial, or other barriers, is very much there for one to see. Books on his life and teachings are being translated from English to various others languages; the translations of *Be the Self*, *The Silent Mind*, *Ramana Gita*, and *Absolute Consciousness* illustrate this. There are Ramana Centers and study circles which have become beacon lights to many earnest seekers.

Ramana's love was universal. It embraced all life, yet it was at the same time particular as well. Every disciple and devotee felt in the past, feels now, and is bound to feel in the future that in some special sense Ramana belongs to them. One relates to him even more intimately than they would to those whom they regard as their near and dear ones. In so many touching ways which baffle understanding, Ramana would demonstrate his love for each person, drawing them to him irresistibly. Eleanor Pauline Noye comes to Ramanasramam in search of a way out of depression. Ramana greets her tenderly and makes some enquiries to put her at ease. "His look of love and compassion was a benediction that went straight to my heart."[7] During her stay of eight months in 1940, she would be moved by his tender acts. Once she kept a beautiful rose as an offering at the small footstool near the couch. Ramana "took and touched it with his forehead and cheeks moving her to tears."[8] At the time of her departure, being fully aware of the emotional turmoil she was undergoing, Ramana read out to her a few comforting passages from Psalms, Chapter 139, Verses 7, 8, 9, and 10.

The mystique of Ramana is inexplicable. The scene is in Yugoslavia. Those are the first few days of NATO's bombing raids. A Ramana devotee, Slobodanka Arunachala, feels as never before Ramana's love for her and an unshaken confidence in his protection. "A feeling which was neither sought nor prayed for but felt." For another devotee, Nebojsa, also in bomb-torn Yugoslavia, "his illusions slowly disappear as he wonders how strange it is that under Ramana's shining sun we are able to value our little selves so much. Above all he discovers that true peace can be found only within, even quickly, and that outer events of life have their own course which need not disturb our inner peace."[9]

Before returning to Bangalore, Ananthamurthy, one of Ramana's biographers, sought Ramana's continued benediction even while at Bangalore. Ramana replied in English, *"What? Is there time, place, or distance for me?"* Is he not the all-pervasive enlightened one, steadily abiding in the Self, beyond time and space?

Notes and References

PUBLISHER'S PREFACE

1. Frithjof Schuon, *Language of the Self*, pp. 40-41.

INTRODUCTION

1. Master Nome: *Timeless Presence*, p.11.
2. Publisher's Note: This, the third book of the trilogy, was eventually published in 2002.
3. Muruganar: "Proper Placing," in *Homage to the Presence*, vv.107-116, pp.9-11.

SECTION I

WHO ARE YOU RAMANA?

1. Bhagavan Ramana: "Miscellaneous Verses," in *Collected Works*, p.150.
2. Muruganar: "Glory of Ramana" (*Ramana Vaibhavam*), in *Songs*, v.1, p.65.
3. Natarajan, A.R. (tr.): *Sat-Darshanam*, v.31, p.35.
4. Refer to "Advent at Arunachala" under Section I.
5. *"From my unthinking childhood, the immensity of Arunachala had shone in my awareness...."*
6. Bhagavan Ramana: "Ashtakam," in *Five Hymns*, v.1, p.124. Narasimha Swami, B.V.: *Self Realization*, pp.106-107.
7. Noye, Eleanor Pauline: "My Pilgrimage to Sri Ramanasramam," *Golden Jubilee Souvenir*, p.447.
8. Iyer, Sundaresa: *At the Feet of Bhagavan*, p.9.
9. Subbaramayya, G.V.: *Sri Ramana Reminiscences*, p.120.
10. Ganapati Muni: *Forty Verses in Praise of Ramana*, p.15.
11-12. Bhagavan Ramana: *Upadesa Undiyar*, p.5.
13. Natarajan. A.R.: *Ramana Gita*, pp.130, 226.
14. Refer to "In Obedience to Father's Command" under Section I.
15. Refer to "Advent to Arunachala" under Section I.
16. Brunton, Paul and Venkataramiah, Munagala (Recorded): *Conscious Immortality*, p.137.
17. Ganapati Muni: *Forty Verses in Praise of Ramana*, p.16.
18. Muruganar: "Ramana Deva Malai," in *The Mountain Path*, v.180.
19. Vinobha Bhave, *The Mountain Path*, v.180.
20. Subbaramayya, G.V.: *Sri Ramana Reminiscences*, p.62.
21. Bhagavan Ramana: "Decad," in *Five Hymns*, v.5, p.104.

TIRUCHUZHIAL—BIRTH PLACE OF SRI RAMANA

1. Bhagavan Ramana: "Occasional Verses," in *Collected Works*, p.152.
2. Rajan, N.N.: "Tiruchuzhi—The Birth Place of Ramana," in *The Mountain Path*, January 1966, p.13.
3. Devasenapathi, Dr. V.: "Tiruchuzial," *The Mountain Path*, January 1986, pp.20, 21.
4. Greenblatt et al: *Bhagavan Sri Ramana*, p.5.

BLISSFUL PARENTS

1. Iyer, Sundaram: "A Schoolmate's Reminiscences," in *The Mountain Path*, January 1980, p.41.
2-4. Iyer, Ramaswamy P.K: "Bhagavan's Father," in *The Mountain Path*, July 1980, p.134.
5. T.P.R.: "Sri. Bhagavan's Father," in *The Mountain Path*, 1989, p.3.
6. Bhagavan Ramana: "Marital Garland of Letters," in *Five Hymns*, v.2, p.23.

BORN WITH A PURPOSE

1. Ramana: "Necklet of Nine Gems," in *Five Hymns,* v.8, p.85.
2. Ganapati Muni: "Life of Sri Ramana Maharshi," in *The Mountain Path*, January 1979, p.11.
3. Osborne, Arthur: *Ramana Maharshi*, p.2.
4. Bhagavan Ramana: "Astakam," in *Five Hymns*, v.1, p.124.
5. Bhagavan Ramana: "Arunachala Mahatmya," in *Collected Works*, p.85.
6. Bhagavan Ramana: "Necklet of Nine Gems," in *Five Hymns*, v.9, p.85.
7. Viswanatha Swami: "Revelations of the Vedic Rishis," in *The Mountain Path*, 1975.
8. Bhagavan Ramana: "Arunachala Mahatmya," in *Collected Works*, pp.84, 85.

EARLY YEARS

1-4. Ganapati Muni: "The Life of Sri Ramana Maharshi," in *The Mountain Path*, pp.8-12.
5. Mudaliar, A. Devaraja: *Day by Day*, entry dt.3.6.46.
6. Osborne, Arthur: *Ramana Maharshi*, p.4.
7. Greenblatt et al: *Pictorial Biography*, p.6.

DINDIGAL—SELF-ENQUIRY BEGINS

1. Mudaliar, A. Devaraja: *Day by Day*, entry dt.1.2.46.
2-3. Ibid, entry dt.31.5.46.
4. Brunton, Paul and Venkataramiah Munagala (Recorded): *Conscious Immortality*, p.68.

MADURAI YEARS

1. Iyer, N.R. Krishnamurthi: "Sri Bhagavan's Boyhood in Madurai," in *Ramana Smrti*, pp.78-80.
2. Greenblatt et al: *Pictorial Biography*, p.9.
3. This was the room in which Ramana became enlightened on July 17, 1896.
4-5. Iyer, N.R. Krishnamurthi: *Ramana Smrti*, pp.78-80.
6. Greenblatt et al: *Pictorial Biography*, p.8.
7. Nagamma, Suri: *Letters* entry dt.8.3.49. In the Vedic hymn "*Namakam*," Rudra (Siva) is called *hiranya bahu* (golden-handed).
8. Greenblatt et al: *Pictorial Biography*, p.9.
9. Osborne, Arthur: *Ramana Maharshi*, p.4.
10. Greenblatt et al: *Pictorial Biography*, p.10.

THE DAY BEFORE

1. Bhagavan Ramana: "Eleven Verses to Sri Arunachala," in *Collected Works*, v.8, pp.105-106.
2. Narasimha Swami, B.V.: *Papers*, an interview with Ramana recorded on 8.1.31.
3. Natarajan, A.R., (tr.): *The Book of Daily Worship (Sri Ramana Astottara)*, p.16. *"The operation of Grace for spiritual ripening is termed* Sakti nipata. *It destroys ignorance and awakens one to the knowledge that the entire universe is permeated by divine light."*
4-5. Refer to chapter "Dindigal—Self-Enquiry Begins" under Section I.
6. Refer to chapter "Born With a Purpose" under Section I.

ENLIGHTENMENT—JULY 17, 1896

1. Narasimha Swami, B.V.: *Self-Realization*, pp.20, 21.
2. Narasimha Swami, B.V.: *Papers*.
3. Mudaliar, A. Devaraja: *Day by Day*, entry dt.22.11.45.
4-6 Narasimha Swami, B.V.: *Papers*.
7. Natarajan, A.R. (tr. and com.): *Sri Ramana Sahasranama*, p.1.
8. Subbaramayya, G.V.: *Sri Ramana Reminiscences*, p.31.
9. Mudaliar, A. Devaraja: *Day By Day*, entry dt.4.10.46.
10. Narasimha Swami, B.V.: *Self-Realization*, p.270.

THE FATHER'S COMMAND

1. Bhagavan Ramana: "Marital Garland of Letters," in *Five Hymns*, v.70, p.47.
2. Narasimha Swami, B.V.: *Self-Realization*, p.28.
3-4. Narasimha Swami, B.V., *Papers*, "Scenes from Ramana's Life," K.K. Ganapati Sastriar, Kapali Sastriar and his wife Parvathiammal, interview dt.14.10.29.

ADVENT AT ARUNACHALA

1. Bhagavan Ramana: "Marital Garland of Letters," in *Five Hymns*, v.108, p.63.
2. Refer to chapter "The Thirties and the Forties," under Section V.
3. Mudaliar, A. Devaraja: *Day by Day*, entry dt.2.9.46.
4-6. Nagamma, Suri: *Letters*, entry dt.12.4.48.

SECTION II

THE PENANCE

1. Ganapati Muni.: *Ramana Gita—Dialogues*, v.18, p.132.
2. Subbaramayya, G.V.: *Sri Ramana Reminiscences*, p.31 and Mudaliar, A. Devaraja, *Day by Day*, entry dt.4.10.46 and 22.11.45.
3. Narasimha Swami, B.V.: *Self-Realization*, p.48.
4-5. Narasimha Swami, B.V.: *Papers*.

GURUMURTAM

1. Ganesan, V.: *Moments Remembered*, pp.105, 106.
2. Narasimha Swami, B.V.: *Self-Realization*, pp.51, 52.
3. Ganesan, V.: *Moments Remembered*, pp.105, 106.
4. Narasimha Swami, B.V.: *Papers*.
5-8. Narasimha Swami, B.V.: *Self-Realization*, pp.52-58.

ARUNAGIRINATHAR TEMPLE—PACHAIAMMAN KOIL

1. Ganapati Muni: *Forty Verses*, v.5.
2. Mudaliar, A. Devaraja: *Day by Day*, entry dt.30.5.46.
3. Nagamma, Suri: *Letters*, entry dt.27.11.47.
4. Ibid, entry dt.27.6.47.
5. Mudaliar, A. Devaraja, *Day by Day*, entry dt.1.2.46, afternoon.

SECTION III

VIRUPAKSHA YEARS, 1899-1916

1. Bhagavan Ramana: "Occasional Verses," in *Collected Works*, p.152.
2. In view of the significance and importance of the relationship between Ramana and mother Azhagammal, and her liberation, a separate chapter on Mother Azhagammal has been included.
3. See chapter "Vasishta Ganapati Muni" under this section.
4. See chapters "Gambhiram Seshier" and "Sivaprakasam Pillai" under this section.

5. Mudaliar, A. Devaraja: *Day by Day*, entry dt.2.5.46, morning.
6. Bhagavan Ramana: "Occasional Verses," in *The Collected Works*, p.94.
7. Mudaliar, A. Devaraja: *Day by Day*, entry dt.26.10.45, morning.
8. Ibid, entry dt.9.12.45, morning.
9. Nagamma, Suri: *Letters*, entry dt.10.10.48.
10. Mudaliar, A. Devaraja: *Day by Day*, entry dt.5.6.45, afternoon.
11. Ibid, entry dt.1.2.46, morning.
12. Ibid, entry dt.5.10.46.
13-14. Nagamma, Suri: *Letters*, entry dt.21.8.46.
15. Mahadevan, T.M.P.: *Ramana Maharshi*, pp.38, 39.
16. Nagamma, Suri: *Letters*, entry dt.25.1.47.
17. Ibid, entry dt.19.8.46.

THE MOST SIGNIFICANT EVENT AFTER ENLIGHTENMENT
1-2. Narasimha Swami, B.V.: *Self-Realization*, pp.269-270.
3. Refer to "Enlightenment, July 17, 1896" under Section I.
4. Cohen, S.S.: "Part II—Talks," in *Guru Ramana*, 25th April, 1937, p.85.

ARUNACHALA
1. Tagare, Dr. G.V. (tr. and annotation): *The Skanda Purana—Part-III*, vv.17-20, p.44.
2. Ibid, Chapter 5, vv. 67b-71, p.30.
3. Ibid, Chapter 7, v. II, p.44.
4. Ibid, Chapter 5, vv.33-39a, p.28.
5. Venkataramiah, Munagala: *Talks*, entry dt.8.5.38.
6. Godman, David: "Bhagavan's Deposition on Arunachala," in *The Mountain Path*, 1990, p.14.
7. Bhagavan Ramana: "Significance of Arunachala," in *Collected Works*, p.84.
8. Bhagavan Ramana: 'Significance of the Beacon,' in *Collected Works*, p.85.
9. Bhagavan Ramana: "Marital Garland of Letters," in *Five Hymns*, v.19, p.29.
10. Ibid, v.63, p.44.
11. Ibid, "Ashtakam," v.1, p.124.
12. Butler, Robert: "Annamalai Venba," in *The Mountain Path*, pp.18-22.
13. Cohen, S.S.: *Guru Ramana*, entry dt.30.10.45.
14. Bhagavan Ramana: "Necklet of Nine Gems," in *Five Hymns*, v.8, p.85.
15. Mahadevan, T.M.P.: *Ramana Maharshi*, p.34.
16. "*A mile per hour alone should all now walk'* said he who over earth and heavens holds sway...."; refer to "Ramana Dasa Sadananda" under chapter "Lesser Known Devotees of Ramana."
17. Nagamma, Suri: *Letters*, entry dt.26.6.49.
18-19. Narasimha Swami, B.V.: *Self-Realization*, pp.173, 180.
20-22. Mudaliar, A. Devaraja: *My Recollections of Bhagavan Sri Ramana*, pp. 69-72.
23. Ibid, p.65.
24. Nagamma, Suri: *Letters*, entry dt.30.11.47.

GAMBHIRAM SESHIER
1-2. "'Self Enquiry' and 'Who am I?': A History and Evaluation," editorial in: *The Mountain Path*, January 1982, pp.1-3.
3-4. Bhagavan Ramana: *Collected Works*, pp.5-6, 12-13.

SIVAPRAKASAM PILLAI
1. "'Self Enquiry' and 'Who am I?': A History and Evaluation," editorial in: *The Mountain Path*, January 1982, pp.1-5.
2. Bhagavan Ramana: *The Collected Works*, pp.39-40.
3. Ibid, p.45.

VASISHTA GANAPATI MUNI
1. Shankaranarayan, S.: *Bhagavan and Nayana*, p.89.
2. Ibid, pp.27, 28.
3. Though greatly drawn to Ramana, because of the luster of his *tapas*, the Muni was not yet ready to surrender to him.
4. Ramaswamy, Dr. S. (tr): *The Guru and the Disciple*; Sastry, Kapali: *Vasishta Vaibhavam*, p.3.
5. Leela S.R. (tr): *Glory of Vasishta Ganapati Muni*; Sastry, Kapali: *Vasishta Vaibhavam*, p.86.
6. Ramaswamy, Dr. S. (tr): *The Guru and the Disciple*, p.7.
7. Natarajan. A.R. (tr): *The Book of Daily Worship*, attribute nos.2, 52, 53, pp.2, 45, 46.
8. Ramaswamy, Dr. S. (tr): *The Guru and the Disciple*, p.7.
9. Natarajan, A.R. (tr. and com.): *Ramana Gita—Dialogues*, Introduction, Natarajan, A.R. p.4.
10. Nagamma, Suri: *Letters*, entry dt.30.4.48.
11. Letter dt.6.6.32 from Kapali Sastri to Viswanatha Swami, Library.
12. Sastry, Kapali: *Vasishta Vaibhavam*, tr. G.V. Kulkarni (unpublished manuscript).
13. Narasimha Swami, B.V.: *Self-Realization*, p.92.

14-15. Sastry, Kapali: *Vasishta Vaibhovam*, tr. G.V. Kulkarni (unpublished manuscript).
16. Natarajan, A.R. (ed.): "Physical Presence at Two Places," in *Miracles*, p.1.
17. Sastry, Kapali: *Vasishta Vaibhavam*, tr. G.V. Kulkarni (unpublished manuscript).
18. Natarajan, A.R. (ed.): "Physical Presence at Two Places," in *Miracles*, p.1.
19. Refer to "Muruganar" under Section V.
20. Natarajan. A. R. (tr. and com.): *Sat-Darshanam*, v.42, p.47.
21. Natarajan, A.R. (tr. and com.): Introduction in *Sat-Darshanam*.
22. Nagamma, Suri: *Letters*, entry dt.18.4.47.
23. Reddy, N. Balarama: *My Reminiscences*, p.63.
24. Venkataramiah, Munagala: *Talks*, entry dt.20.1.37.
25. Natarajan, A.R.: "Muni and the Maharshi," in *The Inner Circle*, p.28.

F.H. HUMPHREYS
1. Humphreys, Frank. H.: *Glimpses*, p.7.
2-3. Narasimha Swami, B.V.: *Self-Realization*, pp.111-112.
4-5. Humphreys, Frank. H.: *Glimpses*, p.19.

LESSER KNOWN DEVOTEES OF RAMANA
1. Sadananda, Ramana Dasa: *Sri Ramana Stuti Dasakam*, p.46.
2. Ibid, pp.33, 34.
3. Narasimha Swami, B.V.: *Papers*. Also see Greenblatt et al, *Pictorial Biography*, p.54.

SACRED HANDS
1. Nagamma, Suri: *Letters*, entry dt.30.12.45.
2. Narasimha Swami, B.V.: *Self-Realization*, p. 47.
3. Nagamma, Suri: *Letters*, entry dt.12.4.48.
4. Narasimha Swami, B.V.: *Self-Realization*, p.49.
5. Ibid, pp.100-102.
6. Nagamma, Suri: *Letters*, entry dt.21.1.46.
7. Godman, David: *Living by the Words of Bhagavan*, p.75.

RAMANA'S MOTHER AZHAGAMMAL
1. Natarajan, A.R.: *Bhagavan Ramana and Mother*, Chapters 1 and 2.
2. Natarajan, A.R.: *Insights*, p.58.
3-4. Narasimha Swami, B.V.: *Self-Realization*, pp.61, 62.
5-6. Nagamma, Suri: *Letters*, pp.358-360.
7-14. Natarajan, A.R.: *Bhagavan Ramana and Mother*, pp.11-31.
15. Ramaswamy, Dr. S. (tr): *The Guru and the Disciple*, p.22.
16. Natarajan, A.R.: *Bhagavan Ramana and Mother*, p.39.
17. See above reference which clarifies this point.
18. Natarajan, A.R.: *Bhagavan Ramana and Mother*, p.40.
19. Godman, David: *Living by the Words of Bhagavan*, p.41.
20. Reddy, N. Balarama: *My Reminiscences*, p.79.
21. Sadhu Arunachala: *Sadhu's Reminiscences*, p.59.
22. Nagamma, Suri: *Letters*, entry dt.25.3.49.
23. Ibid, pp.398-399.
24-25. Sadhu Arunachala: *Sadhu's Reminiscences*, p.60.
26. Sastry T.V. Kapali: "Significance of Maha pooja," in *The Mountain Path*, July 1987, p.170.

SECTION IV
SKANDASRAMAM YEARS, 1916-1922
1. Natarajan, A.R.: *Bhagavan Ramana and Mother*, p.31.
2. Godman, David: "Bhagavan's Deposition on Arunachala," in *The Mountain Path*, p.14.
3. Ananthamurthy, T.S.: *Life and Teachings*, pp.105-107.
4. Mudaliar, A. Devaraja: *Day by Day*, entry dt.25.11.45.
5. Kunju Swami: *Reminiscences*, pp.69, 70.
6. Venkataramiah, Munagala: *Talks*, entry dt.16.10.35.

SADHU NATANANANDA
1. Narasimha Swami, B.V.: *Self-Realization*, pp.217, 223.
2-7. Ibid.
8. Kunju Swami: *Reminiscences*, p.164.
9. Narasimha Swami, B.V.: *Self-Realization*, p.224.
10. Bhagavan Ramana: *Collected Works*, pp.51-79.

SECTION V
THE LIBERTY HALL
1. Nagamma, Suri: *Letters*, entry dt.28.5.46.
2. Narasimha Swami, B.V.: *Self-Realization*, pp.187, 188.
3-4. Brunton, Paul: *A Search in Secret India*, pp. 290-291.
5. Ananthamurthy, T.S.: *Life and Teachings*, p.137.
6. Pillai, Ramaswami: "How I Came to Bhagavan," in *The Mountain Path*, July 1981, pp.145, 146.

7. Refer to "F.H. Humphreys" under Section III, "Virupaksha Years."
8. Narasimha Swami, B.V.: "Scenes from Ramana's Life," in *The Mountain Path*, January 1980, pp.19, 20.
9. Narasimha Swami, B.V.: "Reminiscences of Srinivasa Gopala Iyengar," Narasimha Swami's papers, dt.30.1.30.
10. Narasimha Swami, B.V.: "Scenes from Ramana's Life—III," in *The Mountain Path*, October 1980, p.159.
11. Narasimha Swami, B.V.: "A Dialogue with Maharshi—III," in *The Mountain Path*, January 1983, p.36.
12. Narasimha Swami, B.V.: *Papers*.

ROBBERS WORSHIP RAMANA
1-4. Narasimha Swami, B.V.: *Self-Realization*, pp.153-155.

RAMANA IN THE KITCHEN
1. Subbaramayya, G.V.: *Sri Ramana Reminiscences*, p.72.
2-3. Sampoornamma: *Unforgettable Years*, RMCL, 1997, p.66.
4-6. Santamma: *Unforgettable Years*, pp.71-72.
7. Subbalakshmiamma: *Unforgettable Years*, pp.86-87.
8-10. Ibid, p.92.

EQUALITY IN THE DINING HALL
1. Natarajan, A.R. (ed): *Unforgettable Years*, p.7.
2. Nagamma, Suri: *Letters*, pp.291, 292.
3. Natarajan, A.R. (ed): *Unforgettable Years*, p.73.
4. Ibid, pp.88, 90.
5. Ibid, p.96.
6-8. Yogi; Chhaganlal V.: "Living with Ramana Maharshi," in *Living with Ramana Maharshi*, p.7.

KINDER YOU ARE THAN ONE'S OWN MOTHER
1. Reddy, N. Balarama: "My Recollections of Sri Bhagavan Ramana Maharshi," in *Living with Ramana Maharshi*, p.15.
2. Kunju Swami: *Reminiscences*, p.18.
3, 4, 5, 6, 7 (nos. 8, 9, 10, 13, 16 in the 2002 edition): missing from original text.

IDENTIFICATION WITH THE POOR, HUMBLE, AND THE MEEK
1. Nagamma, Suri: *Letters*, pp.326, 327.
2-3. Ibid, pp.424-427.
4. Chalam: "What I Have Seen and Heard," in *Unforgettable Years*, p.3.
5. Subbaramayya, G.V.: *Sri Ramana Reminiscences*, p.73.
6. Nagamma, Suri: *Letters*, pp.391-394.
7. Iyer, T.P. Ramachandra: *Unforgettable Years*, pp.32-34.

ONE CONSCIOUSNESS
1. Mudaliar A. Devaraja: *Day by Day*, entry dt.26.2.46.
2. Nagamma, Suri: *Letters*, entry dt.24.10.47.
3. On a similar note Ramana would joke, *"When these attendants are immersed in deep meditation, the monkeys come and see to the work of the attendants. Someone has to look after the work. The attendants put the fruits into the basket, the monkeys put the fruit into their stomachs; that is all the difference"* (Nagamma, Suri: *Letters*, entry dt.25.10.47).
4. Narasimha Swami, B.V.: *Self-Realization*, p.168.
5. Nagamma, Suri: *Letters*, entry dt.26.8.48.
6. *The Call Divine* (monthly), M.N. Swami, Bombay, vol.10, p.52.
7. Mallet, Pascaline: "Knowing Eternity," in *Forever is in the Now*, p.113.
8-9. Nagamma, Suri: *Letters*, entry dt.22.5.49.
10-13. Nagamma, Suri: *Letters*, entry dt.20.4.47.
14. Ramana has also described the love that a peahen showed towards him during the Skandasram days. *"The peahen always used to sleep on my lap.... She was very familiar with me. The peacock used to call her to accompany him wherever he went out, but like a little child, she would never leave him and go"* (Nagamma, Suri: *Letters*, entry dt.26.8.48).
15. Iyer, T.K. Sundaresa: *At the Feet of Bhagavan*, pp.48, 49.
16. Nagamma, Suri: *Letters*, entry dt.18.1.46.
17. Mudaliar, A. Devaraja: *Day by Day*, entry dt.22.11.45, afternoon.
18. Osborne, Arthur: *Ramana Maharshi*, p.99.
19. Nagamma, Suri: *Letters*, entry dt.1.1.46.
20. Iyer, T.K. Sundaresa: *At the Feet of Bhagavan*, p.6.
21. Mudaliar, A. Devaraja: *Day by Day*, entry dt.10.12.45.
22. Brunton, Paul and Venkataramaiah, Munagala (recordists): *Conscious Immortality*, p.18.

LIBERATION OF COW LAKSHMI
1. Bhagavan Ramana: *Collected Works*, p.157.
2. Mudaliar, A. Devaraja: *The Cow*, pp.2-3.
3. Mallet, Pascaline: "Knowing Eternity," in *Forever is in the Now*, p.114.
4-5. Nagamma, Suri: *Letters*, pp.328-329.

6: Ibid, pp.330-332.

SOME WESTERN DEVOTEES
1. Brunton, Paul: "Dedication," in *Message of Arunachala*, B.I. Publications, New Delhi.
2. Brunton, Paul: *A Search in Secret India*, p.131.
3. Ibid, p.145.
4. Ibid, p.156.
5. Ibid, p.280.
6. Ibid, p.305.
7. Ibid, p.310.
8-9. Piggot, M.A.: "The Way of the Spirit," in *Forever is in the Now*, pp.132-137.
10. De Acosta, Mercedes: *Here Lies the Heart*, p.294.
11. Ibid, p.296.
12-13. Ibid, pp.299-301.
14. Mudaliar, A. Devaraja: *Day by Day*, entry dt.14.10.46.
15. Osborne, Arthur: *For Those With Little Dust*, Ramana Publications, Florida, 1990, dedication page.
16-17. Ibid, p.5.
18. Ibid, p.8.

THE THIRTIES AND THE FORTIES
1. The record of Ramana's talks with devotees and visitors is covered in the following books:
   a) Venkataramiah, Munagala: *Talks*, SRA.
   b) Brunton, Paul and Venkataramiah, Munagala (recorded by): *Conscious Immortality*, SRA.
   c) Cohen, S.S.: *Guru Ramana*, SRA, *Talks* in Part II (65 pages).
   d) Mudaliar, A. Devaraja: *Day by Day with Bhagavan*, SRA.
   e) Rajan, N.N.: *More Talks with Ramana Maharshi*, RMCL (180 pages).
   f) Annamalai Swami: *Living by the Words of Bhagavan* (45 pages diary), Sri Annamalai Ashram Trust.
2. Sastry, Kapali: "Leaves from a Diary," in *The Maharshi*, entry dt.2.4.50, p.155.
3-4. Rajan, N.N.: *More Talks*, entry dt.18.3.38 to 23.9.38.
5. Subbaramayya, G.V: *Sri Ramana Reminiscences*, p.147.
6. Nagamma, Suri: *Letters*, entry dt.8.9.46.
7. Refer to "Mother Azhagammal" under Section III.

VICARIOUS PENANCE
1. Muruganar: *Sri Ramana Sannidhi Murai*, SRA, 1993, vv.1419, 1420, p.374.
2. Cohen, S.S.: *Guru Ramana*, entry dt.22.2.49.
3. Ibid, entry dt.27.3.49.
4. Ibid, entry dt.18.4.49.
5. Ibid, entry dt.1.5.49.
6. Ibid, entry dt.7.8.49.
7. Ibid, entry dt.19.12.49.

DEVOTEES PANIC—RAMANA'S RESPONSE
1. Cohen, S.S.: *Guru Ramana*, entry dt.6.7.49.
2. Subbaramayya, G.V.: *Sri Ramana Reminiscences*, p.193.
3. Cohen, S.S.: *Guru Ramana*, entry dt.25.6.49.
4. Ibid, entry dt.20.4.49.
5. Narasimha Swami, B.V.: "Sundaresa Iyer— Reminiscences," in *Papers*, statement recorded 14.1.30.
6. Cohen, S.S.: *Guru Ramana*, entry dt.23.1.49.
7. Subbaramayya, G.V: *Sri Ramana Reminiscences*, p.209.
8. Cohen, S.S.: *Guru Ramana*, entry dt.12.4.50.
9-10. Viswanatha Swami: *The Last Days and Mahanirvana*, pp.6, 7.

DID RAMANA SUFFER? HIS ATTITUDE TO *DARSAN*
1. Cohen, S.S.: *Guru Ramana*, *Talks* Part II, XV—The Jnani—The Awakened, June 1938.
2. Iyer, R. Narayana: "The Great Event," in *The Mountain Path*, July 1969, p.182.
3. Cohen, S.S.: *Guru Ramana*, entry dt.12.4.50.
4. Ibid, entry dt.2.8.49.
5. Viswanatha Swami: *Last Days and Mahanirvana*, pp.8, 9.
6. Cohen, S.S.: *Guru Ramana*, entry dt.12.4.50.

MAHANIRVANA
1. Osborne, Arthur: *Ramana Maharshi*, p.174.
2. Swami Satyananda: "How I Have Been Serving Bhagavan," in *The Mountain Path*, January 1973, p.44.
3. Iyer, R. Narayana: "The Great Event," in *The Mountain Path*, July 1969, p.181.

SAMADHI FUNCTION AND THE SIGNIFICANCE OF THE *SAMADHI*
1. Cohen, S.S.: *Guru Ramana*, entry dt.15.4.50.

SECTION VI
THE POST-*NIRVANA* SCENE

1. Osborne, Arthur: *The Last Days and Maha-Nirvana*, p.2.
2. Cohen, S.S.: *Guru Ramana*, entry dt.12.4.50.
3. Keers, Wolter A.: "What of Us, after He Went?" in *The Mountain Path*, July 1975, p.141.

THE CONTINUING STORY
1. Osborne, Arthur: *The Last Days and Maha-Nirvana*, p.31.
2. Brunton, Paul: "The Impact," in *Forever is in the Now*, p.188.
3. Greenlees, Duncan: "The Everpresent," in *The Mountain Path*, 1966, p.109.
4. Cohen S.S.: "Ramana Satguru," in *The Mountain Path*, January, 1966, p.88.

TEACHINGS
1. Bhagavan Ramana: "Eight Verses," in *Five Hymns*, p.128.
2. Bhagavan Ramana: "Five Verses," in *Five Hymns*, v.2, p.138.
3. Bhagavan Ramana: "Self Enquiry," in *The Collected Works*, p.28.
4. Ibid, p.31.
5. Bhagavan Ramana: "Who am I?" in *Collected Works*, pp.39-52.
6. Brunton, Paul and Venkataramiah, Munagala (eds.), *Conscious Immortality*, p.66.
7. Bhagavan Ramana: "Eight Verses," in *Five Hymns*, v.7, p.127.
8. Narasimha Swami, B.V.: *Papers*.
9. Natarajan. A.R. (tr.): *Sat-Darshanam*, v.29, p.35.
10. Ibid, v.30, p.35.
11. Bhagavan Ramana: *Upadesa Saram*, v.10, p.19.
12. Bhagavan Ramana: "Self-Enquiry," in *Collected Works*, p.29.
13. Humphreys, F.H.: *Glimpses*, p.19.
14. "Maharshi in our Midst," in *The Mountain Path*, p.49.
15. Brunton, Paul: *A Search in Secret India*, pp.156, 157.
16. Bhagavan Ramana: "Self-Enquiry," in *Collected Works*, p.30.

SADGURU
1. Bhagavan Ramana: "The Decad," in *Five Hymns*, v.2, p.102.
2. Ibid, v.6, p.104.
3. Bhagavan Ramana: "Spiritual Instruction," in *Collected Works*, p.53.
4. Bhagavan Ramana: *The Collected Works*, Rider, p.45.

5. Mudaliar, A. Devaraja: *My Recollections of Ramana Maharshi*, p.117.
6. Ibid, p.119.
7. Cohen, S.S.: *Guru Ramana*, p.18.
8. Bhagavan Ramana: *Upadesa Saram*, v.13, pp.23-25, also: *Ramana Gita—Dialogues*, chapters VI and VII, pp.62-86.
9. Kunju Swami: *Reminiscences*, p.121.
10. Ganapati Muni: *Forty Verses in Praise of Ramana*, v.22, p.11.
11. Muruganar: "Decad of Journey," in *Songs*, p.77.
12. Butler, Robert (tr.): "Seventy Verses in Praise of the Guru's Holy Feet," in *Non-dual Consciousness*, RMCL, 1998, v.609, p.103.
13. Muruganar: "Magician Ramana," in *Songs*, p.57.

RAMANA'S DAILY MIRACLES
1. Bhagavan Ramana: "Marital Garland of Letters," in *Five Hymns*, p.56.
2. Prof. K. Swaminathan (tr.): *Homage*, p.87.
3. Natarajan, A.R.: "On the Glory of Siddhas," in *Ramana Gita—Dialogues*, v.23, p.229.
4. Natarajan, A.R.: "Invoking Ramana's Grace," in *Insights*, p.103.
5, 6 (13, 14 in the 2002 edition): missing from original text.

TIMELESS IN TIME
1. Natarajan, A.R. (tr.): *Sat-Darshanam*, p.19.
2. Natarajan, A.R.: "The Stamp of Eternity," in *Radiance of the Self*, RMCL, 1998, p.ii.
3. Dr. Sarada: "Falling in Love," in *Radiance of the Self*, p.vi.
4. Viswanatha Swami: *Book of Daily Worship*, p.46.
5. Muruganar: *Non-dual Consciousness*, "Seventy Verses in Praise of the Guru's Holy Feet," vv.625, 629, p.106.
6. Natarajan, A.R.: *Ramana Maharshi—The Living Guru*, pp.1-13.
7. Noye, Eleanor Pauline: "My Pilgrimage to Sri Ramanasramam," in *Golden Jubilee Souvenir*, p.442.
8. Ibid, pp.448, 449.
9. *The Maharshi*, a bi-monthly, New York: Arunachala Ashrama.

BIBLIOGRAPHY
PRIMARY SOURCES (IN THE ORDER REFERRED TO IN THE BOOK)

1. Narasimha Swami, B.V: *Self-Realization—The Life and Teachings of Sri Ramana Maharshi*, Sri Ramanasramam (SRA), Tiruvannamalai, 1996.
2. Osborne, Arthur: *Ramana Maharshi and the Path of Self-Knowledge*, SRA, 1970.
3. Swaminathan, K: *Ramana Maharshi*, National Book Trust, India, 1996.
4. Mahadevan, T.M.P.: *Ramana Maharshi—The Sage of Arunachala*, George Allen & Unwin, London, 1977.
5. Master Nome: *Timeless Presence*, Society for Abidance in Truth, U.S.A, 1996.
6. Muruganar: *Homage to the Presence*, tr. Prof. K. Swaminathan, SRA, 1977.
7. Bhagavan Ramana: *The Collected Works of Ramana Maharshi*, SRA, 1996.
8. Muruganar: *Songs from Sri Muruganar's Ramana Sannidhi Murai*, Ramana Kendra, New Delhi, 1975.
9. Bhagavan Ramana: *Five Hymns to Arunachala and Other Poems of Bhagavan Sri Ramana Maharshi*, tr. Prof. K. Swaminathan, Ramana Kendra, New Delhi, 1977.
10. Natarajan, A.R.: Tr. and commentary, *Sat-Darshanam* (Tamil original, Bhagavan Ramana, Sanskrit rendering, Kavyakanta Ganapati Muni), Ramana Maharshi Centre for Learning (RMCL), Bangalore, 1996.
11. *Golden Jubilee Souvenir*, SRA, 1995.
12. Iyer, T.K. Sundaresa: *At the Feet of Bhagavan*, SRA, 1980.
13. Subbaramayya, G.V.: *Sri Ramana Reminiscences*, SRA, 1994.
14. Ganapati Muni: *Forty Verses in Praise of Ramana*, SRA, 1992.
15. Bhagavan Ramana: *Upadesa Undiyar*, tr. Sadhu Om and Michael James, Sri Kanvasrama Trust, Tiruvannamalai, 1986.
16. Ganapati Muni: *Ramana Gita—Dialogues with Ramana Maharshi*, tr. and commentary by A.R. Natarajan, RMCL, 1990.
17. Natarajan, A.R. (ed.): *Forever is in the Now*, RMCL, 1997.
18. Brunton, Paul and Venkataramaiah, Munagala (recorded by): *Conscious Immortality—Conversations with Sri Ramana Maharshi*, SRA, first edition 1984, revised edition, 1996.
19. *The Mountain Path* (Quarterly), SRA.
20. Greenblatt, Joan and Greenblatt, Mathew: *Bhagavan Sri Ramana—A Pictorial Biography*, SRA, 1981.
21. Mudaliar, A. Devaraja: *Day by Day with Bhagavan*, SRA, 1989.
22. *Ramana Smrti, A Sri Ramana Maharshi Birth Centenary Offering*, SRA, 1980.
23. Nagamma, Suri: *Letters from Sri Ramanasramam*, tr. D.S. Sastri, SRA, 1985.
24. Viswanatha Swami: *The Book of Daily Worship*, tr. A.R. Natarajan, RMCL, 1996.
25. Sastri, Jagadeeswara: *Sri Ramana Sashasranama*, tr. and commentary by A.R. Natarajan, RMCL, 1996.
26. Ganesan, V.: *Moments Remembered*, SRA, 1990.
27. Iyer, Satyamangalam Venkatarama: *Sri Ramana Stuti Panchakam*, SRA, 1977.
28. Cohen, S.S.: *Guru Ramana*, SRA, 1998.
29. Tagare, Dr. G.V.: *The Skanda Purana-Part III*, Motilal Banarsidass, Delhi, 1993.
30. Natarajan, A.R. (ed.): *The Inner Circle*, RMCL, 1996.
31. Shankaranarayan, S: *Bhagavan and Nayana*, SRA, 1997.
32. Humphreys, F.H.: *Glimpses of the Life and Teachings of Bhagavan Sri Ramana Maharshi*, SRA, 1996.
33. Sastry, Kapali: *Vasishta Vaibhavam*, tr. Ramaswamy, Dr. S: *The Guru and the Disciple*, 1998.
34. Sastry, Kapali: *Vasishta Vaibhavam*, tr. Leela, S.R.: *The Glory of Vasishta Ganapati—Biography*, Sri Aurobindo Kapali Sastri Institute of Vedic Culture, Bangalore, 1999.
35. Sastry, Kapali: *Vasishta Vaibhavam*, tr. G.V. Kulkarni (unpublished).
36. Natarajan, A.R. (ed.): *Ramana Maharshi's Miracles—They Happen Everyday*, RMCL, 1995.
37. Reddy, N. Balarama: *My Reminiscences*, SRA, 1997.
38. Venkataramiah, Munagala (Recordist): *Talks with Sri Ramana Maharshi*, SRA, 1984.
39. Godman, David: *Living by the Words of Bhagavan*, Annamalai Swami Ashram Trust, Tiruvannamalai, 1994.
40. Sadananda, Ramana Dasa: *Sri Ramana Stuti Dasakam*, Ramana Dasa Sadananda, Madras, 1933.
41. Natarajan, A.R.: *Bhagavan Ramana and Mother*, RMCL, 1997.
42. Natarajan, A.R.: *Insights*, RMCL, 1996.
43. Kunju Swami: *Reminiscences*, tr. Dr. K. Subrahmaniam, SRA, 1992.
44. Sadhu Arunachala: *Sadhu's Reminiscences*, SRA.
45. Anathamurthy, T.S.: *Life and Teachings of Sri Ramana Maharshi*,

46. Rao, N. Ramachandra: *Bhagavan Sri Ramana Maharshi* (Kannada Biography).
47. Iyer, T.K. Sundaresa: *At the Feet of Bhagavan*, SRA, 1980.
48. Natarajan, A.R. (ed.): *Forever is in the Now*, East-West (Madras) Pvt. Ltd., 1997.
49. Brunton, Paul: *A Search in Secret India*, B.I. Publications Pvt. Ltd., New Delhi, 1990.
50. Natarajan, A.R.: *Ramana's Muruganar*, RMCL, 1992.
51. Muruganar: *The Garland of Guru's Sayings*, tr. Prof. K. Swaminathan, SRA, 1990.
52. Muruganar: *Sri Ramana Gnana Bodham*, Ramana Kendra, New Delhi.
53. Natarajan, A.R. (ed.): *Unforgettable Years*, RMCL, 1997.
54. Natarajan, A.R. (ed.): *Living with Ramana Maharshi*, RMCL, 1996.
55. Mudaliar, A. Devaraja: *The Cow, Lakshmi*, SRA.
56. Rajan, N.N.: *More Talks with Ramana Maharshi*, RMCL, 1996.
57. Sastri, Jagadeeswara: *Swagata Kusumanjali*, SRA, 1999.
58. Godman, David: *Living by the Words of Bhagavan*, Sri Annamalai Swami Ashram Trust.
59. Sastry, Kapali: *The Maharshi*, S.P. Pundit, Sirsi, 1954.
60. Viswanatha Swami: *The Last Days and Mahanirvana of Bhagavan Sri Ramana*, SRA, 1991.
61. Osborne, Arthur: *Ramana Maharshi and the Path of Self-Knowledge*, SRA, 1970.
62. Nambiar, K.K.: *The Guiding Presence of Sri Ramana*, SRA, 1984.
63. Reddy, N. Balarama: *My Recollection of Sri Bhagavan Ramana Maharshi*, SRA, 1997.
64. Natarajan, A.R.: *Insights into the Ramana Way*, RMCL, 1995.
65. Mouni Sadhu: *In Days of Great Peace*, George Allen & Unwin Ltd., 1957.
66. Natarajan, A.R. (Concept): *Radiance of the Self*.

GLOSSARY

Abhishekam: pouring of water over a sacred image.

Advaita: non-duality; a school of *Vedanta* philosophy teaching the oneness of God, soul, and universe, whose chief exponent was Sankaracarya. *See Vedanta.*

Aham Brahmasmi: "Brahma is my Self." Sentence often repeated in the *Upanishads*.

Annamalai: Tamil name for Arunachala.

Appalam: a thin round wafer, made of black *gram* flour, fried crisp.

Atman: Self; the indwelling Divine Presence within every individual.

Bhagavan: a commonly used name for God. The term *Bhagavan* is identified with supreme sages who are recognized as being completely one with God.

Bhakti: devotion; love of God.

Bhiksa: to beg.

Brahma: the Creator God; the first person of the Hindu Trinity, the other two being Visnu and Siva.

Brahman: the Supreme Being; the Absolute; the essence of life.

Chela: disciple.

Choultry: an *asram*, monastery, or community center.

Dakshinamurti: "the South-facing form"; one of the names of Siva.

Darsan: lit. "sight." The blessing derived from beholding a saint or a sacred site.

Dattatreya: famous *yogi*, thought to be an incarnation of Vishnu; attributed as author of *Avhadhuta Upanishad.*

Devasthanam: the statutory authority which manages the affairs of the temple.

Dhyana: contemplation, meditation.

Ganesha: the son of Siva and Parvati, god of wisdom and remover of all obstacles.

Gauri: the "white" goddess; name of Parvati.

Giripradakshina: *giri* means hill, *pradakshina,* going around a holy object or place, keeping the object at one's right. Circumambulation of Arunachala.

Gunas: the three cosmic qualities of *sattva* (purity), *rajas* (passion), and *tamas* (obscurity) of which all of manifestation is constituted.

Hrdaya: the Heart. The seat of Consciousness at the right side of the chest, as experienced and expounded by Bhagavan Sri Ramana.

Iswara: lit. "the Lord of the Universe"; the personal God who manifests in the triple form of Brahma (the Creator), Visnu (the Sustainer), and Siva (the Transformer).

Jaganmaya: universal illusion.

Japa: repetition of a sacred word, syllable, or name of God.

Jayanti: birth anniversary (of a holy person).

Jnana: spiritual wisdom implying the direct cognition of non-duality as the true nature of Reality—the knowledge of the Self.

Jnani: a Self-realized sage; one who has attained realization by the path of knowledge.

Kailasa: a mountain in the Himalayas reputed to be the abode of Siva.

Kamandalams: water jars.

Karma: deeds. The destiny that a person makes for himself by the law of cause and effect.

Khaddar: a coarse homespun cotton cloth.

Koupinam: traditional undergarment.

Kumbhabhisekam: a ritualistic function consecrating a Hindu temple.

Linga: a symbol. Represents Siva or the Absolute.

Maha: great.

Maharshi: great seer, great *rishi*.

Mahasamadhi: lit. "the great absorption." A term used to describe the physical death of a great sage.

Maheswara: "Great Lord"; Siva.

Mandapam: pavillion.

Mandiram: an abode, or temple.

Mantra: a sacred formula or utterance; a prayer.

Maulvi: Islamic cleric or *imam*.

Maya: cosmic illusion; the power (*sakti*) inherent in *Brahman* by which it manifests the world.

Meru: in Puranic legend, the mythical golden mountain; the axis of the world.

Moksa: liberation from *samsara*.

Mouna: silence.

Muni: a holy man given to solitude and contemplation.

Mutt: a meeting place and abode of *sadhus*.

Nadis: channels of flow of subtle vital force (*prana*).

Nataraja: "Lord of the Dance"; one of the names of Siva.

Nirguna: without form or qualities or attributes; opposite to *saguna*.

Nirvana: the extinguishing of earthly attachments and desires; freedom from rebirth. Liberation.

Om: the sacred syllable, the supreme *mantra*, representing the substratum of creative sound which sustains the universe.

Parayana: recitation.

Payasam: sweet rice pudding.

Parsee: member of the Zoroastrian community in India.

Prarabdha: the part of one's *karma* (destiny) to be worked out in this life.

Prasad: food offered to a deity or to a spiritual teacher; this same food distributed to devotees as a blessing.

Puja: ritualistic worship.

Puranas: eighteen sacred books ascribed to Vyasa, which preserve traditions of myth, legend, and rite.

Purushottama: lit. "highest spirit, highest soul"; a term used to refer to the highest Self.

Raja yoga: the principal system of *yoga* as taught by Patanjali.

Rama japa: *mantra* repeating the name of Rama.

Rishi: ancient seer.

Sadhak: a spiritual aspirant.

Sadhana: spiritual practice.

Sadguru: the great master, the true or perfect *guru*.

Saguna: with form, with qualities; opposite of *nirguna*.

Sahaja samadhi: constant and natural absorption in the Self.

Saivite: worshipper of Lord Siva.

Sakti: power or energy; the active feminine aspect of God.

Samadhi: the state in which the meditator and object of meditation, thinker and thought, become one in perfect absorption of the mind.

Samsara: the realm of relativity, transience, and illusion.

Samskaras: innate tendencies, impressions.

Sankalpa: resolution, intentional desire.

Sannyasi: one who has taken formal vows of rennunciation.

Sastras: scriptures.

Sastri: one learned in the *Sastras*.

Sat: Existence; pure Being.

Sattva: purity; one of the three *gunas*.

Shraddha: faith.

Siddha: one endowed with supernatural powers and capable of performing miracles.

Siddhi: supernatural powers; attainment.

Siva: the Destroyer God; the third person of the Hindu Trinity, the other two being Brahma and Visnu.

Siva Panchaksari: *mantra* chanting the name of Siva.

Siva swarupa: lit. "embodiment" or "true form" of Siva. Refers to mountain of Arunachala.

Sivaratri: "the Night of Siva"; traditional Hindu festival.

Sphurana: radiation, emanation, or pulsation.

Sri: lit. "blessed" or "beatific." Used in modern times as a respectful prefix to a name.

Swarupa: lit. "essence, nature."

Swami: lit. "Lord." Used as a sign of respect for a spiritual teacher.

Swaraj: self-rule, self-reliance.

Tapas: religious austerities.

Upadesa: the spiritual guidance or teachings given by a *guru*.

Upanishads: portion of *Vedas* (*Vedanta*) dealing with the ultimate truth and its realization.

Vahana: in Hindu mythology, the object or creature that serves as the vehicle and as the sign of a particular deity.

Vaishnava: a worshipper of Vishnu.

Vasanas: latencies or tendencies inherent in man.

Vedanta: the Absolute Truth as established by the *Upanishads*, *Brahma Sutras,* and *Bhagavad Gita*. The end or consummation of the *Vedas*.

Vedas: The sacred books of the Hindus: *Rig, Yajur, Sama,* and *Atharva*, revealed through the *rishis*.

Vichara: enquiry into the truth of the Self.

Vishnu: the Preserver God; the second person of the Hindu Trinity, the other two being Brahma and Siva.

Yama: the god of death.

Yoga: systems of spiritual techniques and discipline through which the practitioner attains union with God as specifically outlined in the *Yoga Sutras* of Patanajali as well as other yogic and tantric texts.

Yogi: one who follows or has mastered the path of *yoga* (path of Union)

Yogini: woman with yogic attainments.

For a glossary of all key foreign words used in books published by World Wisdom, including metaphysical terms in English, consult: www.DictionaryofSpiritualTerms.com. This on-line Dictionary of Spiritual Terms provides extensive definitions, examples and related terms in other languages.

BIOGRAPHICAL NOTES

A.R. NATARAJAN is the President of the Ramana Maharshi Centre for Learning and the Bhagavan Sri Ramana Maharshi Research Centre, Bangalore. He is also the Vice-President of the Ramana Kendra, Delhi. From June 1982 to January 1986 he was the editor of the quarterly published by Sri Ramanasramam, *The Mountain Path*. His works include commentaries on *Sat-Darshanam; Selections from Ramana Gita; Upadesa Saram*, covering the core of the Maharshi's teachings, and *Bhagavan Ramana and Mother*.

ELIOT DEUTSCH is Professor of Philosophy and Chair of the Department of Philosophy, University of Hawaii. He is an eminent philosopher, teacher, and writer who has made important contributions to the understanding and appreciation of Eastern philosophies in the West through his many works on comparative philosophy and comparative aesthetics. He was editor (1967-1987) of the international journal *Philosophy East and West*, Director of the Sixth Eastern Philosophers conference, and past president of the Society for Asian and Comparative Philosophy. He is the author of 15 books, including, *On Truth: An Ontological Theory* (1979), *Advaita Vedanta: A Philosophical Reconstruction* (1969), *Studies in Comparative Aesthetics* (1975), *Religion and Spirituality* (1995), *Essays on the Nature of Art* (1996), and *The Essential Vedanta* (2004).

Other Titles on Hinduism by World Wisdom

A Guide to Hindu Spirituality,
by Arvind Sharma, 2006

The Essential Sri Anandamayi Ma,
by Alexander Lipsky and Sri Anandamayi Ma, 2007

The Essential Swami Ramdas: Commemorative Edition,
compiled by Susunaga Weeraperuma, 2005

The Essential Vedanta: A New Source Book of Advaita Vedanta,
edited by Eliot Deutsch and Rohit Dalvi, 2004

Hinduism and Buddhism,
by Ananda K. Coomaraswamy, 2007

Introduction to Hindu Dharma: The 68th Jagadguru of Kanchipuram,
edited by Michael Oren Fitzgerald, 2007

Lamp of Non-Dual Knowledge & Cream of Liberation: Two Jewels of Indian Wisdom,
translated by Swami Sri Ramanananda Saraswathi, 2003

Paths to Transcendence: According to Shankara, Ibn Arabi, and Meister Eckhart,
by Reza Shah-Kazemi, 2006

Tripura Rahasya: The Secret of the Supreme Goddess,
translated by Swami Sri Ramanananda Saraswathi, 2002

Unveiling the Garden of Love: Mystical Symbolism in Layla Majnun & Gitagovinda,
by Lalita Sinha, 2007

Timeless in Time: Sri Ramana Maharshi,
by A.R. Natarajan, 2006